Okinawan Karate

Teachers, styles and secret techniques

Mark Bishop

TUTTLE Publishing

Tokyo | Rutland, Vermont | Singapore

"Books to Span the East and West"

Tuttle Publishing was founded in 1832 in the small New England town of Rutland, Vermont [USA]. Our core values remain as strong today as they were then—to publish best-in-class books which bring people together one page at a time. In 1948, we established a publishing office in Japan—and Tuttle is now a leader in publishing English-language books about the arts, languages and cultures of Asia. The world has become a much smaller place today and Asia's economic and cultural influence has grown. Yet the need for meaningful dialogue and information about this diverse region has never been greater. Over the past seven decades, Tuttle has published thousands of books on subjects ranging from martial arts and paper crafts to language learning and literature—and our talented authors, illustrators, designers and photographers have won many prestigious awards. We welcome you to explore the wealth of information available on Asia at www.tuttlepublishing.com.

Disclaimer
Please note that the publisher and author(s) of this instructional book are **NOT RESPONSIBLE** for any injury that may result from practicing the techniques and/or following the instructions given. Martial arts training can be dangerous—both to you and to others—if not practiced safely. You should always consult with a trained martial arts teacher before practicing any of these techniques, and ask them to guide you in the proper techniques to be used. Since the physical activities described herein may be too strenuous in nature for some readers, it is essential that a physician be consulted prior to training.

Published by Tuttle Publishing, an imprint of Periplus Editions (HK) Ltd.

www.tuttlepublishing.com

Library of Congress Cataloging Card No. 99-61561
ISBN 978-0-8048-3205-2

Distributed by:

North America, Latin America & Europe
Tuttle Publishing
364 Innovation Drive, North Clarendon, VT 05759-9436 U.S.A.
Tel: 1 (802) 773-8930 I Fax: 1 (802) 773-6993; info@tuttlepublishing.com I www.tuttlepublishing.com

Japan
Tuttle Publishing
Yaekari Building, 3rd Floor, 5-4-12 Osaki, Shinagawa-ku, Tokyo 141-0032
Tel: (81) 3 5437-0171 I Fax: (81) 3 5437-0755; sales@tuttle.co.jp I www.tuttle.co.jp

Asia Pacific
Berkeley Books Pte. Ltd.
3 Kallang Sector #04-01, Singapore 349278
Tel: (65) 6741-2178 I Fax: (65) 6741-2179; inquiries@periplus.com.sg I www.tuttlepublishing.com

26 25 24 23 22   13 12 11 10 9   2211MP   Printed in Singapore

TUTTLE PUBLISHING® is a registered trademark of Tuttle Publishing, a division of Periplus Editions (HK) Ltd.

Ode to Gabriel

In all the love songs I have sung,
Through all the battles fought and won,
In all the work that must be done,
Your love enriches me.

Mark Bishop
Okinawa, 1987

Contents

Preface to first edition

It has been my fortune (or should I say fate) to spend many years studying fighting arts on Okinawa. During my precious free time, when not working or training, I have made it a rule to visit and interview the most acclaimed karate teachers to record the main technical and often misrepresented historical aspects of the various karate styles.

My use of the term 'misrepresented' is not intended to belittle the sincerity of those Japanese and Western writers who have written extensively about the technical aspects of karate and attempted to dig out the historical details, but to bring the reader's attention to the fact that the origins of Okinawan karate have become unnecessarily shrouded in so much myth. Dispelling a myth is not easy. Finding the basic tools (i.e. the simple facts) to do this is even more difficult; but through my interviews, research of Okinawan literature and a strong desire to tell the Okinawan side of the story, I was finally able to put this work together.

That is not to say that this book is intended to be merely an historical reference work on Okinawan karate. The main purpose of my writing it has been, as the title suggests, to introduce Okinawan karate as broadly as possible through the various characters who have brought it about.

Karate has been defined as a form of combat developed from Chinese boxing by the inhabitants of Okinawa. However, for me it has been more than just a means of self-defence, it has led me to the very roots of Okinawan culture and to a better understanding of life itself. I can only hope that in some small way this work will help others, who are now travelling along the road of martial arts, to reach their final destination.

My sincerest thanks go out to all those teachers who gave quite freely of their time and knowledge – and to everyone else, especially my family, who have helped in making this work possible.

Mark Bishop
Shuri, Okinawa

Preface to second edition

The concept instilled in me more than any other during my long sojourn in Okinawa Prefecture was: *In life, one's greatest adversary is oneself.* It was with this general notion indelibly impressed on my mind that I originally set about writing *Okinawan Karate: Teachers, Styles and Secret Techniques*, for I felt that to give the Okinawan side of the karate story was to highlight this very aspect.

Health and the nurturing of it are just as important now as they were over a quarter of a century ago when I first set foot on Okinawan shores, yet the message that health is of paramount importance, in any martial artist's training, is still sadly lacking. The bare-knuckled facts are that although we train in methods of self-defence, we are far more likely to be hurt in a badly managed dojo than on the street, and we are still more likely to sustain long-term injuries through improper training – even when coached with all sincerity.

In 1976 I returned to my native England for eighteen months and taught Okinawan karate 'for health and self-defence'. However, the one-dimensional approach of learning by rote that was evident there shocked me; the damage that was being done to trainees was frightening. I wanted to help my contemporary karate teachers in Britain to see the reality of what they were doing and to guide them into seeing the likely results if they continued along the same determined path. It was like shouting into a typhoon with deaf ears.

Okinawa, being on the periphery of Japan, was not so affected as the home islands by militaristic indoctrination. Although the karate introduced to mainland Japan from Okinawa was to play a major role in the pre-War militarisation, karate – as it remained on Okinawa – did not suffer this fate to any such degree. Hence the ethos behind any Okinawan *dojo kun*, the underlying, unwritten (often unstated) principle, was to train each other up in a spiritual brotherhood, not to knock each other down in the name of competitive spirit.

Foreigners who trained on Okinawa in the post Second World War era, often failed to adjust to these non-competitive principles and many were disappointed that reality did not live up to preconceived myth. But, in some ways, they were the lucky ones. Those who discovered the true strength of Okinawan karate often had to do so by being confronted directly with its internal, subtle strengths if, for example, a senior were to step in to cool down a potentially aggressive situation. In the unfortunate event of resorting to the physical, one controlled strike would usually suffice to bring home the reality that the negative behavioural trait being expressed was not culturally acceptable. By then, though, unknown to the recipient, it was too late. In the Okinawan dojo, it was the knowledge of the very deathly power of these strikes that prevented chaos and ensured self-discipline, for most Okinawans knew of the delayed havoc reeked within the internal organs of the recipient, like a bomb on a timed fuse. Suffering from a mysterious disease, months or even years later, many an overseas visiting trainee thus found out the hard, cruel way; I was not one of them.

On my final return to England in 1990, most of the teachers and students who had cast a deaf ear and a blind eye to the principles behind long-term, healthy training, the principles that I had been expounding 13 years earlier, were in a sorry state of repair. Since then, through more sensible training regimes, Alternative Exercises and Shiatsu, I have been able to assist in aiding many martial artists back on to a healthier road. There is no doubt that *Okinawan Karate: Teachers, Styles and Secret Techniques* has been a major force in this process of change, both as an initial contact point and as a back-up to my teachings. Much to my regret, though, for some Westerners the message of 'training primarily for health' has come too late and several well-known *karate-ka* (some much younger than myself) have unnecessarily suffered a premature death, or have become physically and emotionally incapacitated. It is disheartening to see budding martial artists, less than half my age, struggle mindlessly through adrenaline-based training programmes, with damaged joints and internal organs crying out for nourishment; even more so to see young children's bodies being irreparably damaged through such mistaken training, while their spiritual development is crushed.

Yet this problem was not so uncommon on Okinawa either. Most of the teachers I interviewed or have represented are now deceased, some having led a full life, others not. For all of them the major issue had been the preservation of vitality and attaining a fruitful old age, where wisdom would rule supreme. For many of them, this book remains the only direct written testament of their achievements and failures, as expressed from their mouths – for it is from our predecessors' past mistakes that wisdom surely develops. Their desire (sometimes outwardly emotional) to pass on to the younger generation of *karate-ka* these life-time experiences – how to avoid the same mistakes that they themselves had made when younger and had, to a lesser or greater extent, suffered from as a result – is the ultimate statement of this work. Therefore, as I dedicate this second edition of *Okinawan Karate* to their memory, I urge you to please listen to the ideals revealed in the wise statements of these teachers and let their words remain a testimony for all time.

Mark Bishop
Sussex, England, 1998

Introduction

Okinawa Prefecture, made up of the Southern and Central Ryukyu Islands, is now politically controlled by and is an integral part of modern Japan. The island of Okinawa, from which the Prefecture derives its name, has been the most important of the Ryukyu Islands, in an economic as well as a cultural sense, from the dawn of history.

The island is by no means large, with a total area of approximately 1,256 sq km (450 sq miles), a length of about 108km (67 miles), and a width varying between 5 and 24km (3 and 14 miles). The sub-tropical marine climate is affected by the warm Kuroshio Current that sweeps up from the Philippines, bringing frequent typhoons between March and September. Northern Okinawa is heavily forested and sparsely populated, whereas the densely populated south, which has recently experienced an economic boom, boasts several cosmopolitan cities; the largest is the sprawling city of Naha. The Greater Naha Area now includes within its boundaries the former towns of Naha, Shuri and Tomari where karate was originally nurtured.

The history of Okinawa

Historically, by the early part of the 14th century, the island of Okinawa, which had been ruled by several feudal lords (anji), became divided into the three states of Hokuzan (in the north), Chuzan (in the middle) and Nanzan (in the south). The Three Kingdoms, as they were known, were united in 1429 under a leader called Sho Hashi who made his capital at Shuri. Sometime later another ruler, Sho Shin (who reigned from 1477 to 1526), put a stop to feudalism, formed a Confucianist state, made the anji move to Shuri, imposed a ban on the wearing of swords and made the private ownership of arms in large quantities illegal.

The Kingdom of Ryukyu, as the country was known, expanded and prospered through trade with China (mostly via Fuchou in Fukien Province), South East Asia, Korea and Japan until 1609 when it was invaded by the Satsuma clan from Southern Kyushu. From then on, although remaining effectively a semi-independent trading nation and keeping close ties with China, Ryukyu was economically milked by Satsuma and gradually declined in wealth. Satsuma reinforced the 'weapons edicts' originally imposed by Sho Shin and in 1699 banned the import of all bladed weapons. In 1724, due to an overexpansion of the Ryukyuan upper classes (shizoku) in Shuri, the latter were permitted to trade, make handicrafts or become pioneer farmers in the countryside or outlying islands; to which many emigrated, taking their culture with them. The overworked peasants however remained in a permanent state of near serfdom, until the Ryukyu Islands were annexed by the post-Restoration government of Japan in 1879 and the Ryukyuan king, Sho Tai, was exiled to Tokyo.

The new Meiji government made the island of Okinawa a part of Okinawa Prefecture and set about Japanising the old Okinawan ways, which were considered to be rather 'foreign'. This trend continued through the Taisho and early Showa Eras as Japan became more and more militaristic, only terminating with the Japanese defeat at the end of the Second World War.

The American occupation of the Ryukyu Islands, which brought about a social and economic revolution, began with their invasion (the Battle of Okinawa) by US forces on 1 April 1945 and, for Okinawa Prefecture, lasted until reversion on 15 May 1972 when political control was returned to Japan, ushering in a new era of peace and prosperity.

Karate on Okinawa

The first recorded advent of karate, or tode as it was then known, is generally agreed to have been in the latter part of the 18th or early 19th century,[1] when a Chinese going by the name of Kusanku (also Ku Shanku or Koso Kun) displayed his Chinese boxing and grappling skills on Okinawa to a delighted audience. Tode (also to-te or tuti, lit. Chinese hand) can be taken to mean Chinese boxing, although it was antedated for several hundred years by a martial art known simply as ti (later this term was Japanised to 'te', meaning hands) which is still in existence and has affected the technical and fighting forms of some modern karate styles. Generally speaking, the introduction of tode (i.e. karate) to Okinawa was effected by either Okinawans who studied Chinese boxing in China or Chinese, like Kusanku, who taught it on Okinawa. Tode began to be called karate in the first half of the 20th century[2] and although its introduction since its debut has been a continuous process, most of the karate which is taught today is, contrary to popular belief, based on the Chinese boxing (mostly from the Fuchou area) that was introduced to Okinawa between the years 1850–1950, reaching its peak of introduction towards the end of the 19th century.

It is necessary to point out here that prior to 1879 martial arts on Okinawa had been reserved solely for the upper-class families and even after that date few ordinary folk were able, if willing, to practise them. I have found not the slightest scrap of historical evidence to even suggest, as is often put forward, that weaponless Okinawan peasants developed fighting systems as a means to overthrow their Satsuma overlords. On the contrary, as will be seen, all evidence demonstrates that after 1609 ti was practised for self-defence and as a personal means of self-development by the nobility. Tode followed suit, developing in the late 19th and early 20th centuries among the shizoku class and their descendants.

Part of the blame for the promulgation of such romantic myths must be put on the Okinawans themselves who, during the pre-war militaristic Japanese administration years, foresaw the role karate could play in the military machine and, with typical propriety, disguised its Chinese roots. This, plus confusion with the Chinese Boxer Rebellion of 1900 and the ever-present vagueness concerning dates (the term 'mukashi' – lit. once upon a time, or a long time ago – is still annoyingly used to date any time from between 10 and 10,000 years ago), gave just the right ingredients. Other factors have been the cultural tendencies stemming from Confucianism which dictate that nothing derogatory should be voiced about social seniors or the deceased; plus the annoying habit of (when not wanting to offend the interviewer) convincingly answering questions by guessing incorrectly, when a simple, 'I'm sorry, I don't know' would more than suffice. During my interviews I was often astounded that whereas a teacher would know all there is to know about his own style, he would know next to nothing about most others. Most karate teachers did not even know that ti still exists, thinking it had been mysteriously absorbed by karate some time in the dim, distant past.

Be that as it may, whereas ti was historically the martial art of the Ryukyuan kings, princes and anji who lived at Shuri, karate, as already mentioned, was developed by shizoku and their descendants in the main population centres of Naha, Tomari and Shuri,[3] becoming categorised by the local townspeople into the somewhat confusing terms of Naha-te, Tomari-te and Shuri-te: i.e. the karate, not the ti, taught respectively at Naha, Tomari and Shuri. Although karate is nowadays taken to mean empty hands, many of the modern styles actually include weapons practice (kobudo) as part of their curriculum.

Because much of modern-day karate cannot be classified as either Naha-te, Tomari-te or Shuri-te, it was decided not to use these out-of-date terms and instead to represent karate, which incidentally has never been unified at any time for any cause, according to its various styles or 'ryu'. Many of the styles were given their names in the social confusion after the Second World War, when financially hard-pressed Okinawans realised karate's commercial value and opened an array of ramshackle private gyms. During the time of the Vietnam War, Okinawa became an important US military supply base and karate became all the more popular among the servicemen, some of whom introduced their styles to the United States and elsewhere. Later, the popularity of Okinawan karate increased world-wide as Okinawans themselves went overseas to teach. However, as the most well-known styles in the West have often been written about and because 'popular' does not necessarily equal 'best' (after all is said and done, a style is only as good as the practitioner), I have tried, whenever information was available, to give more effort and space to introducing the lesser-known styles. I have also avoided introducing karate presently being taught at the island's many US military bases because, although Okinawans teach at these, they are not usually permitted to train at them.

The material is presented in three main divisions: Part I deals with the styles that are claimed to be based on 'complete' Chinese boxing systems: among these is Goju-ryu which was originally called Shorei-ryu and was known locally as Naha-te. In Part II the 'Shorin' group of styles are introduced. On Okinawa the general term used to describe these styles is Shorin-ryu and, as will be seen, the styles are for the most part a mixture of what were known as Tomari-te and Shuri-te. Some of these styles also contain an admixture of Naha-te, i.e. Goju-ryu. Tomari-te is not nowadays taught commercially as a separate style, but has been included as such for its historical significance. Part III consists of the kobu-do and the ti styles. Although all the kobudo styles concentrate on teaching the use of weapons and weapon katas (forms), two of these styles also include empty-hand karate training in their curriculums. Therefore, although it was not my original intention to include the kobudo styles in this work, I have found it nec-essary to give both an historical and modern-day introduction of them, reserving the technical details for a later book on Okinawan weaponry. Likewise, ti is taught side by side with karate and kobudo (ti also has a weapons system peculiar to itself), making an introduction of the ti styles also a necessity.

Many of the 'more dangerous secret techniques' (which were sometimes demonstrated on me with frightening consequences) were passed on to me in confidence on pledges of secrecy; but, as the holding back of knowledge is often more harmful than its release and because one man's secret is general knowledge to another, I have opted to include these. In doing this, however, I accept no responsibility for any injuries that may occur from someone wanting to find out if the techniques really work. Likewise, 'dangerous' vital points were included to demonstrate where and how one should not strike a fellow human being if one wished to seek a long-term friendship with him or her. Included under the term 'secret techniques' are the 'secret principles' which, in some styles, take the form of breathing, relaxation and intrinsic energy circulation exercises that are consid-ered by some to be one thousand times more important than any technique and should be studied carefully.

The barrage of personal and place names (which have been kept to a mini-mum) may be found to be a little confusing, so wherever possible the modern-day Japanised renderings of Okinawan personal names have been used with Okinawan or Chinese nicknames in brackets; honorary titles are in capitals. Easy reference lineage charts have also been included for each style and/or teacher (these charts include the names of students with higher grades regardless of whether or not they operate branch clubs). As far as possible place names have also been written in their modern Japanese rendering and maps are included (Appendix A) for ready location of these. Appendix B is a glossary of the other Japanese, Okinawan and Chinese words used in the text. As the names of katas (as well as their movements) vary from style to style, a list of the katas presently taught on Okinawa (Appendix C) has been included. As weapons also often have several names and because many will be unknown to some readers, a list and description of all those kobudo weapons presently taught on Okinawa (Appendix D) has also been included. Appendices E and F will help the reader to gain an overall picture of the introduction and development of the karate styles; Appendix G shows the vital points for each of the karate styles. Appendix H has information on the respective heads of the styles, their associations and addresses.

REFERENCES

[1] Shoshin Nagamine in *The Essence of Okinawan Karate-Do* gives the exact date as early as 1761.

[2] The term tode was still used by some styles well into the 1960s and one 'new' style, namely Jukendo, has adopted neither term and is still referred to as Chinese boxing.

[3] Naha, Tomari and Shuri are all within a few kilometres of each other.

Part I

Styles based on Chinese boxing systems

Chapter 1
Jukendo

There is always a tendency in dealing with any fighting art for practitioners to reject and unfairly criticise methods that are not known, or are 'new' to them. More so perhaps does this attitude flourish on Okinawa among karate teachers and trainers, who, more often than not, will reject Chinese boxing in general as being 'too soft and flowery'.

Of late, various Chinese boxing styles, like T'ai-chi Chuan (mirroring the world-wide trend), have come to Okinawa and have been taught as such with little or no alteration. But in fact (as already noted in the Introduction), for the past 180 years or so, several Chinese boxing styles have been introduced into Okinawa, modified and taught as karate. To illustrate fully the importance of the influence of Chinese boxing on the development of karate, and to show that the introduction of Chinese boxing has been and still is a continuous process, Jukendo, which has undergone a certain amount of 'karatefication', is first to be introduced in this work.

The style

Jukendo is a Taiwanese-based Chinese boxing system recently introduced to Okinawa Prefecture and taught on Miyako Island by the president of the All Japan Jukendo Association, Akio Kinjo. As a young man, Akio Kinjo learned Goju-ryu from the Higa family, but later studied Jukendo (lit. soft-fist way) under Kinryu, the Golden Dragon (also Tung Chin Tsan), on Taiwan. An introduction to the style is best narrated in Kinjo's own words as translated from a programme for a Jukendo demonstration held at Naha in 1975:

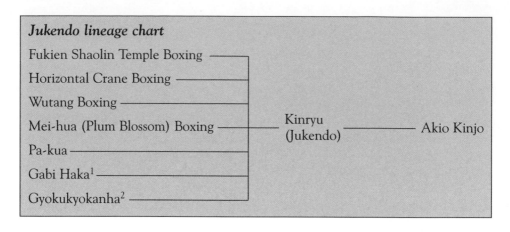

Jukendo lineage chart

Fukien Shaolin Temple Boxing		
Horizontal Crane Boxing		
Wutang Boxing		
Mei-hua (Plum Blossom) Boxing	Kinryu (Jukendo)	Akio Kinjo
Pa-kua		
Gabi Haka[1]		
Gyokukyokanha[2]		

Jukendo is a synthesis of the seven biggest styles of Chinese boxing.

It is a splendid thing that of late Japan has succeeded to great heights of economic growth. However, on the other hand, it is regretful that the human mind has fallen into disuse and there is a tendency to forget to improve oneself in favour of gaining worldly desires.

It is indeed a sad state of affairs when we hear that the youth of today are inactive, irresponsible, indifferent and unreasonable. However cheerful they appear to be, internal cultivation is lacking. They have only momentary pleasures and have no control over spiritual anguish. When there is anything unfavourable they take to destructive group behaviour, etc. Those youths who discard their own individuality and use it enthusiastically for the benefit of society are few.

The history of all ages, East and West, relates the well established fact that unfortunately such spiritually weak societies will certainly collapse. Therefore I earnestly feel that the advancement of spirit and the development of a robust physique is of necessity to the country's youth. The first step to success in leading the youth of Japan was taken with the gathering together of pupils for instruction after the construction of the first dojo (officially called the Kensei Budokan) in my native town of Shimozato, Hirara City, Miyako Island, in June of 1973. The purpose of instruction is to spread the three great objectives: reverence towards the founder, health and self-defence, and the correct use of energy. My disciples are like my own children to me. As if they were close brothers and sisters, I act quite frankly towards them without reserve, sometimes scolding them with a loud voice, sometimes complimenting them and sometimes appeasing them, etc. I affect leadership by means of burning passion and a hint of composure. Those among my disciples who zealously prosecute their studies for more than six months will be seen to change in behaviour, decorum and personal appearance, and have a fresh, lively disposition.

I desire ardently from my heart that everybody can comprehend and will bestow their support on us. Thank you very much for attending this demonstration.

An Outline of Jukendo

Chinese boxing may be roughly classified into two groups, the hard-fist and the soft-fist. The values of the hard-fist systems are external – physical endurance is aimed at, tensing of the body, strengthening of the bones and the flesh, and striking, using only the exterior physical strength of the body, are practised. Technically, from start to finish, there is a general tendency to stress force when striking, kicking and blocking.

On the other hand, the values of the soft-fist systems are internal. Instead of being tense, the body is relaxed and left in its natural state. The internal organs of the body are strengthened by the flow of energy, nerve circulation is regulated, body movements are refined. Rather than using strength for carrying out techniques, the 'mysterious' power of 'ki' (intrinsic energy) is issued from the interior of the body and thrust horizontally and vertically in mutual association to form an outward blow. The skills of the hard-fist are few; they attach much importance to adeptness in striking, thrusting, kicking and blocking, etc. On the other hand, the soft-fist styles have the same thrust, strike, kick and block techniques, but the movements are mainly executed along a circle or curve – and that is not all, all kinds of other important techniques are similarly cultivated, giving an ever-changing appearance.

Actually, there are thousands of schools of boxing described as being hard-fist, a representative list includes: Tai-tsu Ch'ang Chuan, Lohan Chuan (Buddha's Disciples' Boxing), Hung Chia Chuan, Honan Chuan (derived from the original Shaolin Temple Boxing), Yung Ch'un Chuan, Tan T'ui Men Chuan, Tang Lang Chuan (Mantis Boxing), etc. If all were counted they would be found to be innumerable. Technically, among these schools there are hard styles and soft styles which are all, however, generally referred to as being hard. Compared with these there are numerically few soft-fist styles. Historically, 2,000 years ago, after years of refinement and improvement, the leading boxing schools of the country (i.e. China) were Mei Hua and Pa Kua, etc. Although Fukien Shaolin, Yunnan White Crane, Gabi Haka,[3] Gyokukyokanha[4] and the Wutang styles, etc. did not materialise until a long time after this, these styles are accepted as being the most famous. After the Ming dynasty these seven styles were granted highest status by the Chinese Martial Arts Association. Other styles described as being soft are Hsing-i Chuan, Monkey Boxing, Horizontal Crane Boxing and T'ai-chi Chuan.

The honourable founder of Jukendo, Professor Kinryu, had a flair for martial arts from his youngest days. Both his parents were adept at Chinese boxing and quite wealthy. When Kinryu was eight years old a hard-fist master was politely invited to coach at the family mansion. When aged 15 or 16, Kinryu received tuition from Hoa Funsai[5] (Ho Feng of Fukien), originator of the Horizontal White Crane system at the Sazan Kozan[6] Temple in Fukien, where he was struck with admiration by the subtleness and excellence of the soft-fist. At last, when the opportunity arose, Kinryu made up his mind to make a study tour of the central schools and, eventually, after much suffering, blood, sweat and falling tears, he acquired success in all the famous styles.

Teacher's accomplishments in understanding the martial arts can be said to have crystallised from his famous boxing lineage, natural intelligence and wealth of his parents, coupled with his almost insane, super-human enthusiasm for practice.

But in those days, however much enthusiasm and faith one had, in order to be granted instruction in the true techniques of Chinese boxing, one needed to pay a vast fortune to the school. In this respect, when Teacher was initiated into the Mei Hua, Pa Kua and Fukien Shaolin Temple schools, he offered as payment an immense sum (equivalent to eleven two-storey houses) to the respective headquarters of the schools. Whilst doctoring in Chinese medicine at his own clinic, Professor Kinryu synthesised the skills of the seven most famous styles into the Jukendo which he teaches his pupils. It can indeed be said that he is a rare and remarkable person.

Despite Kinjo's obviously flattering words for his teacher, a more down-to-earth introduction to Kinryu is given by Robert W. Smith in his book *Chinese Boxing, Masters and Methods*, under Tung Chin-tsan. Here he states that the Golden Dragon (i.e. Kinryu) spent three years in a Taiwanese corrective labour camp for being implicated with the underworld Black Dragon Society. Smith goes on to say that besides the monk Ho Feng, Kinryu had also learned Chinese boxing from the monk Wei-chen, Ch'en Yu-an, Hsiao Yao-t'ing of Kiangsi, the monk Pai-ho Shou-feng-mu of Yunnan, Lu Ta-ting of Taiwan and some Japanese masters. He had also visited the Shaolin Temple in Fukien. At first Smith had not been impressed by the demonstration given by Kinryu's students, calling what they did 'pseudo judo', but was later reassured of Kinryu's ability when he watched him working out on a wooden dummy, calling his attacks, 'swift and crisp'.

REFERENCES

[1] Japanese pronunciation.
[2] Japanese pronunciation.
[3] Japanese pronunciation.
[4] Japanese pronunciation.
[5] Japanese pronunciation.
[6] Japanese pronunciation.

Chapter 2
Ryuei-ryu; Goju-ryu; Uechi-ryu; Pangai-noon-ryu

To avoid confusion, these styles, excluding modern-day Pangai-noon-ryu, have been arranged in their historical order of introduction to Okinawa, but actually Goju-ryu is the most well known of them in the West. Uechi-ryu, due to the efforts of George E. Mattson, comes a close second, whereas Ryuei-ryu, whose introduction from Fuchou actually preceded the other two, is little known even on Okinawa. The similarities (both historical and technical) between these three styles are obvious, more than suggesting a common root of origin, which is believed by some to have been a derivative form of Pa-kua and Shaolin Temple boxing taught at Fuchou in the second half of the 19th and early 20th centuries.

Ryuei-ryu
Norisato Nakaima (c. 1850–1927)
This little-known style was introduced to Okinawa sometime between the years 1870 to 1880 by Norisato Nakaima (Nakaima PECHIN) who had learned Chinese boxing and Chinese weaponry in China. Born of wealthy parents at Kume, Naha, Norisato was a good scholar and at the age of 19 went to Fuchou in China for advanced studies. Whilst there, a former guard to Chinese

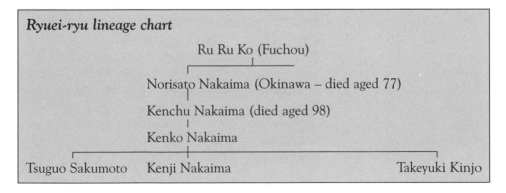

Ryuei-ryu lineage chart

Ru Ru Ko (Fuchou)

Norisato Nakaima (Okinawa – died aged 77)

Kenchu Nakaima (died aged 98)

Kenko Nakaima

Tsuguo Sakumoto   Kenji Nakaima   Takeyuki Kinjo

embassies in Ryukyu introduced him to a Chinese boxing teacher known as Ru Ru Ko. Norisato was accepted as a disciple and after five or six years of practice received a certificate of graduation. Just before leaving China, in order to further his experience of the martial arts, he travelled in the Fukien, Canton and Peking areas where he collected many weapons which he brought home with him. Norisato Nakaima passed his Chinese boxing style in secret to his son Kenchu who taught it only to his son Kenko Nakaima, founder and president of the Ryuei-ryu Karate and Kobudo Preservation Society.

Kenko Nakaima

In 1971, at the age of 60, Kenko Nakaima realised that in today's world there was no longer a necessity to keep his family fighting system secret so, with some hesitation, he took on a group of 20 school teachers as karate students and gave the name Ryuei-ryu to the style. When I visited him at his house near Nago, this powerfully built man was in his late 60s and showed signs of ageing. Also, his sense of guilt over breaking the secrecy pledge he had made to his father was still very obvious.

As a young boy Kenko had started a strict regimen of training in his court-yard, 'by the light of the moon – to preserve the secrecy', which lasted for 37 years, until he had learned all there was to learn. During this time he also trained in kendo under Seibu Tomigawa, Hiroshi Ishihara and Shochoku Ishihara, eventually receiving a kyoshi grade. He also learned Anko Itosu-type karate[1] and Yamani-type kobudo[2] from Chojo Oshiro,[3] as well as Matsumura-type karate from Kentsu Yabu.[4] However, despite his wide experience in the fighting arts, Nakaima takes pride in his claim that he has not altered his grand-father's style (thus Ru Ru Ko's) and does not mix the teaching with that of any other.

Katas

Ryuei-ryu incorporates eleven empty hand katas: Sanchin, Sesan, Niseshi, Sanseru, Seyonchin, Ohan, Pachu, Anan, Paiku, Heiku and Paiho, as well as practice with 14 Chinese weapons: sai, kama, renkuwan, tinbe, gekiguan, kon, bisento, yari, taofua, suruchin, dajio, nunchiku, tankon and gusan. Although sparring is important, students must first learn katas, which consist primarily of flat fist techniques. However, if a student wishes to adopt the foreknuckle or straight fingers strike into his katas, he may do so.

Nakaima told me that the flat fist corkscrew punch is by no means of Okinawan origin, as is often claimed, as this punch is commonly used in China and frequently appears in his system. Sanchin, the basic kata, is virtually the same as that of Goju-ryu and Uechi-ryu, only the finer points are different. The hand forms of Ryuei-ryu's Sanchin can be readily adopted in a fighting situation; the feet are held straight without the toes being turned in, 'as such pigeon-toe-ing,' Nakaima told me, 'makes the Sanchin stance unnatural and impairs manoeuvrability'. On the other hand, if the feet are splayed out one can be easily thrown. One should merely feel that the toes are turned in. Whilst doing Sanchin the breathing is 'natural'; breathing out with a sharp 'hiss' on striking. 'In combat,' Nakaima said, 'your respiration should be undetectable; the proper time to attack is when your opponent is exhaling, as he will not be able to move or dodge out of the way. Always try to dodge an attack either to the rear or side, never use strength when blocking.'

Nakaima does not believe in the hard, so he encourages Ryuei-ryu practitioners to keep their bodies soft and supple, then at the moment of striking, to focus all their energies on the one point. 'Judo and kendo use the same principles,' he told me, 'so be soft.' To illustrate this principle further, he used the analogy of mochi (Japanese rice cake). At first mochi is sticky boiled rice which is pounded until it starts to get lumpy; the pounding continues until the mochi is smooth and soft, but springy to the touch. This is the highest stage of a student's kata development – kata that looks as if it has no strength at all.

'About thirty years ago,' he told me, 'karate tournament competitions became popular on the Japanese mainland and this brought on the onset of a new type of sparring in which the fighters did not wear protectors or gloves but "pulled" their punches. At the same time a new type of kata evolved in which, geared for competition, looks became all important.' Nakaima went on to say that such katas have little to do with the fighting arts; he called them, 'karate dances' and compared them to 'unfinished mochi complete with the lumps'.

Many moves in traditional katas may seem to be unnecessary, but Nakaima warned against altering these, instead 'one should analyse katas to find the good points for use in fighting and feel when and how to use them.'

Protectors

The former headmaster (now retired) of a junior high school, Nakaima has taught Itosu-type katas and free-sparring at schools for more than 30 years. He also did much to encourage the wearing of full protectors (helmet, breastplate and gloves) during free-sparring practice and was one of the leaders behind the movement that brought about the compulsory adoption of protectors for all Okinawan high school karate free-sparring competitions since about 1950 (at present on Okinawa, only the annual Uechi-ryu adult competitions are held without body protectors; in these often bloody bouts the adherents wear mitts and are supposed to pull their punches in the mainland fashion).

Since breaking the family secrecy pledge and teaching Ryuei-ryu publicly, seven North Island high school karate clubs have adopted Ryuei-ryu officially. The emphasis in these clubs is on free-sparring and one of them (Nago High's), Nakaima claims, is a force to be reckoned with in the Kyushu/Okinawa and all Japan full protector free-sparring contests.

Protectors, it was explained to me, allow for full contact without injury to either party; however, strikes to the back, the side of the head or groin and grabbing or throwing are forbidden. The use of these illegal techniques will constitute a foul and possibly result in disqualification.

Some practitioners argue that the breastplate slows them down and that the helmet inhibits vision, but Nakaima said that as both parties have the same disadvantages, they stand on equal ground and if given the choice of fighting with or without, he would choose to wear the protector despite its setbacks, as he considers health to be of prime importance.

As a boy, Nakaima wore a kendo protector during sparring practice and says that there is still need for development, especially on the breastplate, which should be padded with something soft on the inside and something hard like bamboo on the outside. In mainland Japan, where protectors are rarely worn during adult contests, there are, Nakaima told me, many injuries; these do not all materialise immediately, like say a nose bleed, but become apparent after some time. Some more obvious examples are a strike to the ear which may result in deafness, or a strike to the eye which can later result in blindness. Even an unintentional strike to a vital point may result in an illness or premature death as much as several years after the incident actually occurred.

Competition karate

Nakaima claims that Japanese sport karate competitions are unrealistic as speed is all one needs to win; balance, a very important part of any fighting art, thus becomes inconsequential. He would actually like to see matches with full protectors last for a fixed round (say two or three minutes) rather than ending when someone is struck. In this way the contestants could be judged on all their finer points throughout the whole round rather than at one often lucky moment. In his words, 'under the present system, the wrong man often wins'.

During an actual life or death situation, Nakaima cautioned to make sure that one's fists are closed tight shut. 'If the attacker is stronger than oneself stab the foreknuckle into his ribs, because, even if it strikes a rib bone it will roll off the rounded surface into the more vulnerable nerves in the connecting tissue. Always think of attacking vital points as only a tap to the groin, eyes or nose is usually sufficient to disorientate an adversary. Train in manoeuvrability rather than body hardening so that one can avoid any attack instantaneously.'

Nakaima went on to say that karate consists of mostly punching and kicking and so, because it is difficult to throw someone, never try to. 'Throwing takes too much time, during which your opponent will gain an advantage and strike you.' Ryuei-ryu has only two throws, both of which use a body-to-body strike for off-balancing before the actual throw. The makiwara punching board (which Nakaima stated quite firmly is of Chinese origin and not Okinawan as many teachers think) is used for developing a powerful punch, and the chi-ishi (or chikara-ishi) for arm strength. He also told me that until the early part of this century kobudo was known as kobujutsu, the 'jutsu' was changed to 'do' after the introduction of Japanese ken*do* and ju*do*, in imitation of the latters' sport-orientated names. Karate (i.e. tode) jutsu later followed suit, eventually becoming karate-do. Another interesting point that Nakaima mentioned was that although the names may be Okinawanised, all of Ryuei-ryu's weapons and weapon systems are most assuredly of Chinese origin and he explained that they were in no way developed, as some would like to suggest, by Okinawan peasant farmers from agricultural implements.

Nakaima's final advice to me was to 'stick with one style but learn as many fighting techniques as possible from other styles'.

Author's note for the second edition Previously thought of as a lesser-known style, Ryuei-ryu is now well known due to the fame of Tsuguo Sakumoto. It has become established around the San Diego and California areas under the leadership of Tomohiro Arashiro, a former student of Kenko Nakaima's, reportedly from the days when Nakaima informally taught the family style in his courtyard at Nago. Kenko Nakaima passed away in 1989, the very year *Okinawan Karate* was first published, and my regret is that he probably never got to read the write-up on my interview with him. I feel that I did him justice though, especially concerning his insistence that kata, like their exponents, should grow more pliant with age, and that we should be aware of the dangers of competition without wearing full protectors. If he could see what has happened to his family style in recent years, with regard to the hardening process of the form and unprotected 'sportification', I am sure Kenko Nakaima would roll in his tomb many times over. He is succeeded by his son Kenji Nakaima, a Ryukyu University professor, but Kenji does not encourage the contemporary trends in Ryuei-ryu.

Tsuguo Sakumoto

The only one of Kenko Nakaima's disciples presently teaching Ryuei-ryu on a public basis is Tsuguo Sakumoto, a high school sports teacher who teaches Ryuei-ryu karate at the Onna Village Community Hall on Fridays from 6pm to 10pm and in conjunction with Nakaima (who instructs the seniors in weapons) on Tuesdays from 8pm to 10pm. On a visit to one of these classes, I found Sakumoto to be rather boyish and bristling with over-confidence. The sport karate he taught seemed to conflict with all that his teacher had told me about the style, but, like Nakaima, Sakumoto was a fighter who seemed to relish fighting – several times our conversation bordered on a challenge which luckily, for the both of us, never materialised.

Sakumoto's karate is, in his own words, 'hard, scientific and modern'. Geared towards competition, the sparring (without a single protector) was rough and undisciplined and, when seniors opposed juniors, often approached the sadistic. He reflected so clearly the attitude of many young Okinawan karate instructors who feel uncomfortable about 'traditional' karate and pay lip service to the older generation of teachers, placing them on high pedestals of unnecessary respect, out of the reach of most students, while teaching so-called 'modern karate' that, in Sakumoto's case at least, has aptly been defined as an abased form of brutality

disguised as sport. But then who could deny the exact brilliance of his dynami-
cally powerful, machine-like katas that now thrill audiences far and near.

Author's note for the second edition Tsuguo Sakumoto has evidently mel-
lowed since the years I knew him personally, when we were both educators on
the same island and both employed by the Okinawan Prefectural Board of
Education. A sports teacher by profession, my fondest memories are of him leading enthusiastic groups of his high-school students on jogging missions through
the streets of Naha, sporting his unmistakable trade-mark, the shaven head.
Certainly, if one of his aims in life has been to enthuse young people into seeing
the importance of physical training, he has succeeded in much, but my own
views on long-term health remain loyal to those of his teacher Kenko Nakaima.

Goju-ryu

Kanryo Higaonna (1853–1917)

Although Goju-ryu is a popular style taught the world over, there is a noticeable
lack of books on the subject. So, because its history also seems hazy, I have
attempted to present the style in as much detail as possible. 'Goju' literally means
'hard-soft' and was the name given to the style by its formulator, Chojun Miyagi.
Although much credit is given to Miyagi for his work, his teacher, Kanryo
Higaonna, who seems to have been pushed to the background, actually laid the
foundations of the style.

Kanryo Higaonna (sometimes written Higashionna), born at Nishimura,
Naha, was the fourth son of Kanyo Higaonna, the ninth generation successor of
the Shin family line. Kanryo's child name was Moshi but he was also nicknamed
Ushi-chi; the Japanese pronunciation for his Chinese name was Shin Zen Enko.
Due to the poverty of his family, who (despite their being descended from shizoku) transported firewood from the Kerama Islands in a small junk, Kanryo's
academic education was neglected. Described as 'small but fast moving with
powerful hips', he, according to some sources, learned the basics of Okinawan ti
when he was a youth and according to Shoshin Nagamine,[5] from the age of 20
he learned tode from Seisho Arakaki (Maiya Arakachi-gwa) of Kume village,
Naha.

Naha at that time was a comparatively large business centre with many
Chinese and Okinawans involved in the Naha-Fuchou trade. Contact with
the Chinese traders meant that more than a few Okinawans had the chance to
learn Chinese boxing and, among these, some became well known for their
expertise in technique – others, who learned a lot of katas and few fighting
techniques, were known derogatorily as exponents of 'Hanchin-di' ('lazy-man's
boxing'). 'Higaonna,' Eiichi Miyazato (my Goju-ryu teacher) told me, 'often had
the chance to talk with both Chinese and Okinawan practitioners from whom
he learned of the Philosophical attitude and super-human feats associated with
Chinese boxing.' However, Higaonna was hard-pressed to find a good teacher

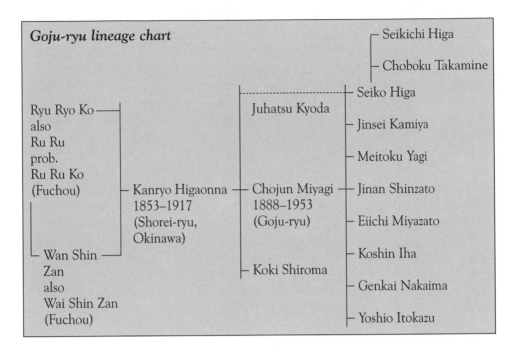

Goju-ryu lineage chart

because boxers of that time were not readily absolved to pass on their secrets and demonstrations of one's technique was considered bad form. According to Miyazato, Higaonna thus decided to journey to China and at the age of 23 or 24 he finally got a passage to Fuchou on an introduction from Yoshimura UDUN.

A slightly different story is presented by Katsumi Murakami in his book *Karate-do to Ryukyu Kobudo*; Murakami was told by his teacher Juhatsu Kyoda (a disciple of Higaonna) that as a young boy Kanryo Higaonna had actually been an aide to Yoshimura UDUN and travelled to China with him several times.

Sources are also a little confused as to who taught Higaonna Chinese boxing in China. After his arrival at Fuchou, Miyazato told me, Higaonna made wicker baskets for a living and became a live-in disciple of a master called Ryu Ryo Ko (whom Miyazato thought was probably the very same Ru Ru Ko of Ryuei-ryu) and his chief assistant Wan Shin Zan. Nagamine assured me that Higaonna had trained under Wan Shin Zan[6] who eventually, after Higaonna had been pledged to secrecy, taught him the essence of Hsing-i boxing. Juhatsu Kyoda told Murakami that Higaonna had learned Chinese boxing from a teacher called Ru Ru.

Training

Be that as it may, at first, although Higaonna found it difficult to understand the local language, he trained in the basic techniques and breathing methods of the style for five or six hours a day. Often he had to cut the grass, tidy the garden and clean the dojo.[7] According to Nagamine, Higaonna often became very despondent with this life and thought of leaving, but remembering a song taught by his seniors, he stayed on; the gist of this song was, 'anybody can put up with a little, but it takes a man to put up with a lot'.

Next, Higaonna learned the basic kata Sanchin and later the open handed katas Seyonchin, Shisounchin, Sanseiru, Sesan, Kururunfua and Suparinpe. 'In fact,' Nagamine told me, 'Higaonna trained so hard that his legs and hips ached and he passed blood with his urine.' With kata practice and weight training, Higaonna gradually became stronger until after five or six years he was able to better most of his fellow students and became an assistant teacher. Later he became well known in boxing circles as Higaonna of Okinawa. Nagamine also told me that Higaonna learned Chinese weaponry and often read the illustrated Chinese boxing manual known in Japanese as Kenpo Haku, 'because he felt that it contained the essence of Chinese boxing'.

Teaching

The time of Higaonna's return to Okinawa is not certain; Miyazato claimed that Higaonna was aged 32 at the time, while Nagamine said that he was 40. Whatever his age, the small amount of education he had managed to gain whilst in China was of little use to him now that Okinawa was rapidly being Japanised, so he returned to his parents' firewood business and, according to Nagamine, became despondent again and took to the then popular habits of drinking and womanising at the Naha red-lantern district of Tsuji. After several years, the interest shown in karate by the Japanese army brought about an upsurge in the popularity of the art amongst youngsters who, until then, had been rather ashamed of its Chinese origins. Higaonna started to take on sons of wealthy Naha families as students, teaching in the courtyard of his parents' home; but he reputedly refused to teach ruffians and would expel any student who showed bad character traits. Eventually his three most notable students emerged as Chojun Miyagi, Koki Shiroma and Juhatsu Kyoda.

Practice at Higaonna's dojo was tedious with the first three or four years being spent doing only Sanchin and, although to those who persisted Higaonna taught much, many students dropped out through plain boredom. According to most sources Higaonna called his style Shorei-ryu[8] (lit. Enlightened Spirit Style); how-ever, it became commonly known as Naha-te, to distinguish it from the karate taught at Tomari and Shuri (i.e. Tomari-te and Shuri-te). 'Juhatsu Kyoda,' Murakami states,[9] 'was often told by Higaonna that karate was not meant for hurting people, but for helping society' and remembered Higaonna's favourite anecdote as being 'karate needs technique and karate needs a purpose'. Higaonna is also sometimes quoted as having said: 'In the martial arts spiritual improvement is important; so remember that if anything in life blocks your way turn aside and go around it.'

Kenko Nakaima of Ryuei-ryu told me that his father often spoke concerning Higaonna who, he said, was a good friend of BUSHI Kunishi.[10] Although they never actually challenged each other, Kunishi once said to Higaonna, 'If I were unlucky enough to be kicked by you, my leg would surely get broken' to which Higaonna replied, 'If I were to be punched by you, I would most certainly be crushed'. Higaonna's sparring was described by Nakaima as 'light with extraordinary footwork and low, fast kicks.' Thus the foot anchoring, solid stances of modern Goju-ryu stand in contrast to Higaonna's style and it seems likely that, like many teachers of his time, he held much back when teaching fighting techniques.

Despite his active life, Kanryo Higaonna died of illness at the early age of 63 and was succeeded by his top disciple, Chojun Miyagi.

Chojun Miyagi (1888–1953)

Chojun Miyagi was born of reasonably wealthy parents at Higashi Machi, Naha. He was strong in body, fond of sports and often earned the reputation of being an unruly youth. He became a student of Kanryo Higaonna at the age of 14, persevered with the initial training and, after much devotion, his technique improved. In May of 1915 Miyagi and a friend called Gokenki went to Fuchou in search of Higaonna's teacher.

They stayed for a year but everything had changed and, although they visited several masters, the old school was no more – possibly as a result of the Boxer Rebellion of 1900. Gokenki actually seems to have played a large role in Miyagi's life and influenced his karate considerably. A Chinese by birth, Gokenki (1886–1940) became a Japanese citizen and adopted the name Yoshikawa. He was a tea importer by profession, but during his spare time he taught the southern Shaolin form of White Crane Boxing at his tea store in Naha, to a group of four or five youngsters. He charged nothing for his services but expected his students to supply the class with fresh eggs; everyone was required to swallow four or five of these raw during the lesson!

Shortly after Miyagi and Gokenki returned from Fuchou, Higaonna died. Miyagi started to take on students and introduced a kata called Tensho which he had adapted from the Rokkishu of White Crane. This kata, although similar to Sanchin in stance and function, contains techniques using the palm and the back of the wrist to block and strike. Miyagi also introduced the kata Saifua (which has hand and leg movements similar to those of White Crane) and sometime later made Gekisai Ichi and Gekisai Ni katas for teaching to young school-age children.

At one time Miyagi explained the intricacies of karate to Kano Jigoro (the founder of Kodokan judo) who was visiting Okinawa. In 1929 Miyagi became karate instructor at the Prefectural Police School dojo and later taught at the Naha Courthouse, the Prefectural Physical Culture Association, the Prefectural Teachers' Training College and at various Japanese universities on the mainland. In April of 1936 he visited Hawaii on a teaching trip and in the same year went to Shanghai accompanied by his old friend Gokenki.

Whilst at Shanghai the two stayed with the Okinawan historian, Kanjun Higaonna, and Miyagi demonstrated karate to the Japanese ambassadorial staff at the Japanese club. One of Gokenki's disciples, who had tagged along, sought out five books on Chinese boxing and gave them to Miyagi who intended to translate them into Japanese. Unfortunately, they were burned, along with Miyagi's other boxing relics, during the October 1944 air-raid on Naha. On another occasion, during a karate demonstration on the mainland at the Dai Nippon Butokukai in 1937, Miyagi's top disciple, Jinan Shinzato (so the story goes), was asked by some of the presiding officials the name of his teacher's style. Not knowing what to answer, Shinzato consulted Miyagi who replied by quoting his favourite clause from the Kenpo Haku, namely 'go-ju, don-tosu' (hard-soft, spit-swallow or exhale-inhale); so the style became known as Goju-ryu.

At the war's end Miyagi was understandably depressed. Along with his other losses, three of his children had died and his smashed homeland was under US military rule. Despite all this he taught karate to the Ryukyu police and opened a dojo at his house in Tsuboya, Naha, where he later died of a cerebral haemorrhage on 8 October 1953, aged 65.

Jinan Shinzato

Jinan Shinzato was born at Kume village in Naha in 1901. He was a small and weak child, but under Miyagi's tuition became strong and healthy, graduating from the Naha Municipal Commercial School to become a bank clerk, a venereal disease inspector and, later, entering the police force where he took up judo. The historian Genkai Nakaima, also a former student of Miyagi, lived next door to Shinzato and remembered him as being something of an acrobat; he was often observed with a white band around his neck doing one-handed pullups on the lintel of his courtyard gate. In 1939 Shinzato received a renshi grade from the Dai Nippon Butokukai and later, after leaving the police force and entering the Prefectural Office, he taught at the karate and judo clubs of the Prefectural Commercial School. Jinan Shinzato stayed with Miyagi until the former was killed at Kin in Northern Okinawa during the early stages of the Battle of Okinawa in 1945.

Training

Among Miyagi's students, Genkai Nakaima remembered that practice sessions were held in Miyagi's courtyard on Mondays, Wednesdays and Fridays from about 3pm to 8pm. The new students practised preparatory exercises for toning up the body; weight training to make a karate physique; and the foot movements of Sanchin, 'up and down, up and down'.

Nakaima said that Miyagi often spoke for hours on such topics as: the features of karate technique, the present state of the karate world, the origins of Chinese boxing, the connections between the latter and Buddhism, and the association between karate and certain aspects of Okinawan culture. 'Sanchin', Miyagi would say, 'should be practised thirty times a day; in fact, if one were to practise Sanchin all one's life, there would be no reason to learn anything else – Sanchin contains everything.' He once remarked that the last two hand actions of Sanchin correspond to those of certain Buddhist statues.

To explain the secrets of his karate, Miyagi used the analogy of a strong wind blowing against a willow tree: the trunk remains firmly rooted whilst the branches flow with the wind and are unaffected by its superior force. Nakaima had once heard that Miyagi could automatically deflect a silent attack from the rear and innocently asked him if he had eyes in the back of his head, to which Miyagi answered that at such times he had a feeling, a kind of sixth sense.

Miyagi would often remark that being without a teacher was like wandering in the dark and in his quest to find a good one visited many masters, including Chomo Hanashiro.[11] Seitoku Higa (one of my ti teachers) told me that on one such quest Chojun Miyagi, Jinan Shinzato, Seiko Higa and some fellow students, on hearing that Matsu Kinjo (Machiya Buntoku) of Itoman had learned the secret principles of Chinese boxing at Fuchou, went to visit the latter.

After introductions and an explanation as to why they had come, they asked for a demonstration. Kinjo tied a hachimaki around his forehead and started what appeared to be a slow zombie-like dance. Seiko Higa, thinking that the poor old man must be senile, held back, but the quick tempered Shinzato sprang to his feet, announced a challenge and immediately attacked Kinjo on the premise that he was trying to make a fool of them. Kinjo, who had actually been quite sincere about his demonstration, parried and bounced Shinzato out of the door and into the garden where he landed heavily, hurting his back. The others departed without further ado and spoke not a word all the way home. Miyagi was later quoted as having said: 'Once again I am groping my way along an unlit road.'

Eiichi Miyazato, who lost his father during the Battle of Okinawa, looked towards Miyagi as a substitute parent as well as a teacher. He told me that although Goju-ryu training had been severe, there was no military-type drilling, as in modern Japanised karate; this was reserved for the junior and senior high schools. At Miyagi's dojo there were about ten students of a night who practised mostly by themselves, overlooked and corrected by Miyagi, who included much weight training in the regimen.

The dojo was typical of those at that time; a small courtyard surrounded by a stone wall and banyan trees and illuminated by oil lamps – rainy days were holidays. When Miyazato joined the small group he spent the first month doing Sanchin walking, the second month walking and blocking and the third month walking, blocking and punching. He later practised sparring with a protector; in fact he told me that Miyagi believed that if karate could be promoted as a sport with the compulsory wearing of protectors, it would soon become popular throughout the world. For this purpose, Miyagi made and tested (on his students!) various protectors but failed in the final stages of development due to the lack of materials in the immediate post-war era. Miyazato also recalled that the secret principles of karate, as related by Miyagi, were 'a humble attitude coupled with hard practice'.

Katas
Kenko Nakaima told me that although Miyagi was his senior he knew him well as they met now and again at Nago when Miyagi toured Okinawa on training courses held at the various police stations. Nakaima remarked that none of Miyagi's students could approach him in technique and that he also performed splendid katas during which he used his powerful hips generously. Nakaima also believed that Miyagi introduced the hard dynamic-tension type of breathing into the style. Yuchoku Higa of Shorin-ryu (Kobayashi), whose parents were very close to Chojun Miyagi, said that Miyagi did katas with large, powerful, circular hip movements and 'was a strict teacher who made sure you did it right'. Higa had been so beloved of Miyagi that on hearing the news of his death this hitherto non-smoker lit up a cigarette and has not stopped smoking since.

Altogether, Miyagi taught twelve katas which still form the basis of modern day Goju-ryu. These are namely: Sanchin, Gekisai-ichi, Gekisai-ni, Saifua, Seiyonchin, Shisouchin, Sanseiru, Sepai, Kururunfua, Sesan, Suparinpe and Tensho.

After the death of Miyagi, Gogen Yamaguchi carried on his work on the Japanese mainland. On Okinawa three of Miyagi's disciples, Eiichi Miyazato, Meitoku Yagi and Seiko Higa, opened karate clubs and taught Goju-ryu.

Eiichi Miyazato
Eiichi Miyazato's father, a merchant by trade, had at one time been a student of Kanryo Higaonna and so, on his father's introduction, Miyazato entered Miyagi's dojo in 1935 at the age of 13. Except for a brief respite during the Second World War, when he was posted to Manchuria, he never left his teacher's side. Miyazato assisted Miyagi at the Tsuboya dojo until the latter's death when, at the request of his fellow students and Miyagi's family, he assumed teaching responsibilities and remained until the construction of his first gym, the Jundokan, at Asato, Naha in 1957.

Miyazato also succeeded Miyagi as chief karate instructor of the police school where he taught self-defence and judo. He had started judo training at the age of 14 under a local teacher called Shoko Itokazu and later was able to train for a while at the Kodokan in Tokyo, eventually gaining a 6th Dan grade in judo. At one time Miyazato was the all Okinawa judo champion and the all Japan police judo champion; currently he is president of the Okinawa Judo Federation.

In 1969 Miyazato built the present Jundokan, a well-equipped gym with changing rooms and hot and cold showers. In 1971, as rumour has it, he resigned from the police school due to a hush-hush scandal involving some underworld associates and became the director of a small haulage company.

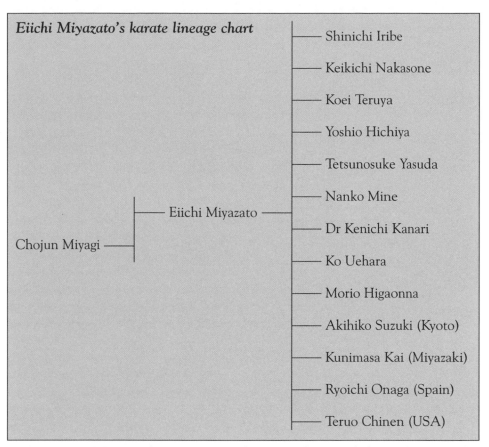

Eiichi Miyazato's karate lineage chart

Chojun Miyagi — Eiichi Miyazato —
- Shinichi Iribe
- Keikichi Nakasone
- Koei Teruya
- Yoshio Hichiya
- Tetsunosuke Yasuda
- Nanko Mine
- Dr Kenichi Kanari
- Ko Uehara
- Morio Higaonna
- Akihiko Suzuki (Kyoto)
- Kunimasa Kai (Miyazaki)
- Ryoichi Onaga (Spain)
- Teruo Chinen (USA)

At present, Miyazato has approximately 500 students and claims that over the years since 1953 he has trained more than 12,000 karate-ka. Among his notables is the dynamic Morio Higaonna who used to run a small but much respected dojo in a dingy part of Yoyogi in Tokyo, but who now teaches at his new dojo in Tsuboya, Naha. I trained for a year at the Yoyogi dojo and it was on Higaonna's introduction that I originally journeyed to Okinawa and enrolled at Miyazato's Jundokan where I remained for five years. The atmosphere at the Jundokan was relaxed and polite but friendly. We, the students, worked mostly by ourselves and were free to learn as many of the katas as we were able. Several senior students, whose valuable advice was readily given on request, were always on hand, with Miyazato at the ready to settle any differences of opinion over technique.

Katas were polished and repolished. Sparring consisted of fixed forms and light free fighting; often judo, aikido and ti techniques crept into the regimen. We practised a hard form of sticky hands, known as 'kakie', during which the two practitioners stand opposite each other in the Sanchin stance with palms open, pushing back and forth against the other's extended forearm; the purpose being to develop blocking, pushing and grabbing techniques and, like an octopus using its tentacles, get the feel of the opponent's movements.

Hohan Soken[12] once remarked to me that Miyazato was a good judo-ka but not so good at karate; however, Miyazato often warned me against using judo techniques such as makikomi as they are of little use for self-defence (being meant for sport), leaving one wide open to strikes. Miyazato deprecated sport karate and referred to it as 'silly and unfair', because a fast punch is not easily seen by the judges and they have no means of measuring its power or the ability of someone to receive a strike without injury. Likewise he felt that the use of high kicks made the user open to counters, 'karate' he would say, 'is a defence against four antagonists, not one'.

Built like a rhinoceros, Miyazato's movements are small, soft and seemingly ineffective to the casual observer, but woe be he at the receiving end. Once he corrected my form by 'lightly' jabbing his fingers into the small of my back; I shall never forget the sensation of having heavy iron bars drilled into my spine and have never made the same mistake again. On another occasion he demonstrated an elbow lock on my elbow and, just as it was on the point of breaking, I felt so unnerved that I wanted to scream, but was powerless even to do that; I never again asked for a practical demonstration of joint techniques.

Meditation

Miyazato taught me that karate and meditation go hand in hand and he named four types of the latter: sitting (or kneeling), standing, laying down and moving. Karate should be moving meditation. This attitude, plus the presence of a dojo shrine, gave the teaching a semi-religious element. Likewise, Sanchin and Tensho katas equal Zen – these katas are the most important aspect of his Goju-ryu.

When practising these katas Miyazato's advice was to make sure that the chin is tucked in and the spine is held straight as a rod and vertical – one must be natural, so do not hunch the back or shoulders or depress the chest. Primarily, the energy should be sunk to the tanden (i.e. the lower navel) and issued out to the limbs; never exert strength at the shoulders. Inhale slowly through the nose using the lower abdominal muscles and in the same way gently ease the air out through the mouth with a guttural 'hiss'. This sound is coincidental to the breathing and should not be made on purpose. The feet are at shoulder width with the heel of the forward foot in line with the big toe of the rear foot. At first the stance is pigeon-toed (to 'shut off' the inside of the legs) and awkward, but after some time the feet develop a more natural attitude.

Weight training

Another important aspect of Goju-ryu is weight training with the use of traditional and modern appliances. Chojun Miyagi had encouraged and developed weight training because he felt that many young Okinawans, although fast moving, lacked weight and power. Miyazato told me that the most important parts of the body to train are the hips, waist and legs; not the shoulders, chest and arms. Likewise, the makiwara is used to develop powerful hips, not to make calloused fists.

The essence of Miyazato's karate is best summed up by his dojo kun, here translated by a senior student, Tetsunosuke Yasuda, a yoga instructor who used to teach Goju-ryu at the Schilling Recreation Center on Kadena Air Base.

– Be mindful of your courtesy with humbleness.
– Train yourself considering physical strength.
– Study and contrive seriously.
– Be calm in mind and swift in action.
– Take care of yourself.
– Live a plain and simple life.
– Do not be too proud of yourself.
– Continue training with patience and humbleness.

Author's note for the second edition Presently spearheading the Jundokan Goju-ryu drive in the USA is Teruo Chinen, head of the large Jundokan International organisation and Eiichi Miyazato's senior student in North America. In a letter to me Chinen congratulated me on the publication of the original edition of *Okinawan Karate* and kindly enclosed the following information. 'During the period 1946 to 1953, I lived two houses away from [Chojun] Miyagi Sensei's home in Tsuboya-Cho, and trained at that location in his back-yard dojo from 1950 until his death in 1953. I then continued my training under Eiichi Miyazato at the Jundokan Dojo until 1958, when I was sent to the Yoyogi Dojo in Tokyo to assist Morio Higaonna.' Personally, I remember Teruo Chinen as a masterful and helpful senior at the Jundokan, where we often trained together and attended connected functions along with Morio Higaonna. Chinen's contact address is: 614 East 7th Street, Spokane, WA 99202 (tel: 509 838 4941).

Meitoku Yagi

Meitoku Yagi, who believes that 'karate is for fighting and not for talking about', runs a small wooden dojo at Kume in Naha. He was first introduced to Chojun Miyagi by his uncle and somewhat reluctantly started karate practice when aged 13. Yagi is not the sort of man one can say one enjoys being with; Miyazato openly disliked him, claiming that 'he is unqualified to teach Goju-ryu because before the War Yagi had stayed only two years with Miyagi before being called up for military service. Then at the War's end he became a policeman and was posted to a country district, rarely if ever meeting his teacher'.

The practice session that I witnessed at the Meibukan (Yagi's gym) consisted mostly of drilling; the students started with basics, marching up and down to a cassette tape-recorder blaring 'ichi (one), ni (two), san (three), etc.'. The tape (or was it the students?) had not been carefully prepared and the students embarrassingly came to the end of the gym before the tape did, causing a bit of a muddle. Next the students performed disciplined katas with stiff, straight movements. By this time the smell of sweat pervaded the stuffy dojo air as the students dug into a gruelling display of fixed- and free-sparring which lasted until the session ended with kneeling meditation.

Yagi then mysteriously disappeared saying barely a word and left the students to themselves. They, anticipating an interesting evening's chat with the bearded foreigner, sat themselves in a circle on the uneven floor that had been stained dark brown and polished over the years by their own bare feet and elbow grease. I took up my position among them only to be instantly challenged to a sport bout by Yagi's tall, skinny son who claimed to be a university student. At this, most of the others in silent demonstration, got up and left; I immediately followed suit pondering whether Yagi's not wishing to talk was somehow connected with his having nothing to talk about.

Despite all this (or, should I say, in the absence of all this?), I did manage to ascertain that, like many Okinawan karate teachers, Yagi believes that competition fighting is a good thing but feels that the present Japanese rules are inadequate. He also believes that karate and meditation are one 'Ken to Zen wa ichi'; 'Thus, if the soul is perfected the body will follow suit'.

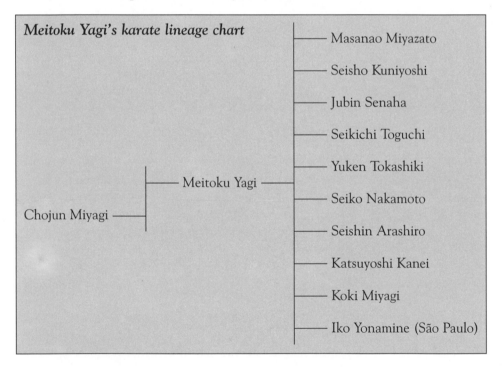

Meitoku Yagi's karate lineage chart

Chojun Miyagi —— Meitoku Yagi ——
- Masanao Miyazato
- Seisho Kuniyoshi
- Jubin Senaha
- Seikichi Toguchi
- Yuken Tokashiki
- Seiko Nakamoto
- Seishin Arashiro
- Katsuyoshi Kanei
- Koki Miyagi
- Iko Yonamine (São Paulo)

Seiko Higa (1898–1966)

Seiko Higa entered Kanryo Higaonna's dojo when aged 13 and remained until the latter's death in 1917, when he became a student of Chojun Miyagi. On graduating from the Prefectural Oceanographic School, Higa became an elementary school teacher and later entered the police force teaching karate in his spare time. In 1931 he left the police and opened a dojo at Shioizumi village, Naha, then two years later he moved this to Matsushita village, Naha. From 1937 to 1939 he visited the South Pacific island of Saipan where he taught Goju-ryu and on his return received a renshi grade from the Dai Nippon Butokukai. After the Second World War, Higa opened a dojo at Itoman in Southern Okinawa and taught karate at the Itoman High School, the Ryukyu University at Shuri and the Naha prison.

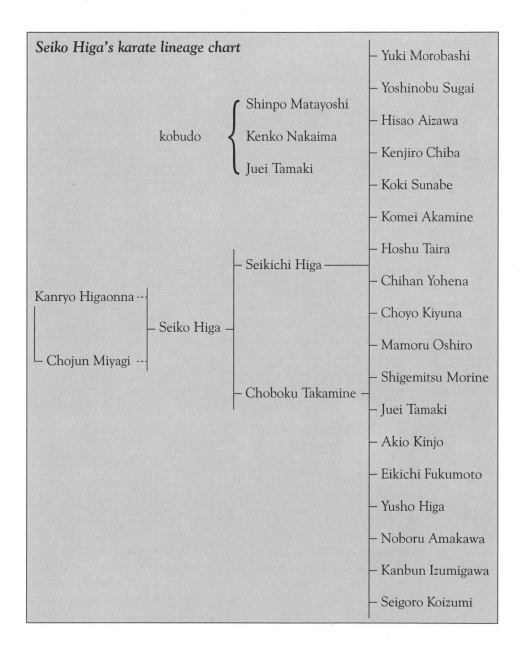

Seiko Higa's karate lineage chart

In 1956 Higa became one of the first vice-presidents of the newly formed
Okinawa Karate-do Federation and two years later became president receiving,
by mutual agreement of the other self-acclaimed members, a hanshi grade.
During the same year he built the Shodokan dojo and formed his own organisation, The International Karate and Kobudo Federation, with the aim of research-
ing Goju-ryu and unifying the katas. Higa was of course president of this federation, with Kenko Taira and the kobudo instructor Juei Tamaki as vice-presidents
– Shinpo Matayoshi[13] became the kobudo instructor on his return from
Kawasaki in 1960.

Choboku Takamine, who had trained under Seiko Higa since 1927, took over
the presidentship of the International Karate and Kobudo Federation on Higa's
death in 1966. Seiko Higa's son, Seikichi Higa, is presently head teacher of the
Shodokan, and Kenko Nakaima of Ryuei-ryu occasionally teaches kobudo.

Goju-ryu and health

During the course of my research I met quite a few karate teachers who berated
Goju-ryu for its general hardness and warned me to discontinue the training
(which I eventually did) or face high blood pressure-related illnesses and a premature death. These critics gained much of their visual evidence from watching
unskilled practitioners doing dynamic-tension demonstrations of Sanchin. In this
exercise all the body muscles are hardened into one rigid structure as the sweating demonstrator performs the Sanchin moves as if pushing against a heavy
weight, whilst being punched and kicked by an associate and issuing a loud guttural 'hiss'.

During the Sanchin exercise, I was told, certain blood vessels are shut off at
the limb joints, the blood cannot flow freely, reverses and accumulates around
the chest, neck and shoulders causing a red flush in that area. Blood vessels of
the neck and arms become swollen as the heart tries in vain to keep the circulation going and forces the blood up to the brain. The result of the exertion on the
heart, blood vessels and internal organs is not considered by the critics to be
good for the health, and regular daily practice is said to be the cause of high
blood pressure and obesity amongst Goju-ryu practitioners over the age of 40.
Rumour also has it that some older practitioners have difficulty lifting their arms
higher than their shoulders.

Although this type of dynamic-tension Sanchin training is fast becoming popular, I could find no really convincing explanations for its practice, apart from its
being a crowd gatherer and a somewhat dangerous body builder. Whether or not
Chojun Miyagi encouraged dynamic-tension and the resulting overall hardening
process of Goju-ryu is not clear, but the fact that premature deaths through illnesses associated with high blood pressure are common among Goju-ryu practitioners cannot be disputed.

The following is a generalisation of other 'evidence' passed on to me by those
who believed Goju-ryu practice to be coincidental with poor health:

1. In order to harden the buttocks during the Sanchin exercise, forceful closing of the anal sphincter is practised. This, I was assured, will result in haemorrhoids after only two or three years of regular practice.
2. When blocking, the thumb side of the fist is forced sideways towards the forearm, causing pressure to be exerted on a vital point at the side of the wrist. This point may be detected by relaxing the left hand and running the thumb of the right hand to the base of the left thumb until a hollow is found. Even slight pressure at this point will bring pain. In actual fact, an abnormal amount of pressure should not be exerted here as, I was assured, it will have adverse effects on the lungs which may result in various lung complaints, including TB and asthma.
3. The testing of Sanchin 'hardness', by punching and kicking the abdomen, will have adverse effects on the intestines and may result in stomach cancer.

Yoshio Itokazu

Of course, there is always the exception to the rule: Yoshio Itokazu was that exception. I paid him a visit one hot and humid summer afternoon at the quiet village of Funakoshi, where he now grows vegetables to help supplement his income. At the age of 81, Itokazu, having practised Goju-ryu for 65 years, was in the prime of health and, unlike other Goju-ryu teachers I interviewed, was open-minded, jolly and alert.

Between the ages of 17 and 21 he had learned Goju-ryu from Chojun Miyagi. Then he was drafted into the Japanese army, saw action in Siberia and was decorated for valour. On leaving the service at the age of 25, he worked on the mainland at Osaka and learned karate for two and a half years from Kanyei Uechi.[14] Itokazu started teaching Goju-ryu and remained in Osaka until he was 70 years old, when he returned to his native Okinawa. He opened a dojo at Sobe in Naha but, feeling that 'karate is for the young', he passed control of this to his students, whom he visits now and again. The students from his still-functioning Osaka dojos pay him regular visits and likewise he makes the odd call to Osaka.

As a young man, Itokazu had large muscles from regularly practising with stone weights (sashi) and earthenware pots (kame), but he said that he left off

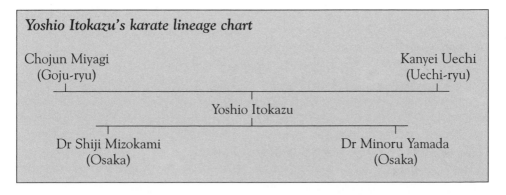

Yoshio Itokazu's karate lineage chart

Chojun Miyagi (Goju-ryu) — Kanyei Uechi (Uechi-ryu) — Yoshio Itokazu — Dr Shiji Mizokami (Osaka) — Dr Minoru Yamada (Osaka)

such practice because 'on reaching the sixties age group Goju-ryu practitioners change physically, lose their strength and become weak again like children, lacking both co-ordination and balance'. Itokazu used to perform Sanchin at an annual sumo contest in Osaka and, during the course of the demonstration, a burly sumo wrestler would strike him full force in the abdomen without Itokazu feeling the slightest pain or losing balance. He did this every year until he was 57 and claims to have suffered absolutely no ill effects as a result.

'Sanchin,' Itokazu said, 'is the most important exercise in Goju-ryu and should be practised daily even if one becomes weak from old age.' During Sanchin practice one should breathe 'so that everyone can see what you are doing', but in a fight one's respiration 'should be undetectable'. Although during the demonstration of Sanchin he did for me he was a little unsteady on his feet, the echoing sound that accompanied his exhalations, and seemed to come from the very inside of his abdomen, was uncanny. His Sanchin looked even softer than Eiichi Miyazato's, but he demonstrated the 'internal' hardness of his abdomen by allowing me to prod it whilst he was talking naturally. 'This "internal hardening",' he told me, 'came about naturally from tightening the inside of the legs, not the buttocks and anal sphincter.' He denied that Sanchin was bad for the health, but in the next breath stated that he never touches alcohol, avoids dynamic-tension exercises and leads a steady life.

Yoshio Itokazu's routine for good health is this: he gets up at 5 o'clock in the morning and, bare-footed on the gravel road outside his house, does deep-breathing exercises three times. Then he performs a series of stretching exercises whilst standing and finishes off with none other than Sanchin.

Itokazu cautioned me that during free-sparring practice one should try to avoid harming one's partner, by merely imagining the location of his vital points, without actually striking them. 'Reigi (courtesy),' he said, 'does not mean bowing, as this is merely a greeting; reigi means respect for one's teacher and seniors and most important of all reigi means that seniors should be gentle, kind and understanding in their attitude toward juniors.' Finally, he stated that all karate is the same, only the names of the styles are different: 'like men with different names, they are all men – the important thing is to practise safely and diligently.'

Uechi-ryu

Kanbun Uechi (1877–1948)

Historically, the foundations of Uechi-ryu were introduced to Okinawa by Kanbun Uechi who, like Kanryo Higaonna and Norisato Nakaima, studied Chinese boxing at Fuchou.

According to his son Kanyei Uechi, Kanbun Uechi was the eldest son of Kantoku Uechi who, born into the shizoku class, had moved from Shuri to Izumi on the Motobu Peninsula to become a pioneer farmer. In 1897, when aged 20, Kanbun Uechi travelled to Fuchou[15] and learned a form of Chinese boxing called Pangai-noon (also pronounced Pan Ying Jen or Pan Ying Gut) from a medicine hawker going by the name of Shu Shi Wa.

At first Uechi had entered the Kojo dojo at Fuchou[16] with an acquaintance, Tokusaburo Matsuda, but due to a speech impediment of Uechi's, the dojo's chief assistant Makabe UDUN took him for a fool and nicknamed him Uechi Watabu-gwa meaning Big Belly or Good-for-nothing Uechi. Offended by this insult, Uechi left the Kojo dojo and was not seen there for three years. When on returning he explained that he was now a disciple of Shu Shi Wa and demonstrated Sanchin, he was praised by the surprised Makabe.

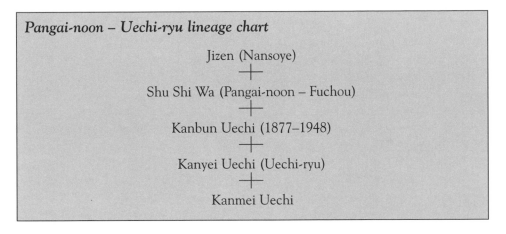

Pangai-noon – Uechi-ryu lineage chart

Jizen (Nansoye)

Shu Shi Wa (Pangai-noon – Fuchou)

Kanbun Uechi (1877–1948)

Kanyei Uechi (Uechi-ryu)

Kanmei Uechi

The life of Shu Shi Wa (or Chu Chi Wo) is something of a mystery, due to his probable connections with the Chinese secret societies who sought to overthrow the Ching and return the Ming. Although Shu Shi Wa made his living by making and selling herbal medicines, he claimed to be the son of a farmer and it is believed that he had been a 'priest' (using the name Sosei) at the central temple at Nansoye (or Nansei), a little to the south of Fuchou. His teacher at this 'temple' is thought to have been a 'priest' named Jizen and as Shu Shi Wa was at one time known to have been sought by the authorities, it has been put forward that the Nansoye Shaolin Temple was actually a cover for a secret society and its history had been purposely clouded. One theory is that the 'temple' had been built in 1768 and was actually a kind of village for society members who had fled persecution in the North.

In order to support himself, Kanbun Uechi helped Shu Shi Wa with the medicine hawking business. Kanyei Uechi told me how his father had gathered herbs in the mountains and made herbal medicines, 'to cure all kinds of illnesses'. Then Kanbun Uechi had to carry the heavy box of medicines on his shoulder to an appropriate spot where he would display the goods. Uechi and Shu Shi Wa would next attract a crowd with a kung-fu demonstration and sell as much as they could before moving on to a new spot. Later Uechi was able to make and sell the medicines by himself.

Shu Shi Wa's Pangai-noon (which means hard-soft) was based on the principle of hard attacks and soft blocks. Kanbun Uechi learned the three katas: Sanchin, Sesan and Sanseryu, but did not have enough time to take in the fourth kata, Suparinpe. On gaining his shihan (master) grade in 1904, he travelled south to Nansoye where he opened a dojo, revisiting his teacher at Fuchou every year for about ten days at a time. In 1909 he made his way back to Okinawa and farmed the family land at Motobu, refusing to take on students.

Gokenki, the White Crane boxing master who ran a tea business at Naha,[17] had met Uechi and Shu Shi Wa at Fuchou as well as at Nansoye and often told interested customers about Uechi. Some of these sought Kanbun Uechi out, but when they asked for tuition he would scoff and send them away; one rumour has it that the reason for his behaviour was that Uechi, or one of his students, had killed a man in Nansoye and as a result he had vowed never to teach again.

In 1924, due to the unemployment problem on Okinawa, Kanbun Uechi took his family to the Japanese mainland and found work in a clothing factory at Wakayama. A year later, at the request of two Okinawan workmates, he started teaching in the evenings and finally in 1932 opened the Pangai-noon-ryu Karate Jutsu Club at Heiwa Road, Wakayama. He finally returned to Okinawa in 1946 and remained until his death in 1948 at the age of 71.

Kanyei Uechi

Kanyei Uechi is president of the Uechi-ryu Karate-do Association, a world-wide organisation with clubs on the Japanese mainland as well as in the USA, Australia, New Zealand, Great Britain, Yugoslavia, France, Argentina, Brazil and Mexico. He was born the eldest son of Kanbun Uechi at Izumi, Motobu and when aged 13 travelled with his father to Wakayama where, four years later, he started to train in Pangai-noon-ryu. In 1937, after ten years of practice, Kanyei Uechi opened his own dojo at Osaka where he taught for two and a half years before returning to Okinawa. Here he opened the Uechi-ryu Karate-jutsu Research Club at Miyazato village, near Nago – the style having been renamed by Kanbun himself. After his father's death, Kanyei Uechi moved his dojo to a makeshift shack at Nodake in Ginowan ('for commercial reasons') and later built the present concrete gym nearby at the strategically located boom town of Futenma.

I found Kanyei Uechi to be a quiet, modest and sincere man who was not afraid of telling the truth. A family man, his three sons and daughter all practise Uechi-ryu and assist with the instruction; in fact, upon his death, Uechi would like to pass control of his association to his eldest son, Kanmei.

In the dojo Uechi personally takes charge of the group training sessions and then corrects the students' katas individually, paying special attention to correct form and balance. More than likely a typical training session would probably be described by keep-fit addicts as 'a good workout with a lot of enjoyable sweat'.

Uechi believes that sport competition helped to popularise karate but,

Uechi-ryu Karate-do Association lineage chart

- Kanbun Uechi
  - Kanyei Uechi
    - Saburo Uehara
      - Noboru Miyagi
      - Takenobu Uehara
    - Shuei Sakiyama
      - Jiro Uehara
    - Kata Yamashiro
      - Seisaburo Miyagi
    - Natsukichi Shimabuku
      - Isamu Uehara (Tokyo)
        - Yasuo Shimoji (Tokyo)
        - Saburo Miyagi (Argentina)
        - Shusei Maeshiro
      - Takashi Kinjo
    - Noboru Uchima
      - Seiki Itokazu
    - Susumu Tamamura
      - Seisho Komesu
    - Kazuo Kishimoto
      - Seisho Yonaha
    - Kayei Akamine
      - Seishin Shirado
    - Ryuyu Tomoyose
      - Katsuhiko Minowa
      - Seiyu Arashiro
        - Seiki Ire
        - Tsutomu Nakahodo
      - Masamitsu Kinjo
      - Kanmei Uechi
      - Kansei Uechi
      - Kanbun Uechi (Jnr)
      - Kiyoshi Komesu
      - Seiko Itokazu
      - Shinsei Omine
      - Soryu Furugen
      - Kosuke Yonamine ——— Shoji Arasaki
      - Shigeru Takamiyagi
      - Hiroshi Sugihara
      - Koichi Mori
      - Satoru Araki (Osaka)
      - Ryokichi Tomoyose (Wakayama)
      - Kosuke Henna (Mexico)
      - Takeo Hiyagon (Brazil)
      - Koshin Shimabukuro (France)
      - Mario Topolsek (Yugoslavia)
      - David Scot (Great Britain)
      - Robert Donnely (Australia)
      - George E. Mattson (USA)

although his association sponsors an annual free-fighting competition, he admits that the traditional forms are superior. Modern Uechi-ryu contains the three original Pangai-noon katas with the addition of five others, namely: Kanshiwa, Kanchin, Seryu (which were made by Kanyei Uechi), Kanshu or Dai Ni Sesan (which was made by Uechi's student, Saburo Uehara) and Sechin (which was made by another student – Seiki Itokazu). These eight katas, which contain forms imitating the crane, tiger, cat and the swimming action of the carp, are taught in the following order: Sanchin, Kanshiwa, Kanshu, Sechin, Sesan, Seryu, Kanchin and Sanseryu.

In the kata Sanchin the fingers are held straight and when striking are corkscrewed into a vital point just below the nipple on an imaginary opponent's chest. There is a small hollow at this point. When practising this kata one should breathe in through the nose without making the abdomen move and breathe out naturally through the mouth with a sharp 'hiss'. The movements of Sanchin are done at normal speed; they are light and not forced. The other katas (at least when performed by Kanyei Uechi) appeared to be soft and pliable, with one technique flowing into another.

External body hardening techniques are emphasised in Uechi-ryu. These include: kotekitai (a form of sticky hands in which the two opponents' forearms are rubbed together with the fists clenched), striking a makiwara bound with straw, thrusting the extended fingers into a pail of small pebbles and the forceful kicking of each other's legs. In another form of practice the exponents stand facing each other and take it in turn to punch and block in a set sequence. Speed is essential to proficiency in Uechi-ryu fighting techniques and Kanyei Uechi told me that Pangai-noon had been the fastest of the seven then popular Chinese styles. Uechi-ryu has both close-in- and distant-fighting techniques and incorporates free- and fixed-sparring. The front snap kick is a speciality and makes good use of the tip of the big toe for striking; exponents can break four boards using this technique.

On asking if Uechi-ryu has secret principles, Kanyei Uechi answered that it does: 'but these are not really so secret and are not taught as such. They are discovered through long and constant practice.'

Author's note for the second edition In 1991 Kanyei Uechi passed away at the ripe age of 80. I believe that my interviews with him were extremely relevant, because at the time the author Shigeru Takamiyagi, who I also interviewed, was seemingly trying to create a more mythological history for Uechi-ryu – albeit along more traditional Ryukyuan thought patterns of subjectively wishing to embellish the past. Kanyei Uechi's down-to-earth insistence to me, for example, that his father Kanbun had been a street-side medicine hawker and that he had practised body hardening techniques to attract crowds of prospective buyers, was iterated and reiterated. Objective writing in the modern world means that a balanced, informative text is more appreciated by the majority, although it is accepted that a few may be offended by reality. Although, therefore, it has been brought to my attention that some Uechi family members were offended to read that Kanbun Uechi may have possibly been responsible for another man's death, the inclusion of this reported rumour remains. Cultural sensibilities can sometimes suppress positive progression towards greater understanding.

Pangai-noon-ryu

Pangai-noon-ryu was reformed in October of 1978 by a breakaway group of Kanyei Uechi's disciples headed by Seiko Itokazu and Takashi Kinjo. From what I could gather this group felt restricted by the silly, 'politically' orientated squabbling centring around another student and the set standards of Uechi-ryu. Also they wanted to include kobudo as well as other fighting arts in their own dojo training curriculum. In this new style Uechi-ryu, karate and other fighting systems are taught along with Matayoshi-type kobudo.

REFERENCES
[1] See Shorin-ryu, page 88.
[2] See Yamani-ryu, page 120.
[3] Chojo Oshiro taught at the Prefectural Teachers' Training College; he died at the early age of 40.
[4] See Matsumura Orthodox Shorin-ryu, under Sokon Matsumura, page 55.
[5] See Matsubayashi-ryu, page 76.
[6] Also sometimes referred to as Wai Shin Zan. Gichin Funakoshi in *Karate-do Kyohan* writes that Wai Shin Zan was a military attaché and had other Okinawan students going by the names: Shimabuku, Higa, Senaha, Gushi, Nagahama, Arakaki and Kuwae.
[7] A martial arts school, training area or gym.
[8] Kafu Kojo of Kojo-ryu told me that Shorei-ryu had originated in the Shorei Temple, said to have been in Fukien Province, China.
[9] In *Karate-do to Ryukyu Kobudo*.
[10] See Okinawa Kenpo, page 114.
[11] See Matsumura Orthodox Shorin-ryu, under Sokon Matsumura, page 55.
[12] See Matsumura Orthodox Shorin-ryu, page 57.
[13] See Matayoshi kobudo, page 128.
[14] See Uechi-ryu, page 40.
[15] Eiichi Miyazato told me a popular romantic rumour that has Uechi fleeing military service by stowing away on a junk bound for China only to be ship-wrecked off the Fukien coast and washed ashore on to a beach near Fuchou, where he was helped by the locals who taught him Chinese boxing.
[16] See Kojo-ryu, page 46.
[17] See Goju-ryu, under Chojun Miyagi, page 27.

Chapter 3
Kojo-ryu

Although Kojo-ryu was not named until after the Second World War, the roots of this style go back through several generations of the Kojo (also pronounced Koshiro, Kogusuku or Kugushiku) family. Such was the fame of this family that it gave birth to such expressions as: 'To talk of karate is to talk of Kojo, to talk of Kojo is to talk of a fine martial arts family'; and, 'One Kojo is equal to three of any other'. The present head of the Kojo family, Kafu Kojo (to whom fighting is a science), lost all of his family records during the war, but kindly supplied me with the following information that he was able to remember.

History
The Kojo family, from whom Kojo-ryu derived its name, lived at Kume village, Naha and were descended from one of the 'thirty-six families' of Chinese immigrants who settled at Kume in 1393; the Chinese family name being Sai. As family members often visited Fuchou for work and academic studies, close ties with China were not lost until the 20th century.

Family tradition holds that in the 1700s Kojo UEKATA (Ko Sai) learned Chinese weaponry, grappling (which Kojo told me was used during battle should one's weapons be lost or broken) and other martial arts in China and that on returning to Okinawa instructed male family members in these systems.

1st generation
Although Kojo UEKATA is considered to be at the head of the Kojo family-style lineage, the first generation is counted from Kojo PECHIN. In the late 18th century, Kojo PECHIN (nicknamed Nmari BUSHI) learned grappling from his father and developed many new techniques.

2nd generation
Shoi Sai (1816–1906), nicknamed Seijin TANMEI (meaning – wise old man) was well known for his expertise with the staff and stick and is credited with

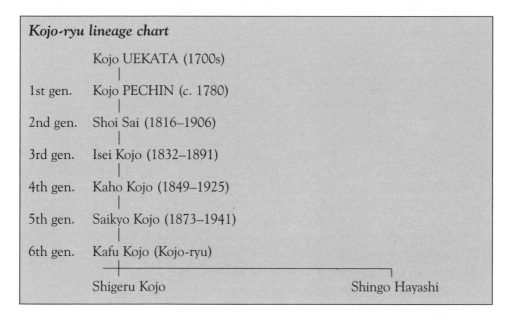

Kojo-ryu lineage chart

	Kojo UEKATA (1700s)
1st gen.	Kojo PECHIN (*c.* 1780)
2nd gen.	Shoi Sai (1816–1906)
3rd gen.	Isei Kojo (1832–1891)
4th gen.	Kaho Kojo (1849–1925)
5th gen.	Saikyo Kojo (1873–1941)
6th gen.	Kafu Kojo (Kojo-ryu)

Shigeru Kojo   Shingo Hayashi

having introduced the staff and sword concealing techniques into the family system. He spent some time in Fuchou where he learned grappling and Chinese weaponry but, on his return, he never worked and spent most of the time 'fishing'. One day he saw two Satsuma samurai attempting to rape an Okinawan woman at Tsuji. He entered the house where they had dragged her and opposed the two rapists who tried to draw their swords. In a flash it was all over and Shoi Sai was seen leaving the premises with one dead and one half-dead samurai slumped over his shoulders. He presented these trophies to the local chikusaji (constable) but was called before a magistrate and stripped of all state monetary privileges. After that he returned to Fuchou where he ended his days in comparative poverty.

3rd generation

Shoi Sai's son, Isei Kojo (1832–1891), travelled to Fuchou with his father at the age of 16 to study Confucianism and Chinese weaponry, later becoming known for his skill with the hand spear and the bow and arrow. He learned Chinese boxing from a military attaché called Iwah and later became assistant at the latter's dojo. At the age of 36, Isei Kojo returned to Okinawa, having spent a total of 20 years at Fuchou, and now and again demonstrated his skills.

Once, when wishing to cross the Hija river and being a long way from the bridge, he threw some bundles of firewood into the water and, using a body-lightening technique, proceeded to skip from one bundle to the other until he had crossed to the opposite bank of the river. On another occasion he virtually levitated 5m (5yds) into the air, then kicked and broke a tile on the Gate of

Courtesy at Shuri castle. Next he did a handstand on a patio at the castle, balancing on his thumbs and index fingers. Then, lifting one hand, he struck a 7cm (3in) thick paving slab with his thumb and cracked it.

Isei would also practise running up a high wall and sliding down the other side. This technique, he would explain, prevented one from being impaled by a waiting enemy's spear. Although the Chinese boxing that Isei Kojo learned from Iwah (probably a form of Fukien Shaolin Temple boxing) became the basis of present-day Kojo-ryu, he failed to pass on two of the style's secrets due to his sudden death from a cerebral haemorrhage at the age of 59.

Isei Kojo had a cousin named Taitei Kojo (1837–1917 – he was nicknamed Goken or Hard-fist TAMEI). The two were in Fuchou together and Taitei, like Isei, studied Confucianism, the hand spear and the bow and arrow, but learned Chinese boxing from Wan Shin Zan.[1] On his return to Okinawa, Taitei Kojo brought back with him a large book on the Chinese martial arts and some Chinese weapons, which he thoughtfully concealed from the Satsuma agents.

He is also said to have had long arguments about Sanchin with his contemporary, Kanryo Higaonna.[2] Taitei Kojo's younger brother, Jiro Kojo, was another notable. In the latter part of the 19th century he emigrated to Hawaii, but whilst *en route* the ship was captured by pirates whom Jiro Kojo subdued single-handedly and promptly threw overboard, making a bit of a name for himself on arrival at his new homeland.

4th generation
Kaho Kojo (1849–1925) seems to have been born after his father Isei Kojo had departed for Fuchou and he was brought up in Kume village. Once when Iwah came to Okinawa on official duty, he met the young Kaho and, seeing that he would make a promising student, took the lad back to Fuchou and taught him Chinese boxing. On being granted independence from Iwah, Kaho Kojo opened a dojo at Fuchou with an Okinawan called Makabe UDUN[3] as chief assistant. The dojo became well known and Kanbun Uechi[4] trained there for a brief period. Kaho Kojo was a noted calligrapher and introduced the stick into the family fighting system.

5th generation
Saikyo Kojo (1873–1941 – nicknamed Kumejima O) learned his father's style of Chinese boxing, the staff and stick, and passed these on to Kafu Kojo.

6th generation
Kafu Kojo's young life was spartan with little freedom. From the age of 12 he started a tough and disciplined routine of karate training under his grandfather, Kaho Kojo. On the latter's death in 1925, Kafu Kojo's father and uncle, Shuren Kojo, took over the teaching responsibilities. Kafu Kojo recalled that Shuren Kojo had been the first police inspector on Okinawa and had received the nick-

name Oni Bucho – or Demon Chief. Shuren had learned Chinese boxing from
Kaho Kojo and Ranho Maezato (BUSHI Maezato) who had, in turn, studied
under Iwah when the latter stayed at Kume village.

One teaching exercise, Kafu painfully recalled, was playing catch with his
uncle using two 10kg (22lb) stone slabs. They both held a slab in their respective
right hands and simultaneously lobbed them at each other, catching the other's
slab with their left hands – and so forth. Kafu's back often ached from such practice and the bruises he got on his legs, from failing to catch the slabs, were
numerous.

After the Second World War Kafu Kojo opened a dojo at Makishi, Naha in
conjunction with his eldest son, Shigeru, but due to the latter's ill health this was
closed in 1975 and the building is now used for raising chickens. Kojo-ryu is
presently taught publicly at only one location, that being on the Japanese mainland at Totori City in Totori Prefecture. The instructor, Shingo Hayashi, was a
former student at the Makishi dojo during his university days. He is now a den-
tist and teaches Kojo-ryu to all-comers at the Totori Budokan, charging nothing
for his services.

The style

Kojo-ryu practice consists of 70 per cent sparring and 30 per cent kata. There are
six empty hand katas, one staff kata and one stick kata. Three of the empty hand
katas are named after and imitate the action of animals, namely: Hakuryu
(White Dragon), Hako (White Tiger) and Hakutsuru (White Crane). The other
three empty hand katas, Ten, Ku and Chi contain twelve Kamaes (ready-to-fight
postures), representing the twelve animals of the Chinese zodiac.

'Kamaes,' Kojo told me, 'should always be relaxed to allow for speed when
countering and attacking.' Each kamae in Kojo-ryu has its own special function.
For example the Chiseigan kamae is used against an opponent who attacks with
his legs; all one has to do is kamae, wait until the opponent kicks, then move in
and throw him. The Fudo kamae gives one a solid appearance (like a bull) and is
used to deter a would-be attacker.

The three 'animal' katas also have kamaes. Hakutsuru has the Namigaeshi
kamae (which looks like a crane spreading its wings) and is used against a threat
by four to six assailants, so as to allow them no place of entry. Kafu Kojo told me
that actually one of the old boxing secrets had been that there is no kamae, but
he admitted that in some cases they do indeed have a function and are helpful
when training. During the Second World War he was posted to the Philippines
and once, whilst walking through the jungle on his own, he was suddenly surrounded by a group of about 20 Filipino guerrillas. His immediate reaction was to
kamae and give a loud shout, at which one of the Filipinos ran off, hotly pursued
by the bewildered others. Kojo ran in the other direction, rolled down a slope
and got away.

Kata	*Kamae*	*Zodiacal sign*
	Seishin	Ne (rat)
	Fudo	Ushi (bull)
TEN (heaven – upper)	Jinpu	Tora (tiger)
	Jumonji	U (rabbit)
	Unryu	Tatsu (dragon)
	Aiki	Mi (snake)
KU (sky – middle)	Katate seigan	Uma (horse)
	Seiha	Hitsuji (sheep)
	Tenchi	Saru (monkey)
	Suika	Tori (cock)
CHI (earth – lower)	Chiseigan	Inu (dog)
	Ichimonji	I (boar)

The movements of the Kojo-ryu katas can be used in a fighting situation with little or no alteration. Movements should always be relaxed and appear light. Speed is essential and, during a fight, movements should be kept small until an opening is found, 'then immediately go in and finish off with one powerful strike'.

The basic rules for sparring and fighting are:

– never attack with a large technique
– move as if you have springs on the soles of your feet
– block and strike simultaneously.

Kafu Kojo thinks that the Goju-ryu and Uechi-ryu blocks are too big to be effective, but believes that the corkscrew punch is quite powerful when used by someone with large shoulder and chest development and that it tightens the muscles which protect the vital points at the side of the rib cage. But despite this, he prefers to use the standing fist as it is more natural and probably more effective. A unique Kojo-ryu technique is the tatsumaki (tornado) block; the use of which, Kojo claims, prevents any frontal unarmed attack from coming home. However, this block is not easy to master. Both hands, palms facing out, simultaneously draw a figure of eight in opposite directions in front of the body (when the outer hand is rising up, the inner is dropping), the feet slide and kick alternately as the whole seething mass slowly progresses forward.

Kojo told me that any attack can be foiled and used advantageously. If during sparring practice you are struck, think over and analyse the sequence of events concerning the incident, as a seemingly minor error is often the cause. Practical experience of many free-sparring bouts is essential to progress in Kojo-ryu and over the years a natural intuition develops; intuition being the mobilising factor behind success in the martial arts. Intuition is like a reflex action that develops naturally through constant and dedicated practice. In this respect Kafu Kojo claims that he can tell instinctively if someone is going to attack him, even if the would-be attacker is hidden from sight.

Training

In training, a student's 'good points' should be sought out and developed and his/her health should be of great concern. To avoid injuries during free-sparring practice, the base of the palm is gently used to slap the opponent. Students are usually paired beginner with expert – with one student attacking and the other blocking. Overly rough students are expelled. In a real fight, when using the butt of the palm, bend the finger tips over and snap the base of the palm forward on to the target. This will add power to the strike. If the fingers are held straight when striking with this technique, the power will be dispersed into the finger tips. 'The flat fist also disperses the power of a strike and is suitable for children' Kojo claims.

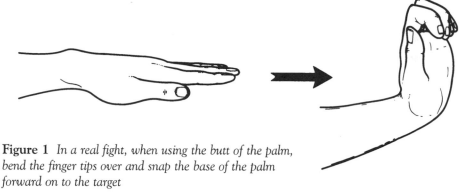

Figure 1 *In a real fight, when using the butt of the palm, bend the finger tips over and snap the base of the palm forward on to the target*

Although Kojo-ryu contains 180 hand and joint techniques, it is better to learn ten of these well than 50 badly. Techniques must become part of the practitioner and be used spontaneously. 'Karate,' Kojo told me, 'is not just kicking and punching – this is for beginners. Karate is a fighting art – not a sport – so one can use any part of the body for striking, grappling and throwing. Always remember: never grab and hold or you will be an easy target for countering, train constantly so that eventually you will be able to think up your own techniques. The basic rule for striking is: hard (foreknuckles, etc.) strikes soft area – soft (butt of the palm, etc.) strikes hard area.'

With Kojo-ryu weight training, the student is free to train to his liking; however, Kafu Kojo stresses that overdoing things causes harm to the body. It is better to move a small weight 30 times than a large weight three times. Lifting too heavy a weight will harm the sinews and make them stiff – sinews must be pliable. In this respect Akahige Kojo (i.e. Red Beard), who did back somersaults on his 70th birthday, believed that a boxer gets stronger with age. When Akahige eventually died his body was entombed (as was the custom) for three years, but when the senior female members of the family came to wash the bones in alcohol before placing them in the burial urn they found that, although Akahige's flesh had deteriorated, his sinews were still firmly anchored to his bones and when pulled were like strong elastic.

Also Sanchin training, as in Goju-ryu will, Kojo remarked, make the body hard, strong and muscular but the breathing is unnatural and causes the sinews to lose their pliability. After weight training or any good workout, always wipe the sweat from the body and allow it to cool naturally before taking a cold shower. Never take a cold shower directly after exercising, as it will damage the muscles and probably make them ache.

Kojo-ryu muscle breathing exercises help to 'harden' the body internally and, through regular practice of these, Kafu Kojo has developed the ability to take a punch on most body surfaces. He admits that although the skin hurts a little on the impact of a strike the force does not penetrate, because his energy is automatically focused at the point of impact. With this technique he also claims to be able to break the wrist of someone striking his abdomen. Other training techniques are used to strengthen the grip so that, although the body may become weak through old age, the fingers always retain their gripping power.

General knowledge

After about eight to ten years of practice Kojo-ryu exponents start to learn the relationships of five general knowledge subjects to the martial arts. These subjects are:

1. Shakaigaku — practical knowledge (social studies)
2. Igaku — traditional Chinese medicine
3. Sugaku — mathematics
4. Butsurigaku — physics
5. Tetsugaku — philosophy.

1. Practical knowledge, or using one's head, consists of common sense aspects of learning. For example, during the Second World War, Kafu Kojo was hiding in a cave when four or five armed American soldiers entered in search of the enemy. The unarmed and frightened Kojo picked up an unopened can of food and threw it in the direction of the soldiers, where it landed with a heavy metallic thud. Thinking that it was a hand grenade, the Americans ran helter-skelter out of the cave and never came back.

2. Traditional Chinese medicine includes a working knowledge of the weak and strong points of the human body and ways of healing it. For example, after a bad knock, to avoid bruising and subsequent damage to the internal organs from a blood clot, the affected area should be pricked all over with a needle and the 'bad' blood sucked out. If it is not possible to suck, a small hollow vessel in which a partial vacuum has been made (by placing a burning substance inside or by heating it and allowing it to cool) may be tightly sealed over the area.

3. Mathematics includes the judging of the distance of an adversary under various circumstances and simple computations such as: if someone grabs you with one hand he will have only three usable limbs as opposed to your four – therefore you are at an advantage of 4 to 3.

4. Physics (or more properly physical aspects) is taught during practice on natural terrain. For example, if you are accosted on a sandy beach, slowly grind your feet into the sand to form a solid foothold. In doing this, some sand will inevitably fall across the toes and this can easily be flicked into the antagonist's eyes.

5. Philosophy deals with such topics as: karate being for the benefit of society, practitioners should be 'Christian-like' in their attitude towards people.

The secrets

Traditionally, the secrets of Kojo-ryu have been passed down through the Kojo family by word of mouth, but some of these 'family secrets' Kafu Kojo realises, are not really all that secret. Once, whilst practising Sekiguchi jujitsu at Tokyo in his younger days, he was surprised to learn a technique that has been an old closely guarded Kojo family secret. Namely: if someone applies a strangle hold on your neck, push the tip of your tongue up hard against your front upper palate and tuck your chin in; this will give you enough time to find a way out of the hold. Shigeru Kojo claimed that, using this very technique, he had remained unaffected for 30 seconds with a judo belt twisted around his neck, whilst a man pulled each end of the belt as hard as he could.

Another Kojo 'family secret' is a form of striking using the first knuckle of the thumb.[5] The thumb is concealed behind the fingers and is used to attack vital points. In pre-war days, when street fights at Naha's red-lantern district of Tsuji were quite commonplace, such strikes were used to fool any bystanders, who may have witnessed the fight, into believing that nothing violent had taken place. However, the recipients of such strikes often became listless and died some time later.

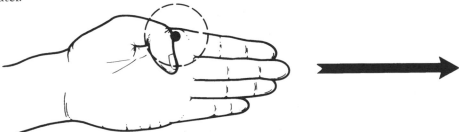

Figure 2 *The first-knuckle-of-the-thumb strike*

'Vital points,' Kojo told me, 'can be detected with the finger tips.' These points are numerous, but very small (and painful) and the surrounding area feels soft and slightly indented. Like most teachers on Okinawa, Kafu Kojo does not usually teach vital points to his students, mostly from fear of police reprisal should a nasty incident involving their use occur. Be that as it may, he did pass on a few of these to me, namely:

1. to paralyse the leg, strike at the vital point just below the calf muscle.

2. demobilise the arm for a fraction of a second by inserting your extended thumb into the opponent's armpit, then strike between the ribs with the other hand.

3. strike the point on the upper arm at the base of the shoulder muscle with your foreknuckle or the side of your hand, to give a 'dead arm'.

4. if a point at the side of the chest on a line with the nipple is struck hard enough, 'the victim will turn three full circles with his arms outstretched and fall down foaming at the mouth'. Even a light strike here will cause the opposite side of the chest to ache the next day; so take extreme care.

5. another extremely dangerous vital point is the soft area just under the tip of the jaw. This can be struck with the finger tips, extended thumb or the tip of the big toe. Kafu Kojo saw someone nearly die from this strike during a brotherly squabble.

6. on folding the ear forward the tip comes directly over a vital point on the side of the head which coincides with a joint of the skull (in Kojo-ryu the skull is divided into eight parts) that can be attacked with the side of the hand.

7. if a line is drawn between the bottom of the shoulder blades, it coincides with a vital point on the spine which, if struck with force, can cause listlessness and eventual death two or three years later. This is most effective when struck with the heel if the victim happens to be in the unlikely position of lying sprawled on his chest with his arms outstretched above his head.

8. not all vital points are quite so nasty as these; in fact, most of them, if massaged lightly, are good for the health.[6] For example, the point at the base of the thumb and index finger may be rubbed to relieve toothaches and headaches.

To sum up, I would personally class Kojo-ryu as a style with a lot of substance, as well as having much historical interest. It will be of note to know that Shigeru Kojo, having recovered from his illness, is thinking of teaching again and would welcome the chance to do so in Europe or the USA.

REFERENCES

[1] See Goju-ryu, under Kanryo Higaonna, page 25.

[2] See Goju-ryu, under Kanryo Higaonna, page 24.

[3] Katsuya Miyahira of Shorin-ryu (Kobayashi) told me that Makabe UDUN was actually Choken Makabe (or Chan-gwa) and that he was very small and light.

[4] See Uechi-ryu, page 39.

[5] This striking technique is also seen in Goju-ryu and Uechi-ryu, but is generally disguised as a 'finger-jab' or 'butt-of-the-hand strike', probably due to its dangerous nature.

[6] See Bugeikan, page 136.

Part II
The Shorin styles

Chapter 4
Matsumura Orthodox Shorin-ryu; Ishimine-ryu

The beginnings of the so-called 'Shorin styles' originate with one man, Sokon Matsumura. A short biography of him has been included under Matsumura Orthodox Shorin-ryu, but it should be noted that, to a greater or lesser extent, his influence can be seen in all of the styles included in Part II, except for Tomari-te.

Matsumura Orthodox Shorin-ryu
Sokon Matsumura (c.1809–1901)
Sokon Matsumura (also called Buseitatsu, Unyu, BUSHI Matsumura or Bucho) was born into a well-known shizoku family at Yamagawa village, Shuri. He was a good scholar, as well as a noted calligrapher, and from an early age he, like many Shuri youths, learned the basics of ti. Later he is said to have learned the use of the staff from Sakugawa SATUNUSHI (Tode Sakugawa) who had studied the art in China and was then living at Akata village, Shuri.

Whilst working as a bodyguard to the last three successive Ryukyuan kings,[1] Sho Ko, Sho Iku and Sho Tai, Matsumura twice visited Fuchou and Satsuma as an envoy on affairs of state. At Fuchou he was able to visit several Chinese boxing schools and study under the military attachés, Ason[2] and Iwah. According to Hohan Soken and Chozo Nakama, he had even taken time off to visit the Fukien Shaolin Temple. At Satsuma, Matsumura is said to have been initiated into the Jigen-ryu sword fighting system under the master, Yashichiro Ijuin.

The 'Shorin styles' chart (simplified)

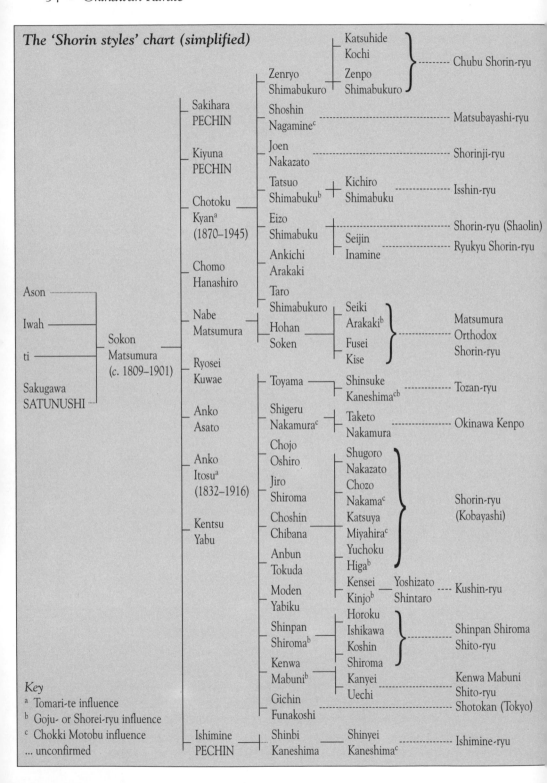

Key
[a] Tomari-te influence
[b] Goju- or Shorei-ryu influence
[c] Chokki Motobu influence
... unconfirmed

After retirement, Matsumura taught karate at an open space in Sakiyama village, Shuri. Among his students were:

Anko Itosu (1832–1916)
Kentsu Yabu (1866–1937)[3]
Chomo Hanashiro (1869–1945)[3]
Gichin Funakoshi (1868–1957)[3]
Chotoku Kyan (1870–1945)

Anko Asato
Kiyuna PECHIN
Sakihara PECHIN
Ryosei Kuwae (1853–?)

It is difficult to decipher Matsumura's character. In his book *Karate-do, My Way of Life*, Gichin Funakoshi, true to Okinawan form, gives Matsumura almost super-human qualities, but Shoshin Nagamine told me a brutish story about Matsumura having subdued a tethered bull by repeatedly banging the poor animal on the forehead for over a week with a heavy stick. A more credible story was related by Joen Nakazato of Shorinji-ryu who, as a boy, had heard it from his teacher Chotoku Kyan:

Sokon Matsumura and some disciples (including Kyan) had just left a tea house at Tsuji and were returning home when, feeling for their aged teacher's safety, Matsumura's disciples, realising that they would have to pass close-by five drunken seamen who were causing a disturbance by shouting abuses at passersby, suggested that they take an alternative route home. However, Matsumura decided the issue by obstinately stating that they would take their originally intended route and, as was expected, the five seamen set upon Matsumura with a flourish of kicks and punches. Whilst the shocked disciples were wondering what they should do next, they saw their teacher curl up in a ball in the middle of the road apparently unaffected by the beating. At this the attackers, realising that this was no ordinary old man, became wary and drew back. Matsumura stood up and straightened his clothing but on feeling his topknot he found that his silver hairpin had fallen out and was lying near the now frightened seamen who quickly returned the missing article with an excuse of an apology and took to their heels.

Sokon Matsumura's wife is said to have had qualities that most men would envy. The daughter of a wealthy Yonabaru merchant, she was fond of sumo, arm-wrestling and weight-lifting contests in which, until she met Matsumura, she often challenged and bettered would-be suitors. Nakazato told me that Chotoku Kyan remembered seeing her pick up a 60kg (132lb) bag of rice with one hand, just to sweep under it.

The exact dates of Matsumura's birth and death are uncertain. Shoshin Nagamine's enquiries revealed that Matsumura had had his 88th birthday party in 1897 and thus calculated his birth year as 1809. Katsuya Miyahira of Shorin-ryu (kobayashi) and others claimed that Matsumura died aged 92 so, taking 1809 as his birth year, a simple calculation gives his death in approximately 1901. Sometime before he died, however, Matsumura presented a letter to his pupil

Ryosei Kuwae who in turn passed it on to his eldest son. This letter is of some importance as an insight into the mentality of the times, and is one of the few old Okinawan manuscripts to have survived intact to the present day. Although it has been published in Japanese several times, this is probably the first time it has ever been translated and published in English:

If you want to practise fighting arts, you must know the true meaning of them, therefore I have resolved to state the facts; please examine them closely.

So, the way of learning and the way of fighting arts have one and the same purpose. There are respectively three kinds of learning and fighting arts.

The three kinds of learning are namely:

1. reading, writing and arithmetic – the three Rs
2. exegetics
3. the study of Confucianism.

The three Rs include calligraphy, composing words into sentences and being able to calculate the totals of rice stipends required by important people. Exegetics is the teaching to people the sense of duty ascertained through the Chinese classics, having the way of profound knowledge and teaching by example. Both the former schools of learning are distinctive as being just literary arts, however Confucianist learning brings about sincerity, pureness of heart and a sense of propriety in all things. Hence the governing of one's house (and even one's country) well, will result in world peace. This is true knowledge, Confucian knowledge.

The three kinds of fighting arts are:

1. those of court instructors
2. nominal styles
3. the true fighting arts.

The court instructors' styles are practised in a very unusual way; movements are never the same, formless and light, becoming (like women) more and more dance-like as the proponents mature.[4] The exponents of nominal styles do not practise regularly, they come and go here and there, contriving how to win, quarreling with and perhaps inconveniencing people. Most serious of all they cause bodily harm, making their parents and family ashamed of them. With the true fighting arts you will not be distracted, so contrive for achievement, govern your own heart and wait for your enemy to be disarrayed; quieten yourself and wait for your enemy to become agitated; snatch your enemy's heart and you will conquer him. As your proficiency increases distinctiveness will come, you will be capable of everything, you will not be disorientated, you will know the place of filial piety. The spirit of a ferocious tiger and the speed of a flying swift will develop naturally so that you will be able to overpower any aggressor.

A wise sage wrote in the Chudokansha the following so called 'Seven Martial Virtues': Martial artists are forbidden to act in an unruly manner; soldiers should practise admonition, help people, distinguish themselves and safeguard the people so that the populace can live in peace and have abundant wealth. Therefore learning and fighting arts have the way of truth. Court instructors' styles and nominal styles are useless, so consider the true fighting arts carefully. I think you should seize the opportunity to act accordingly with restraint, so that if you practise with the previous mentioned facts in mind, it has been said that, the lower abdomen will become the storehouse of one's energy.

Hohan Soken

Hohan Soken, the oldest karate practitioner on Okinawa, claims to be the third generation successor to Sokon Matsumura; the latter having taught karate to his grandson, Nabe Matsumura (Nabi TANMEI), who in turn instructed Soken. When I interviewed Hohan Soken he was in his late 80s, slightly senile and a little hard to comprehend; quite the opposite to when I had seen him do a brilliant kama (sickle) kata demonstration in Naha four years earlier.

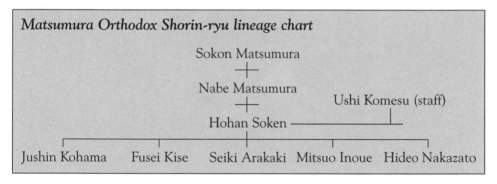

Matsumura Orthodox Shorin-ryu lineage chart

Soken told me that during the late 19th century his father had left Tera village in Shuri to become a farmer in Gaja, Nishihara, where Soken was born. Soken's mother was Nabe Matsumura's sister (making Nabe Matsumura Hohan Soken's uncle) and through her introduction Soken started karate training at the age of 13.

Despite Nabe Matsumura's shizoku background he, like many of his social class at that time, had taken to pulling a rickshaw for his living and was also employed to guard the village of Gaja and surrounding farmland against thieves and poachers.

Katas and weapons

Hohan Soken told me that Nabe Matsumura taught him the katas: Naihanchi Shodan, Naihanchi Nidan, Naihanchi Sandan, Pinan Shodan, Pinan Nidan, Passai Sho, Passai Dai, Chinto, Kusanku, Gojushiho, Sesan, Rohai Jo, Rohai Chu, Rohai Ge and, finally, at the age of 23, Hakutsuru (White Crane). Nabe is supposed to have learned all of these katas from his grandfather, Sokon Matsumura; however, Soken later ambiguously informed me that Sokon

Matsumura had taught Hakutsuru only to his son. This would seem to indicate that Nabe Matsumura had learned Hakutsuru and perhaps other katas from sources other than his grandfather. Be that as it may, these katas became the foundation of Soken's karate system.

'The kata Hakutsuru,' Soken reminisced, 'was often practised on a 30cm (1ft) wide plank stretched over a fish pond.' Many of the ballet-like movements of the kata are done on the balls of the feet with the arms unfolding sideways from the elbow in imitation of a crane's unfurling wings. Breathing is an important aspect of Hakutsuru and develops a 'martial strength' (bu no chikara)[5] that cannot be detected by the eye and is totally different from normal muscular strength, 'it is a "soft" strength that collects in the lower abdomen (tanden) and is directed by the mind'.

From Nabe Matsumura, Soken also learned the use of the weapons: sai, kama, kusarigama, tuifa, suruchin and the nunchaku. From an old local, known as Ushi Komesu TANMEI of Nishihara, he learned the staff kata, Tsuken no Bo. It is interesting to note that few karate practitioners learned kobudo when Soken was a boy and that much of the kobudo taught today is, Soken felt, derived from that originally taught by Sokon Matsumura.

The style

Due to the ever-present work shortage on Okinawa, Soken emigrated to Argentina in 1920 where he worked as a farm labourer. He returned to Okinawa in 1952 and started teaching karate, calling his style Matsumura Orthodox Shorin-ryu,[6] choosing the Chinese characters for Shaolin to write Shorin – Shorin being the Japanese pronunciation of Shaolin.

Amidst much celebration Soken recently visited the USA, accompanied by his student Fusei Kise and, although he has had many invitations to return, his age restricts him from doing so. However, he still teaches karate to a group of senior students at his home on Mondays, Wednesdays and Fridays.

Unlike Goju-ryu which, Soken told me, 'is too "hard" and harmful to children', Shorin-ryu is a 'natural style' that is taught according to each individual student's attributes. His style has many holds and release techniques that incorporate using the thumb to bring pressure on vital points. These techniques were originally taught in secret and do not appear in the karate katas, suggesting that they were derived from Okinawan ti. A basic rule for applying these holds is 'grasp a weak opponent firmly and a strong opponent lightly' . Some 'safe' vital points for use with the extended thumb are:

1. a point at the base of the thumb and index finger (on the back of the hand)
2. a point on the outside of the elbow
3. a point on the shoulder joint between the chest and the shoulder
4. a point on the front of the neck just above the collar bone.

Another interesting technique, that actually appears in several of the Shorin styles, is the use of the outer muscular area of the forearm in a one action block and strike, as opposed to the more common middle and upper block with the bony side area of the forearm near the wrist.

Last of all, Hohan Soken told me that when he was a young man karate practitioners could, on permission of their teachers, visit other masters to learn their specialities. Nowadays, however, Soken believes that due to the commercialisation of karate the students are encouraged to learn only the one style, resulting in too narrow a scope of training that could eventually lead to an overall stagnation of the fighting art.

Author's note for the second edition Soken Hohan passed away in 1982 (or 1983 according to some sources), not so long after I called on him for a final interview. I remember that he was not too pleased at my impromptu visit, partly I presumed because I broke Okinawan protocol by being very informal, and partly because I was insistent on trying to resolve my dilemma of from whom Nabe Matsumura had learned Hakutsuru. The issue was never resolved and I felt a tinge of dishonesty. Was there a connection with the tea merchant Gokenki (see Chojun Miyagi, under Goju-ryu), or was there was a Ryukyuan ti connection? – especially because, as described to me, Hakutsuru resembles the ti-based, meditative dance Washin'tui (Jap. Washi no tori), or Dance of the Eagle. According to an interesting article in Bugeisha magazine, 'Village Kobudo' by John Sells (Issue #2, March 1997), Hohan's other recorded teacher, Ushi Komesu, had been a student of Tsuken Hantaka (or Chikin Kuraka, 1829–1898), evidently the creator of the staff kata Tsuken Bo, alias Chikin no Kon.

Seiki Arakaki

Recently, four of Hohan Soken's students, Seiki Arakaki, Mitsuo Inoue, Jushin Kohama and Hideo Nakazato, formed The Matsumura Shorin-ryu Karate-do Association with the aim of preserving orthodox Matsumura karate. Seiki Arakaki, being Soken's longest serving student, became president of the association and posted himself as Soken's top disciple. Soken told me however that he did not sanction this, stating that Arakaki's katas were now substantially different from those he originally taught him.

Despite the latter circumstances Seiki Arakaki is a karate-ka in his own right. Like many pre-war youngsters he learned Itosu-type karate[7] from various teachers whilst at school. He also learned sai techniques from his father who, like Arakaki's grandfather, was an expert with this weapon. Later, Seiki Arakaki learned Goju-ryu from Seiko Higa and, on Hohan Soken's return to Okinawa from Argentina, Arakaki, also being a native of Gaja village, started to train under him.

At his modern concrete gym Arakaki teaches Matsumura Orthodox Shorin-ryu katas with the addition of the two basic katas, Fukyu Ichi and Fukyu Ni. These two katas were, he told me, made up in order to teach karate to junior-

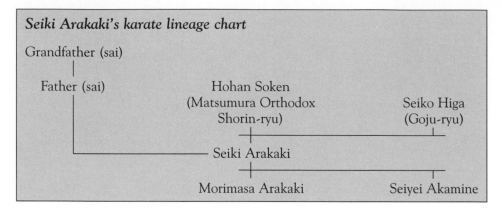

Seiki Arakaki's karate lineage chart

Grandfather (sai)
|
Father (sai)   Hohan Soken   Seiko Higa
                   (Matsumura Orthodox   (Goju-ryu)
                      Shorin-ryu)
                 └─────── Seiki Arakaki
                 Morimasa Arakaki   Seiyei Akamine

high-school boys; Fukyu Ni being the Goju-ryu kata, Gekisai Ichi. He also teaches three staff katas: Tsuken Bo Ichi, Tsuken Bo Ni and Tsuken Bo San, as well as one sai kata, Uhuchiku no Sai.[8] The staff katas, he thought, came from Tsuken Island, having originally been introduced there by Tsuken Akachu (Red Man Tsuken) who had been deported from Shuri.

Although Goju-ryu's name means 'hard-soft', Arakaki told me that actually all karate is hard and soft (several other teachers also held this opinion) and that Eiichi Miyazato had once suggested to him that the concept of karate styles was silly and should be abandoned in favour of the old, pre-war system when all karate was just simply tode. Arakaki remembered that when he was a young boy there were many man-to-man street fights often ending in death for one or both of the opponents and for this reason he, like many teachers, 'disguises' the instruction, rarely, if ever, teaching the real vital points or 'death blows'. 'In true martial arts, unlike sports, there are no rules. That is why in the past teachers carefully chose their students – sometimes during the interview of a prospective student, a teacher would throw his cup of tea into the young applicant's face to see if he would anger easily.' Arakaki in a way regrets the modern trend towards sports and commercialisation and recalled the days when there were no high kicks or upper punches, when pupils were taught to imagine attacking the groin and vital rib areas.

'Although large karate stances look powerful,' Arakaki explained, 'they should actually be kept small. These large stances were developed of late by Japanese who consider looks to be all important. They (the Japanese) also brought about the modern trend towards terminology of karate, but in fact when I was a boy this was lacking.' Other advice given to me was: 'when sparring one should not overly rotate the hips as an opponent will be able to "read" your moves.' He also said that: 'Lower your hips and bend your legs', is a good rule for Okinawan sumo as well as for karate; the same applies for bull- and cock-fighting: 'Ushi sageru hō was katsu (The lowest bull will win).' 'Always remember, if someone pushes your left shoulder don't oppose the thrust, go with it and counter with your right fist.'

The dojo kun

Another important aspect of Arakaki's teaching is 'reigi', the meaning of which he quoted as 'Waza migaitte, kokoro migaitte (Polish your technique, polish your mind)' and told me that it was also the basis of his dojo kun, as follows:

1. all students should practise politeness
2. bow before you start to practise and after you (have) practise(d)
3. do your best whenever you practise; lazy practice will disturb your progress
4. follow the instructions of your instructor and your seniors
5. see and hear the instructors' forms and their instructions
6. practise continually even for a while, interruptions (will) disturb your progress
7. learn the main part of karate and watch your own heart, find your (own) way to make progress
8. be moderate in your daily life. Abnormal eating and drinking (will) disturb your progress
9. try to make progress always and don't lose yourself
10. a loose mind is one of the weakest points in karate practice
11. karate practice has no limit in progress; practice makes you complete.

The makiwara

Lastly, he told me of the pros and cons of the makiwara punching board or post. 'A makiwara should be springy with a generous amount of give or the constant striking of it will damage the striker's wrists. There were, and still are, basically two types of makiwara, the flat board and the round post. The flat one is used for

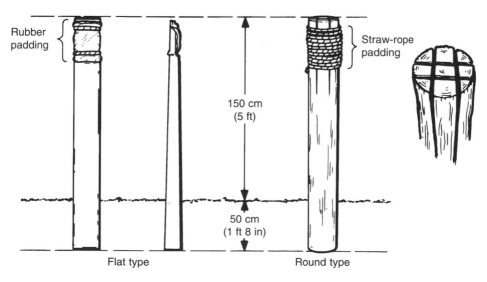

Figure 3 *Makiwaras*

practising the straight corkscrew punch and the round one, which has one or two splits to halfway down the middle, is used for training the fist, elbow and the side of the hand. Makiwaras should always be padded with something soft like straw-rope, rubber or carpet, to cushion the impact of the strike.'

Arakaki has invented another kind of makiwara with a large, flat surface area padded with rubber. This is suitable for children, as many youngsters damage their knuckles when practising on the usual ones. The large makiwara is also useful for practising side and jump kicks. When first using a makiwara, one should punch softly then gradually increase the power day-by-day.

Arakaki's father often warned him about making large black callouses on his knuckles. One reason was that, as his father was a merchant, customers would, on seeing the swollen and deformed hands, be easily frightened away. Another reason was that local ruffians would often try to pick fights on pseudo-karate-ka who flouted such grotesque trophies. 'After practice on the makiwara,' Arakaki told me, 'it is a good idea to wash one's hands in salt water (or urine) and then alcohol; if the skin is cut, always carefully sterilise the affected area.'

Author's note for the second edition Since my interview with Seiki Arakaki, he has reportedly passed away.

Ishimine-ryu

Shinyei Kaneshima

Shinyei Kaneshima, an 80-year-old lawyer, is president and founder of the Ishimine-ryu Karate-do Preservation Society. He named his style after a teacher he called Old Man Ishimine (Ishimine O) who, although once well known on Okinawa, is today little remembered. Kaneshima does not know who Old Man Ishimine's teacher was but other sources suggest that this Ishimine was, in fact, Ishimine PECHIN who had at one time been a student of Sokon Matsumura.

Ishimine PECHIN is described as having been very small with spindly legs. Once, on his way home to Shuri from a night out at Tsuji, he neared a big, powerful man known as Tamanaha who was taking a rest after the long, uphill climb. Ishimine asked Tamanaha for a light for his pipe and the two started up a friendly conversation as they set out together for the remainder of the trip. When Tamanaha realised that his skinny companion was the famous Ishimine he fancied his chances and thought of a way to anger him. As there was a slight drizzle, Tamanaha opened his paper umbrella and asked Ishimine to hold it for him. Ishimine complied with the cheeky request, but when Tamanaha next passed him his muddy straw sandals, Ishimine promptly threw them over a roadside hedge.

A fight thus being provoked, the two squared off. The weighty Tamanaha attacked with one mighty punch but the light-footed Ishimine quickly sprang to one side kicking his opponent with the tip of his big toe at a vital point on the lower rib-cage. Tamanaha immediately passed out and, after a futile attempt to revive him, Ishimine slung the gross piece of flesh over his shoulders and carried him home. Two days later Ishimine, feeling sorry for the harm he had caused, paid a sick call on Tamanaha and started to apologise, but the now feeble Tamanaha would have none of it and excused Ishimine from any blame saying the fault was entirely his own. Tamanaha died a few days later.

Shinyei Kaneshima's father, Shinbi Kaneshima (c.1868–1921), had been a student of Old Man Ishimine, having started training under him at the age of 16. Shinbi Kaneshima later became a Tokyo-to-Naha steamship stoker and during their valuable free time together he managed to pass on the essence of Ishimine's style to Shinyei, but died at the early age of 53 when Shinyei was only 21.

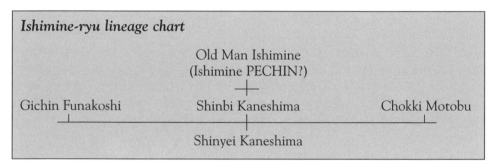

Ishimine-ryu lineage chart

Old Man Ishimine
(Ishimine PECHIN?)

Gichin Funakoshi   Shinbi Kaneshima   Chokki Motobu

Shinyei Kaneshima

Shinyei Kaneshima had reluctantly started karate and makiwara training at the age of seven under his father who made a point of saying that such practice was for the sake of health, not for fighting. Every morning Shinyei would get up, wash his face and go directly to the round makiwara post in the courtyard of his home and perform 10 right-hand and 20 left-hand strikes.

At the age of 19 he went to Tokyo as a student but later became a policeman and trained under the famous teachers, Gichin Funakoshi and Chokki Motobu. 'Funakoshi,' Kaneshima remembered, 'was well educated and a good youth leader; his famous adage "Karate ni sente nashi" had meant that one should never attack and if attacked, be only defensive.' Kaneshima also remembered the part he personally played in the popularising of karate on the mainland of Japan, by taking part in demonstrations at Tokyo and the surrounding areas with a school teacher named Kanken Oyadomari. In 1946 Kaneshima returned to Okinawa and demonstrated karate to the despondent post-war population at schools and village halls around Naha.

Ishimine-ryu has only three katas, Kuma-te (or Kuma-di) Sanchin, Naihanchi and Passai. Kuma-te Sanchin is unique to this style and is imitative of the bear (kuma). The stance is solid and bigger than in the Sanchin katas of other styles. The movements also resemble those of a bear; for example one of the arm movements is representative of a bear scooping a fish from water. The butt of the palm is the primary weapon and, because the finger tips are curled over, the hand resembles a bear's paw. Even the fighting strategy is based on that of a bear; for example, when a bear attacks a bull it supposedly strikes the bull in the face to stun it, then moves behind to finish it off.

Shinyei Kaneshima feels that of late there is too much emphasis on competition in karate and does not see the point of training to keep healthy and fit, only to get beaten up in some free-sparring contest. He feels that damage to the body is greatly reduced if the practitioners of such bouts wear full protectors. Although Kaneshima said that he has no actual disciples, he sometimes coaches the occasional interested visitor. His main interest is classical Okinawan painting and calligraphy, in which field he is one of only five or six such masters alive today. He hopes to publish his works in an effort to preserve the mood of the Okinawa he once knew; indeed the paintings he showed me reflected the quiet dignity of his character and of a bygone Ryukyu.

REFERENCES

[1] Some authorities claim that he was also a court instructor.

[2] According to Chozo Nakama of Shorin-ryu (Kobayashi). Gichin Funakoshi in *Karate-do Kyohan* also lists Sakiyama, Gushi and Tomoyore as having studied under Ason.

[3] Later became students of Anko Itosu.

[4] Probably a reference to ti. See Motobu-ryu, page 130.

[5] Another expression used by other teachers to explain martial strength was 'heavy fist'.

[6] i.e. Matsumura Seito Shorin-ryu.

[7] See Shorin-ryu (Kobayashi), page 88.

[8] See Uhuchiku Kobudo, page 122.

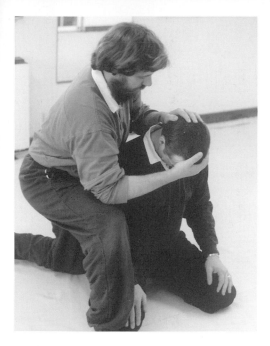

Above The author giving a te-based Shiatsu treatment for release of stress

Above right Getting ready for a bout. Contestants at the annual Shuri Festival karate competition

Right Jukendo's Golden Dragon

Below Ryuei-ryu kata demonstration

Above Rare photograph of Meitoku Yagi testing hardness in Sanchin kata

Above right Kenko Nakaima

Right Wooden statue of a Chinese martial arts deity at the Jundokan

Below The first Annual All Okinawa (non-protector) Free Sparring Contest, sponsored by the Uechi-ryu Karate-do Association. Tsugo Sakumoto (*seated referee*) earnestly watches as one of his karate students (*right*) avoids a powerful strike from a member of the US team, and drives his knee into his opponent's groin

Kanryo Higaonna

Seiko Higa

Jinan Shinzato

Chojun Miyagi

Above Training inside the Jundokan

Left Training apparatus used in the Jundokan

Below left Training at Meitoku Yagi's dojo

Below Eiichi Miyazato demonstrating the kata Tensho

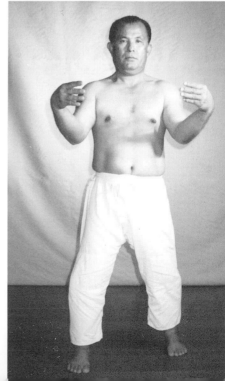

Kanyei Uechi performing a kata

Kanyei Uechi teaching at his dojo

Meitoku Yagi

Kanbun Uechi

Kafu Kojo (*centre*) with Shingo Hayashi (*front right*), Hideki Kojo (*front left*), Tatsumi Kojo (*rear left*) and Kaoru Kojo (*rear right*)

Uechi-ryu weight training

Hakutsuru Kamae

Seishin Kamae

Fudo Kamae

Jinpu Kamae

Jumonji Kamae

Unryu Kamae

Aiki Kamae

Katate Seigan Kamae

Seiha Kamae

Tenchi Kamae

Suika Kamae

Chiseigan Kamae

Ichimonji Kamae

Above Hohan Soken

Above right Nabe Matsumura

Right Sokon Matsumura

Below Seiki Arakaki (*kneeling centre*) with students at his dojo

Above left Seiki Arakaki in his dojo

Above right Shinyei Kaneshima demonstrating Kuma-te Sanchin

Left Hohan Soken in his latter years

Below Arakaki's large makiwara

Above left Chotoku Kyan
Above centre Joen Nakazato practising 'secret
techniques' with Bunei Okuhira, December
1931
Above right Chokki Motobu in fighting pose

Right Kosaku Matsumora

Below Chotoku Kyan with students (*left to
right*) Joen Nakazato, Kyan, Matsumoto,
Nishihara and Kurato (c. 1940)

Shorinji-ryu speciality,
the standing-fist punch

Takayoshi Nagamine

Kata practice overlooked by Joen Nakazato

Above Shoshin Nagamine (*left*) practising Zen meditation with some students at his dojo, the Kodokan

Right Kichiro Shimabukuro of Isshin-ryu

Below left Shoshin Nagamine

Below right Young students practising at the Chubu Shorin-ryu Meibukan

Above left Katsuhide Kochi

Above right Katsuhide Kochi demonstrating the kata Aran

Left Matsubayashi-ryu lineage: *(from left to right)* Chokki Motobu, Ankichi Arakaki and Chotoku Kyan; *(below)* Shoshin Nagamine

Right Isshin-ryu world headquarters dojo in 1979

Left Seijin Inamine

Above Kata practice overlooked by Inamine

Right Line up of karate teachers.
Upper row (*from left to right*): Shinpan Shiroma, Chitose, Choshin Chibana, Genwa Nakasone.
Bottom row (*from left to right*): Chotoku Kyan, Kentsu Yabu,
Chomo Hanashiro,
Chojun Miyagi

Right Gokenki (*seated centre*) with some students

Chapter 5
Tomari-te

Tomari-te was the karate (or tode) taught at Tomari village and, although nowadays it is not taught commercially as a system unto itself, the katas and some techniques, which once made up the major part of it, are to be found in most of the Shorin styles.

Kafu Kojo of Kojo-ryu called Tomari-te 'a hotch potch of various Shaolin katas' and stated that the shizoku of Tomari were of the lowest order. One of the few surviving Tomari-te practitioners, Seikichi Hokama (born in 1896), told me that when he was a boy the katas were fairly universally spread amongst the various teachers. This is not surprising as Tomari at that time was little more than a village and the mainstay of Tomari-te was passed on by two late 19th-century contemporaries, Kokan Oyadomari and Kosaku Matsumora, whom it seems were on very good terms with each other.

Oyadomari-type Tomari-te
During an interview with Seikichi Hokama, he told me how he had learned the katas: Naihanchi Shodan, Naihanchi Nidan, Passai, Wanshu, Rohai, Wankan, Kusanku Sho and Kusanku Dai, from the brothers Kotsu Oyadomari and Konin Oyadomari. The style incorporating these katas had been handed down from Kokan Oyadomari through the Oyadomari family from father to son for three

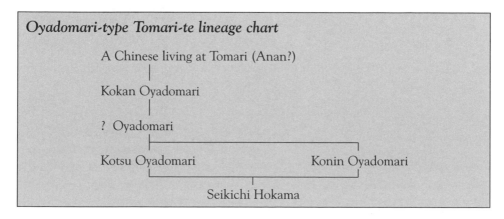

Oyadomari-type Tomari-te lineage chart

A Chinese living at Tomari (Anan?)
|
Kokan Oyadomari
|
? Oyadomari
|
Kotsu Oyadomari   Konin Oyadomari
|
Seikichi Hokama

generations, Kokan Oyadomari having originally learned Chinese boxing from a Chinese living at Tomari 'who used very light techniques'.

Seikichi Hokama recalled that at the age of 16 he had been skinny, often bedridden and suffered from a stomach complaint. A local doctor diagnosed tuberculosis and gave Hokama some medicine which he promptly discarded 'because it tasted nasty'. Next, Hokama was introduced to Kotsu Oyadomari, a friend of the family, who diagnosed lack of exercise and set the lad to work on the makiwara. At first Hokama did ten strikes a day, gradually building up to 20, and then 30 several times a day. His health rapidly improved until in under a year he was quite well. He stayed under the guidance of the Oyadomari brothers until he was 25, but during this time he also studied now and again under Kodatsu Iha, Kama Higa and One-Eyed Toguchi – all of Matsumora-type Tomari-te. A Chinese merchant, called Ten Senshi, who had a tea business at Tomari and employed Hokama as a watchman for his store, taught him a punching technique.

The Oyadomaris taught that the drinking of alcohol and smoking of tobacco were not conducive to karate practice. They also would often preach that: 'Because our parents went to a lot of time and trouble to bring us up to be healthy adults, we owe it to them to defer from anything that may impair our health, so if you get into a fight remember that your opponent's life is in your hands, and yours in his – a slight mistake can be fatal to either party.' Then he warned that if the opponent is bigger than yourself: 'Spring in like a cat and do not give him a chance to catch hold of you.'

When Hokama was younger he refused to teach anyone Tomari-te because he thought that it was too dangerous, but now, being still healthy and in his 80s, he feels rather sorry for not having done so. 'Before the Second World War,' he told me, 'many a fine young man was killed in a fight due to his being overconfident after only two or three years of karate practice, so remember, there is always someone stronger than yourself.'

Matsumora-type Tomari-te

Seikichi Hokama suggested that I pay a visit to Seiyu Nakasone for information on Matsumora-type Tomari-te, but unfortunately, due to the poor health of Nakasone, I was unable to arrange an interview with him. However, I was able to ascertain that Kosaku Matsumora (1829–1898) had learned the secret principles of Chinese boxing from a Chinese who was living the life of a derelict amongst the graves in a hillock cave near Tomari[1] that has now succumbed to bulldozers.

Matsumora and some acquaintances had often seen the Chinese practising a form of Chinese boxing and one day decided to ask for tuition. The Chinese consented and taught the group in the courtyard of a tomb near his cave. Before leaving Okinawa the Chinese presented Matsumora with a scroll painting of a woman in a kamae posture holding a willow twig, which represented the secret principles of his Chinese boxing – however, even if he had learned them, Matsumora never taught these secret principles.

Katsuya Miyahira of Shorin-ryu (Kobayashi) told me of a similar story of a Chinese from Fuchou called Anan who was shipwrecked in the Ryukyus and ended up in Tomari where he taught Chinese boxing to Shiroma of Tomari, Kinjo, Kosaku Matsumora and others. In his book *Karate-do Kyohan*, Gichin Funakoshi relates that he had heard that a teacher of Gusukuma (Shiroma), Kinjo, Yamada, Nakazato, Yamazato, Toguchi, Matsumora and Oyadomari (all of Tomari), had trained under a southern Chinese who had drifted ashore at Okinawa. This would suggest that Kokan Oyadomari's teacher, who used light techniques, and Kosaku Matsumora's teacher were actually one and the same. However, Matsumora also learned a fighting art from two Okinawan teachers going by the names of Ki Teruya and Karyu Uku.

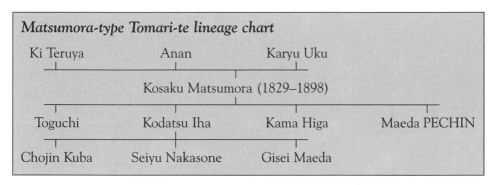

Matsumora-type Tomari-te lineage chart

Ki Teruya   Anan   Karyu Uku

Kosaku Matsumora (1829–1898)

Toguchi   Kodatsu Iha   Kama Higa   Maeda PECHIN

Chojin Kuba   Seiyu Nakasone   Gisei Maeda

During his younger days, Seiyu Nakasone had been a well-known karate-ka throughout the Shuri, Naha and Tomari areas where he was nicknamed Nakasone 'Kaka' because of his uncontrollable stutter and, although usually a passive person, he would strike out at anyone who inadvertently called him by this name. Hokama remembered that Nakasone was two years his senior and that they sometimes practised together under Matsumora's top disciple, Kodatsu Iha. Nakasone had had a powerful punch which he often demonstrated by break-ing boards and tiles. Once he killed a goat that was being prepared for a feast by punching the poor beast on the head and kicking it in the chest, breaking its skull and some of its ribs. Another of his 'tricks' was to chop the neck off a standing beer bottle with the side of his hand, without knocking the bottle over.

The style

'Practice of Tomari-te,' Hokama told me, 'was hard work and done in semi-secre-cy behind slatted bamboo fencing, high stone walls, or in the hillocks then sur-rounding Tomari.' He described Tomari-te as having been 'soft', not 'jerky' like modern-day karate; the Chinese, he thought, still understand this concept well. The full-corkscrew punch was not encouraged as it leaves the vulnerable back of the hand open to a rap-with-the-knuckles strike that can render the attacker's hand inoperative. The rising-standing-fist punch, which is aligned with the cen-tre of the opponent's body, was preferred because it could be readily adapted for the foreknuckle-strike. By utilising the opponent's strength, the rising block was used to 'open up' the opponent's vital chest areas so that the foreknuckle-jab could be used most effectively.

Although Tomari-te and Shuri-te were similar, they differed in several minor ways. One example was in the kata Naihanchi, in which Shuri-te incorporated a high stance known as 'kiba dachi', whereas Tomari-te incorporated a lower stance called 'shiko dachi'. To practise shiko dachi a student had to walk up and down the dojo area with another student standing on his outspread thighs. The kata Kusanku was very acrobatic and was derived from the Chinese of the same name who demonstrated and taught Chinese boxing on Okinawa in the late 18th or early 19th centuries. The kata Wansu (or Wanshu) is said to have been taught to Matsumora and Oyadomari by a Chinese military attaché of that name who came to Okinawa with the military attaché, Ason.

Chokki Motobu (1871–1944)

Chokki Motobu is credited with having learned karate from Anko Itosu,[2] Tokumine PECHIN and Kosaku Matsumora (some sources also include Sokon Matsumura) but, in Higa Yuchoku's[3] words, 'He was no one's disciple'. Due to Chokki Motobu's connections with Tomari, I have classified him under Tomari-te, but actually the style he taught reflected more his own unique personality than any established system.

According to Chozo Nakama,[4] Chokki Motobu, or Motobu Saru (Motobu the Monkey), as he became known, was born at Akahira village, Shuri, the third son of Motobu UDUN, a high ranking Anji.[5]

Whereas Chokki's elder brother Choyu, the eldest son of the family,[6] received a fine education and was taught the secrets of his family's ti system by his father as was customary, Chokki, whose education was rather neglected, grew up with his mother and gained the reputation of being an uncontrollable child. However, he picked up some of the basics of ti and regularly practised with the then fashionable makiwara punching board, gradually forming a fighting system of his own fashion.

On reaching manhood, Chokki Motobu took it upon himself to visit Tsuji and challenge strong-looking young men. He was rarely defeated and gradually, from practical experience of many such fights, adopted and developed all kinds of techniques into his system, earning himself a reputation for being rather aggressive. He entered Anko Itosu's dojo but was soon expelled because of his attitude of always wanting to prove himself.

Next he drifted to Tokumine PECHIN who was well known for his karate, bojutsu (staff fighting) and habitual drinking. Motobu conveniently paid for his nightly tuition with the odd flask of awamori rice wine, but the set-up did not last long because Tokumine, having bettered 30 constables in a fight at Tsuji, was considered by the local magistrate to be an undesirable and was promptly exiled to the Yaeyama Islands. Tokumine no Kun, Tokumine's staff kata, is still said to exist there.

Nakama also related how Motobu had knocked on Kosaku Matsumora's door, but, because of his own bad reputation, Motobu disguised his identity and used his mother's surname, Sesoko. The ploy did not last long and Matsumora soon discovered Motobu's true identity, but allowed him to stay on anyway.

Seikichi Hokama told me a slightly different story of how Motobu and two of his pals had cockily approached Matsumora for tuition upon which the latter sat down on the edge of his verandah and instructed the three to attack him. Thinking that this would be an easy victory, Motobu and pals jumped at the opportunity and lodged a simultaneous attack on Matsumora. Without flinching, Matsumora caught one of the attacker's arms by the wrist, flicked and painfully disabled it; he caught another attacker's arm with a circular block and trapped the hand under his armpit; the third attacker came in with a 'chop' to Matsumora's neck, but the latter merely pinned the attacker's hand between his neck and shoulder. Everyone thus knew quite clearly where they all stood and never caused any more trouble.

Motobu's fight

In 1921, due to the failure of his horse-drawn taxi business, Chokki Motobu went to Osaka with his family in search of work and was taken on as a night watchman in a spinning company. Whilst there he gained countrywide recognition by defeating a big foreign boxer in a much publicised challenge match. I heard the story of this fight from several sources but the facts always differed slightly. Some said dubiously that the foreigner was the world boxing champion; most agreed that he was a Russian and some gave the unlikely name of John Ken Taro.

Chozo Nakama said that Motobu had told him the foreigner's name was Johnson (Seikichi Uehara of Motobu-ryu claimed it was George) and that Motobu's landlord had arranged the challenge bout in answer to a newspaper advertisement for challengers. Nakama also said that during the fight Motobu managed to dodge his opponent for the first round and did not counter. Then in the second round the foreigner became over-confident and went for an all-out attack, but at the same instant Motobu jumped and struck the foreigner behind the ear with a typical ti foreknuckle strike, knocking him out cold – some authorities say that he never completely recovered. Although members of the audience were at a loss as to what had happened and were puzzled by the sup-posedly new fighting art, the technique that Motobu was supposed to have used was typical of his repertoire. The publicity from the bout later brought about much interest in the then fairly unknown art of Okinawan karate and Motobu became a full-time teacher.

In about 1938 Chokki Motobu left his family at Osaka and made one of his return trips to Okinawa, later opening a dojo at Nishin-machi (in modern-day Kume-cho), Naha in about 1940. Once, a visiting Japanese judo expert, called Sudo, challenged Motobu to a friendly match. Motobu agreed and at the appointed time they squared off and faced each other without moving an eyelid for two full minutes, upon which Sudo declared that he could not find an open-ing and gave up. In another story I heard, Motobu, feeling confident over his win at Osaka, decided to try his skills out on his elder brother Choyu[7] but it in no way diminishes Chokki to say that Choyu toyed with him ('as if dancing') and threw Chokki about as if he were a child. Realising the brilliance of Choyu's technique Chokki humbled himself and adopted many new ti forms.

Nakama insisted that Chokki Motobu was not the ruffian he was often made out to be; in fact, he was quite the gentleman befitting his social background. His speech (Okinawan dialect) was polite, authoritative, as well as masculine and he always taught his students the essence and necessity of good manners. However, his Japanese was lacking somewhat and when teaching at mainland universities he always used an Okinawan interpreter; indeed, due to the dictates of the times, his noble birthright made it quite unnecessary for him to assume a humble attitude.

Motobu could neither save money nor run a business efficiently. When in Okinawa he lived at Tomari with his mistress who, because she thought that he had no sense of the value of money whatsoever, would carefully account his daily needs and pass him the exact amount of cash explaining, as one would do for a little child, precisely what each sum was for.

Whilst in Okinawa, Motobu dictated many notes on karate to Chozo Nakama, who carefully wrote them down and compiled them into book form in his spare time. The final manuscript contained passages on the history of karate, names of katas, kata explanations and Motobu's own free-fighting development, 'henshu'. On a return trip to Osaka, Motobu sent a letter to Nakama requesting him to forward the manuscript immediately as he needed the money to pay hos-pital fees. Motobu sold the book to an unknown publisher and Nakama has never heard of it since; his own copy was burned during the Second World War. Despite this, the author later found out that Motobu did in fact publish a book, but whether or not this is the book that Nakama compiled is uncertain; it was published by the Tode-jutsu Popularisation Society and called *Okinawa Kenpo Tode-jutsu*, Kumite Edition.

Although he knew two karate katas, Naihanchi and Passai, Motobu usually only taught his own interpretation of Naihanchi that included ti-like grappling and throwing techniques. Much more than his katas, though, it is the part he played in the development of karate sparring for which he is best remembered. Such was the fame of his sparring that students of other teachers were often referred to him in order to learn these special techniques. Among his many sur-viving Okinawan students are Shoshin Nagamine (Matsubayashi-ryu), Shinsuke Kaneshima (Tozan-ryu), Shinyei Kaneshima (Ishimine-ryu), Katsuya Miyahira (Shorin-ryu – Kobayashi) and Chozo Nakama.

In September of 1944 Chokki Motobu died in the home of his mistress at Tomari aged 73, in Chozo Nakama's words, 'still looking for the essence of karate'.

REFERENCES

[1] The tomb-pocked hills to the north of Tomari are even today the haunt of many a homeless derelict.

[2] See Shorin-ryu (Kobayashi), page 88.

[3] See Shorin-ryu (Kobayashi), page 94.

[4] See Shorin-ryu (Kobayashi), page 99.

[5] See Motobu-ryu, page 130.

[6] See Motobu-ryu, page 130.

[7] See Motobu-ryu, page 130.

Chapter 6
Shorinji-ryu; Matsubayashi-ryu; Chubu Shorin-ryu; Isshin-ryu; Shorin-ryu (Shaolin); Ryukyu Shorin-ryu

The styles included in this chapter have all been heavily influenced by Chotoku Kyan who, according to Shoshin Nagamine, was the third son of Chofu Kyan (Joen Nakazato told the author he was the fourth), an eleventh generation successor of the Ryukyuan king, Sho Sei.

Shorinji-ryu
Chotoku Kyan (1870–1945)
Chotoku Kyan's father, Chofu Kyan, was steward to the last Ryukyuan king, Sho Tai, and accompanied the latter when he was exiled to Tokyo. The young Chotoku also journeyed to Tokyo, where he received much of his academic education, and later, after returning to Okinawa, he was able to learn karate from several teachers to whom he had been introduced by his father. According to Joen Nakazato, Chotoku Kyan, at one time or another, learned the katas:

Sesan, Naifuanchi and Gojushiho – from Sokon Matsumura (Shuri-te);
Kusanku – from Yara Chatan (Shuri-te), who had migrated from Shuri to settle in Yomitan village;
Passai – from Kokan Oyadomari (Tomari-te);
Wanshu – from Maeda PECHIN (Tomari-te), a student of Kosaku Matsumora;

Chinto – from Kosaku Matsumora (Tomari-te);
Ananku – from a Taiwanese who visited Okinawa[1] (another claim is that he brought this kata back with him as a souvenir of a trip to Taiwan);
and the staff kata, Tokumine no Kun, from Tokumine PECHIN in Yaeyama.

Chozo Nakama told me that actually when Kyan visited Yaeyama he found that Tokumine had already died. However, before his death, Tokumine had taught his landlord the kata Tokumine no Kun and the landlord, who was by then an old man, kindly consented to teach the kata to Kyan.

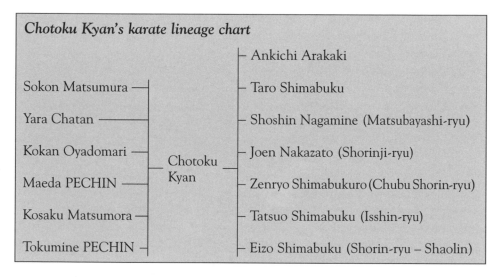

Chotoku Kyan's karate lineage chart

Sokon Matsumura — ┐
Yara Chatan ─────┤
Kokan Oyadomari ─┤ Chotoku
Maeda PECHIN ───┤ Kyan
Kosaku Matsumora ┤
Tokumine PECHIN ┘

├ Ankichi Arakaki
├ Taro Shimabuku
├ Shoshin Nagamine (Matsubayashi-ryu)
├ Joen Nakazato (Shorinji-ryu)
├ Zenryo Shimabukuro (Chubu Shorin-ryu)
├ Tatsuo Shimabuku (Isshin-ryu)
└ Eizo Shimabuku (Shorin-ryu – Shaolin)

Chotoku Kyan was small, thin and nicknamed Chan Mi-gwa (Small-eyed Kyan) because of his permanent squint. According to Nagamine, Kyan's adult life was miserably poverty stricken, but Katsumi Murakami in his *Karate-do to Ryukyu Kobudo* states that Choshin Chibana[2] had told him that Kyan frequented the Tsuji brothels and was fond of travelling. To raise money for these activities Kyan used various ploys; once his wife bought a pig and whenever it gave birth to piglets Kyan would sell them and deceive his trusting spouse by giving her less than he had received, keeping the difference for himself. Kyan is also said to have been an asthmatic and often bedridden.

Two rather undisciplined students of Kyan's, Ankichi Arakaki and Taro Shimabuku, often accompanied him on his excursions. Once they went for a 'martial arts' trip to the northern Japanese island of Hokkaido and advertised that they would accept any challenges. During such contests Kyan always warned the two to use one-strike-knock-out punches should the challenger manage to force them to the edge of the arena. When visiting Tsuji, Kyan taught his two disciples that karate practice alone was not enough and that they should engage in drinking bouts and associate with prostitutes to fulfil their martial-arts training!

Kyan loved cockfighting and often took his two disciples along with him to the various village cockfights. Whilst at one such meeting, where many village youths were gathered, Arakaki and Shimabuku, wanting to test the strength of their teacher, started a scrap then ran off and hid themselves. Kyan, still clutching his precious prize cock under one arm, fought the attackers off with his free arm to the amazement of his two disciples who were silently watching the scuffle from their hiding place.

Ankichi Arakaki, who was the eldest son of a Shuri rice wine brewer, is still remembered by the old folk of Shuri for his debonair antics. Strong, good-looking young men like him were the local stars of the times and a topic of many a conversation. The sons of former shizoku families, they found it difficult to adapt to the plebeian way of life and were constantly seeking outlets for their frustrations. Arakaki is often credited with having killed a large sumo wrestler at Tsuji with his famous tip-of-the-toe kick, but rumour has it that the cause of his own untimely death at the age of 28 was brought about when he went out of his depth and challenged Nago no Agarie.[3]

Kyan taught karate at his home near the Hija Bridge in Yomitan ward and later became karate instructor at the Okinawa Prefectural Agricultural School and the Kadena Police Station. Among his other students were Joen Nakazato, Shosin Nagamine, Zenryo Shimabukuro, Tatsuo Shimabuku and Eizo Shimabuku. He sometimes did karate demonstrations with Choshin Chibana and, in 1942, at the opening of Shoshin Nagamine's dojo, Kyan demonstrated his karate before Admiral Kenwa Kanna. In 1943 Kyan and three of his students did demonstrations at the Motobu and Nakijin elementary schools to help improve the morale of families who had lost young sons during the long, bitter war. Kyan was 73 at the time and thrilled the audience by breaking some boards. He always denied however that he could peel the bark from a pine tree with his bare hands, 'as the skin of the hands,' he would explain, 'is too soft'.

Kyan taught an adaptation of the standing fist which, he told his students, should be used to strike the upper parts of someone taller than oneself. Despite his small stature he was never defeated in his many challenge matches because he always used evasive tactics. He often warned his students that if two young oak saplings are banged together only the bark is damaged, but if two fresh eggs are rolled together they will both crack open. 'There is nothing more frightening than karate,' he would say, 'so experts try not to fight.'

Chotoku Kyan survived the holocaust of the Battle of Okinawa, but died shortly after in the north of the island from fatigue and malnutrition at the age of 76.

Joen Nakazato

Shorinji-ryu contains the essence of Chotoku Kyan's style. Joen Nakazato, the founder and president of the All Okinawa Shorinji Association, studied karate under Kyan (between the ages of 13 and 20) whilst attending the Okinawa

Prefectural Agricultural School and later the Kadena Teachers' Training College. In 1942 Nakazato was drafted into the army and posted to the north of China. At the war's end he found himself in the Siamese Highlands and his division was placed under the custody of an English army overseer. Nakazato remembered that at the mountain camp he built a makeshift karate dojo, demonstrated karate at camp variety shows and, in the evenings, staff in hand, helped to guard the camp.

On his return to Japan, Nakazato opened a dojo at Matsubashi, Kumamoto Prefecture and demonstrated karate and kobudo with Bunyei Okuhara, Matsuo Kawada and Juhatsu Kyoda[4] at the Kumamoto City Kabukiza. In March of 1947 Nakazato returned to Okinawa and opened a dojo in the courtyard of his old home at his native village of Chinen, where he resides and teaches to this day.

On finding that his teacher had died, Nakazato first thought of calling the style Kyan-ryu, but after much deliberation decided on the name Shorinji because of the historical connections between karate and the Shaolin Temple in China (Shorinji being the Japanese pronunciation of the Chinese characters for Shaolin tzu, i.e. Shaolin Temple).

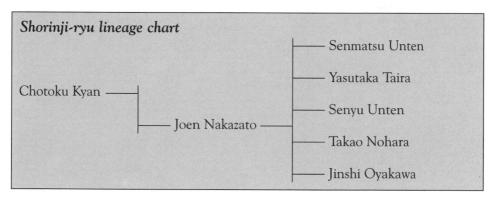

Shorinji-ryu lineage chart

Chotoku Kyan —— Joen Nakazato ——
- Senmatsu Unten
- Yasutaka Taira
- Senyu Unten
- Takao Nohara
- Jinshi Oyakawa

Katas and training

Because Nakazato wants to pass on Kyan's style in its entirety, he teaches Kyan's nine katas in their unaltered forms. These katas are performed with hard, powerful movements and contain many 'disguised' techniques. For example, an ordinary middle block can be made into a backfist. Sesan is taught as a basic kata and is practised with dynamic tension in a similar way to the Sanchin kata of Goju-ryu; breathing in naturally with the lower abdomen, then out, in conjunction with slow, forceful movements. Nakazato explained that this exercise does not pose a danger to health, provided one does not hold the breath whilst the body is in tension. 'This breathing exercise,' he told me, 'is used naturally by human beings when at work, as when stone masons break large rocks; however, punching the abdomen to test hardness should be avoided at all times.'

I found Nakazato to be a stocky, good-natured, modest and friendly man. The deputy headmaster of an elementary school, he has several karate students who are teachers, and who captain Shorinji-ryu karate clubs at their respective high schools. Shorinji-ryu is a style to be reckoned with at the various high-school sports competitions in which full protectors are compulsory.

'During sparring practice at Kyan's dojo,' Nakazato remembered, 'the students sometimes wore protectors but at other times sparred without them.' To test if their strikes (during the non-protector bouts) were accurate, the students would dip their finger tips in soot and touch (rather than strike) their opponents, later assessing their success or failure by examining the soot marks on their opponents' bodies. The main target areas were along a broad line following the inside of the arms, down along the side of the chest to the floating ribs and along the inside of the legs from the ankle to the groin. Except for those of the head, the other vital points were not considered to be so important as they could easily be protected by merely hardening the body at that point.

Inside Nakazato's breeze-block and corrugated-iron-roofed dojo, makiwaras take a prominent position, and the swollen knuckles of many of his students testify to much work on these. Due to the distance of Chinen village from the main city centres, Nakazato has comparatively few students; however, he has instructed students from the Japanese mainland and would not object to taking on interested visitors from overseas.

Matsubayashi-ryu

Shoshin Nagamine

The founder of Matsubayashi-ryu, Shoshin Nagamine, is one of the few Okinawans to have written at any length about karate. In his excellent book, *The Essence of Okinawan Karate-do*, Nagamine gives a thorough historical and technical description of the style, as well as a brief history of karate and his thoughts on the tournament system. The son of a farmer, Nagamine suffered from poor health as a young boy but, from the age of 17, he started karate training under Chojin Kuba of Tomari-te and his health gradually improved. Next, Nagamine learned karate from Chotoku Kyan's young disciples, Taro Shimabuku and Ankichi Arakaki. At the same time, whilst he was captain of his school karate club, he trained under Kodatsu Iha of Tomari-te.

In 1928 Nagamine was drafted into the army and posted to China. In 1931, after returning to Okinawa, he entered the police force and was appointed to the Kadena police station for four years, where he received karate instruction from Chotoku Kyan. Whilst studying at the Metropolitan Police Academy at Tokyo in 1936, Nagamine had the opportunity to learn sparring and practical fighting under Chokki Motobu; he also met Sokon Matsumura's and Anko Itosu's disciples, Chomo Hanashiro and Kentsu Yabu, who warned him that the karate katas at Tokyo had changed considerably and that Nagamine should take pains to keep the katas he taught in their original form.

Later, in 1940, Nagamine received a Renshi grade in karate (on the recommendation of Chojun Miyagi[5]) and a 3rd Dan in kendo at the Japanese Martial

Matsubayashi-ryu lineage chart

Chotoku Kyan
Ankichi Arakaki
Taro Shimabuku
Chojin Kuba
Kodatsu Iha
Chokki Motobu
— Shoshin Nagamine —

Takashi Kiokawa
Masaru Takamura
Narihiko Takamura
Seiyei Miyagi
Shinyei Kyan
Takayoshi Nagamine
Jokei Kushi
Seigi Nakamura
Kaoru Kinjo
Shinsaku Minami
Masakatsu Inezuka
Yoshiaki Iwanishi
Masao Mizutani
Ichiro Shirasaka
Toshizo Egawa
Masao Kobayashi
Tadashi Nakagawa
Masanori Ishikawa
Isoroku Katagiri
Keiichi Suji
Takasuga Kitamura
Yukio Adachi
Harumi Takami
Kunihiro Kato
Kazuo Tabata

Arts Festival held at Kyoto. In 1941 he made up the kata Fukyu Ichi, for the purpose of teaching karate to young school children, and in 1942 he opened his first dojo at Tomari. After the Battle of Okinawa, Nagamine felt a need to help the disconcerted youth of the island and decided to build another karate dojo (the first one having been destroyed) but in 1951, before realising his dream, he was promoted to police superintendent and became head of the police station at

Motobu in northern Okinawa. The following year he trained the winning judo team for the All Okinawa Judo Tournament, then in 1953 he resigned from the police force and built his present gym, The Kodokan (originally naming it the Kodokan Karate-do and Kobujutsu Dojo), at Naha.

On the formation of the Okinawa Karate-do Federation (an umbrella organisation that originally included the styles: Goju-ryu, Uechi-ryu, Shorin-ryu (Kobayashi) and Matsubayashi-ryu) in May of 1956, Nagamine became the first vice-president and later an adviser. In 1969 he started a study of the Myoshinji School of Zen Buddhism under the priest Keisei Okamoto, as well as the Enkakuji School of Buddhism under the priest Sogen Sakiyama and has since included Zen meditation as an integral part of Matsubayashi-ryu.

The style

Matsubayashi-ryu (sometimes also confusingly pronounced Shorin-ryu) was so named in 1947 by its formulator, Shoshin Nagamine, in honour of Kosaku Matsumora and Sokon Matsumura whose teachings have heavily influenced the style. Matsubayashi-ryu contains 18 katas: Fukyu Ichi, Fukyu Ni (or Gekisai Ichi), Pinan Shodan, Pinan Nidan, Pinan Sandan, Pinan Yondan, Pinan Godan, Naihanchi Shodan, Naihanchi Nidan, Naihanchi Sandan, Ananku, Wankan, Rohai, Wanshu, Passai, Gojushiho, Chinto and Kusanku; as well as the five weapons: bo, nunchaku, tuifa, sai and kama (the kama – sickle – is, for obvious reasons, taught only to black belt-Dan-holders).

Lessons are held three times a day, with Nagamine taking the morning sessions from 7.30am to 9.00am and the afternoon sessions from 2.30pm to 4.00pm, whilst his son, Takayoshi, takes the popular evening classes from 6.30pm to 8.30pm. A typical lesson starts with 15 minutes of cross-legged meditation in front of the dojo shrine which, Nagamine told me: 'Is merely symbolic and may just as well be a Christian cross!' His key to successful meditation is quite simple:

1. assume the correct posture
2. take deep, quiet breaths
3. count the breaths in your mind and concentrate on one thing.

The lesson continues with warming-up exercises which include running around the dojo 20 times, followed by punch, block and kick practice. Then come physical exercises followed by katas and sparring; the latter being divided into fixed- and free-sparring. Next is weight training using traditional as well as Western tools. Then, last of all, comes another 15 minutes' meditation.

Although his physical strength has obviously declined, Nagamine is still a strict disciplinarian who firmly believes in formal etiquette at all times. 'To keep fit,' he told me, 'I get out of bed at 5.30 every morning and run a 5-kilometre (3-mile) marathon.' He believes in hard work-outs and sweat and, during the hot summer months, the stuffy corrugated-iron-roofed dojo becomes like an oven, producing an abundance of the latter.

Nagamine has 30 branch dojos in Japan. In the USA, which he has visited twice, he boasts 40. He also has branch dojos in Canada, Australia and Argentina; 'In all,' he claims, 'my students total more than 10 thousand!'

Author's note for the second edition Shoshin Nagamine led a long and fruitful life, recently passing away in 1997 at the age of 90. Much admired on Okinawa for his karate, dance and Zen-Buddhist related work and research, he was seen abroad as one of the great grand-masters of the twentieth century. It is claimed that it was he who developed Fukyu[gata] Ichi in 1940, on request of the then Japanese military governor of Okinawa, General Hayakawa. The kata remains a standard for popular en masse karate demonstrations. In December of 1996 Nagamine made one last visit abroad, to Hawaii, where he was reportedly given the honorary Zen-Buddhist name of Kenzan by the Chozenji International Zen Dojo. To mark the occasion, he made a speech which he titled 'Okinawan Karate and World Peace'. This exemplified the spiritual psychology behind all martial arts, which is to disarm without resorting to the physical, to train our minds to bring forth life and not destroy it with our fists. Before his death, Nagamine managed to finish one more book, *Tales of Okinawa's Great Masters*. However, my personal view is that (judging also from previous books and newspaper articles), one should read works on 'eminent masters' with a pinch of salt, taking into consideration the generation time-frame of the writer. For people of Shoshin Nagamine's age group, exultation and veneration of the deceased is far more important, for a happy eternal life in karate Heaven, than is the recording of objective facts; yet many younger writers have been highly influenced by mythical works, mistaking descriptive, poetic fantasy for unbiased information.

Takayoshi Nagamine

Shoshin Nagamine's son, Takayoshi Nagamine, spent eight years (between the ages of 23 and 31) teaching karate in Ohio, USA, but returned to Okinawa because of family responsibilities and to help his father with the running of the Naha dojo. On my meeting Takayoshi he invited me to watch an evening training session at the dojo, during which I noted that, although his behaviour seemed artificial, he gave personal instruction to new students and was very patient.

Takayoshi had fast, snappy movements and an exceptional side kick. After the session he kindly introduced me to his beautiful wife and then took me out to his 'secret bar' complete with not-so-pretty hostesses. Then, after the consumption of a few whiskies, he told me that he was actually a criminal investigator in the Criminal Investigation Division of the United States Marine Corps, and thus sees much of the seedier side of Okinawan/American life where drugs, gangsters, M-16 rifles and smuggling are common topics of interest. He felt that 'Americans have a shallow culture' and seemed to blame the American involvement in the Ryukyus for Okinawa's modern-day woes, or as he put it, 'the recent decline in cultural values among Okinawans'.

He told me that, when teaching in the United States, he originally had some 300 students, but gradually weeded out what he termed 'the trouble makers' until he had 'a select group' of 40 students, 'with exceptional mental and physical abilities'. 'Many instructors in the United States,' he stated, 'are stupid and out for the money,' but he admitted that there are also 'some good ones'. He called the Japan Karate Association 'a bit waki-waki', meaning not really up to scratch, and finally told me that it is important for young instructors to set a good example and train even harder than their students. Takayoshi Nagamine's ultimate aim in life is simply, 'to be a good man'.

Author's note for the second edition Takayoshi Nagamine is now head of Matsubayashi-ryu worldwide.

Chubu Shorin-ryu
Zenryo Shimabukuro (1904–1969)
Like many well-known karate teachers, Zenryo Shimabukuro was born at Shuri. At the age of 24 he moved to Chatan village to start a bakery and later a tatami-mat workshop. Whilst there he was introduced to Chotoku Kyan and began karate practice at the latter's house, continuing with him until 1944. Shimabukuro started his own dojo in 1947 because he thought that as Kyan was then dead and he himself was thus without a teacher, it would be the best way to keep up his training. His first students were some nephews and his eldest son Zenpo, but gradually other school-aged children and older students enrolled. One of these students, who had a connection with the US Army's 503rd Airborne Division, arranged to have Shimabukuro teach the paratroopers and later some of these young American servicemen introduced Shimabukuro's karate to the United States.

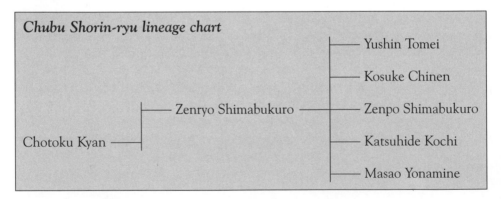

Chubu Shorin-ryu lineage chart

Chotoku Kyan —— Zenryo Shimabukuro ——
- Yushin Tomei
- Kosuke Chinen
- Zenpo Shimabukuro
- Katsuhide Kochi
- Masao Yonamine

In May of 1960, Zenryo Shimabukuro joined The All Japan Karate-do Federation and became president of the Okinawa regional headquarters. Joen Nakazato of Shorinji-ryu was vice-president, with the advisers Shigeru Nakamura of Okinawa Kenpo, Shinsuke Kaneshima of Tozan-ryu and the musician Seiyu Yonaha. Five-man teams were sent to the All Kyushu Open Free-sparring Championships and annual tournaments were held in Okinawa between the approximately 15 Okinawan member dojos. However, due to petty squabbling in The All Japan Karate Federation, the Okinawan branch resigned after only two years of membership and formed the Okinawa Karate-do United Association with the same officials as before. The annual inter-association tournaments were continued with Shimabukuro's dojo frequently gaining first, second and third places.

In 1967 the Okinawa Karate-do United Association combined with the Okinawa Karate-do Federation (which had been formed in 1956[6]) to form the All Okinawa Karate-do Federation, with the aim of preserving the 'traditional' karate forms as a cultural asset for the sake of peace, development of the mind and co-operation between styles. Shoshin Nagamine was president with vice-presidents Meitoku Yagi of Goju-ryu, Kanyei Uechi of Uechi-ryu and Zenryo Shimabukuro – Yuchoku Higa of Shorin-ryu (Kobayashi) was the director general.

Zenryo Shimabukuro, Joen Nakazato and others decided to divide the member Shorin styles into two geographically divided branch associations. Nakazato's Shorinji-ryu came under the South Island (Nanbu) Shorin branch and Shimabukuro's style, then known as simply Shorin-ryu, came under the Middle Island (Chubu) Shorin branch. Zenryo Shimabukuro died in 1969 and was succeeded by his son Zenpo. Two years later the Nanbu and Chubu Shorin branches of the All Okinawa Karate-do Federation amalgamated into the Chubu Karate-do United Association with Zenryo Shimabukuro's former student Katsuhide Kochi as president. Chinsaku Kinjo was vice-president with advisers Seiki Arakaki of Matsumura Orthodox Shorin-ryu, Shinsuke Kaneshima and Joen Nakazato.

Typically, this situation did not last long and the Chubu Karate-do United Association was soon disbanded, the former members forming their own organisations that, except for Chinsaku Kinjo's and Shinsuke Kaneshima's, have remained as branches of the still functioning All Okinawa Karate-do Federation.[7] Katsuhide Kochi became president of the newly formed Chubu Shorin-ryu Karate-do Association and the style became known as Chubu Shorin-ryu. Zenryo Shimabukuro's other former students, Kosuke Chinen, Yushin Tomei and Masao Yonamine, along with Shimabukuro's son, Zenpo, also became members.

At his dojo, the Seibukan, Zenryo Shimabukuro taught Chotoku Kyan's katas: Naihanchi Shodan (i.e. Naifuanchi), Wanshu, Passai, Gojushiho, Chinto, Sesan, Kusanku and Ananku, with the addition of Naihanchi Nidan, Naihanchi Sandan, Pinan Shodan, Pinan Nidan, Pinan Sandan, Pinan Yondan and Pinan Godan. Shimabukuro learned the five Pinan katas along with Chokki Motobu's fighting from Chozo Nakama of Shorin-ryu (Kobayashi), who was an old friend of the family.

Katsuhide Kochi

When I visited Katsuhide Kochi one warm Autumn night, he told me that for 'various reasons' he no longer taught karate; however, he granted me an interview and supplied much of the information on Chubu Shorin-ryu.

Katsuhide Kochi was the third son of Katsumori Kochi who had learned both Shuri-te and Tomari-te. Katsumori had also had dealings with many Chinese boxers and there was said to be something unique about his style. When young, Katsuhide Kochi trained with his father for over ten years and after the war he gained experience from other masters, last of whom was Zenryo Shimabukuro. In 1955 he opened a dojo at Ageda in Koza and worked hard to promote Chubu Shorin-ryu. He taught Shimabukuro's katas with the addition of his father's special kata, Aran.

Zenpo Shimabukuro

Zenryo Shimabukuro's son, Zenpo Shimabukuro, believes in both modern and traditional karate and feels that the individual trainee should decide the happy balance: 'Just because one believes in the modern, one should not forget the old.' He told me that he wants to make all his students 'happy' and so he gives 'all his body and mind when teaching', but even then students 'change' suddenly and leave; a situation that he finds 'heartbreaking'.

Zenpo Shimabukuro started his karate training under his father at the age of ten. Between the years 1963 to 1966 he stayed at and taught karate in Pennsylvania, USA and had nine clubs spreading from California to New York, with one in Mexico. He revisited these in 1975, but felt disappointed at the modern trend towards commercialisation and admitted that he had trouble keeping his organisation together. 'Karate teachers,' Shimabukuro said, 'should be sharp, have good character and teach by example.' He thought that teachers in the United States had no discipline and the sports contests that they sponsored looked like fashion shows complete with long hair and multi-coloured karate uniforms.

In a way he felt that young Okinawan teachers are to blame for these trends and are ruining the 'good impression of karate'. He claimed that many of these teachers are not qualified and teach only for financial profit, giving black belts away too easily. 'Most GIs,' he said, 'spend only two years on Okinawa, so they tend to train with teachers who guarantee them a black belt after a given amount of time.' Once a GI, who had a 2nd Dan grade, came to Shimabukuro for instruction but, feeling that the young man was overgraded, Shimabukuro told him that he would first have to forfeit his black belt. The GI could not settle for this, although he admitted that the standard at Shimabukuro's dojo was very high.

Shimabukuro felt that if 'good' Okinawan instructors were to teach abroad the standard of karate overseas would naturally go up. Exactly who the 'goodies' and the 'baddies' were, I was unable to ascertain, but it was obvious that

Shimabukuro did not get on too well with some of the other All Okinawa Karate-do Federation members – a character trait that did not seem to be uncommon among other teachers. He openly disliked Shoshin Nagamine who, he said he had been told by his father (who had heard from Chotoku Kyan), was 'stuck up'. Shimabukuro also declared that many of Nagamine's day-time students had left him because he had arranged, for a small fee, to have daily coach loads of Japanese mainland tourists come in the dojo and ogle at the students practising a set routine of exercises dictated by the tour company! 'Yuchoku Higa,' Shimabukuro whispered, 'uses karate to increase his political power.'

When younger, Zenpo Shimabukuro had the ambition of spreading karate all over the world, but, when I interviewed him, he felt that too big an organisation would be uncontrollable and so settled for about 20 dojos which he kept, 'like a family'. He had no true disciples on Okinawa (which was not surprising), but supplied me with a list of some of his American 'followers', namely: Edward Takae, Walter P. Dalley, Jack Mark, Kim Diginakis, Steve Waters, Larry Hall, Don Kennedy and Noboru Isakawa in Mexico.

The Seibukan is a tidy, well-lit, concrete gym. Practice is on Mondays, Wednesdays and Fridays from 7pm to 9pm. Shimabukuro teaches his father's style of karate intact and his movements are fast, angular and to the point. As a teacher he was a tough perfectionist. On an evening about 20 to 30 students gather for instruction but, because of the hard work and the constant drilling of basics, many drop out after only two or three months' practice. Taking this to heart, Shimabukuro said: 'Why should I beat my body up for them and later have them pass me by on the street unnoticed.' 'In sparring,' I was assured, 'a student's good points are sought out and developed.' However, the sparring session that I witnessed sometimes lapsed into barbarism, as when two young boys of unequal size and age were forced to fight each other despite the smaller one's protestations of unwillingness and eventual brutal defeat in tears.

'Seibukan,' Shimabukuro informed me, 'means Holy Art School, and was so named because the students' minds are developed in a spiritual way – it is not how many students one has, it is how good they are.'

Isshin-ryu

Kichiro and Tatsuo Shimabuku

There are approximately 336 branches of Isshin-ryu throughout the world, most of which are concentrated in the USA. I met the president of the Isshin-ryu World Karate Association, Kichiro Shimabuku, at his headquarters dojo at Kyan in Gushikawa, but as he was 'a very busy man' he could spare me only a little of his 'precious time'; consequently my notes on Isshin-ryu may seem to be lacking in detail.

Kichiro Shimabuku, being short, plump and bald with an effeminate, squeaky voice, is not what most people imagine a karate teacher to be like. During his elementary school days he started karate and kobujutsu training under his father and, when older, taught karate near Camp Hansen Marine Base at Kin.

Kichiro's father, Tatsuo Shimabuku, had enrolled at Chojun Miyagi's dojo[8] in 1919, at the age of 13, and later, whilst studying at the Okinawa Prefectural Agricultural School, learned karate from Chotoku Kyan. In 1956 he combined what he considered to be the best points of both his teachers' styles and formed the Isshin-ryu Karate-do Association. As the emblem for Isshin-ryu, Tatsuo Shimabuku chose a half-sea-snake half-woman deity called Mizugami, whom he had seen in a vision. She represents the strength of a snake and the quiet character of a woman, thus expressing the essence of the style. Among Tatsuo Shimabuku's katas were Sanchin, Seienchin and Sunsu.

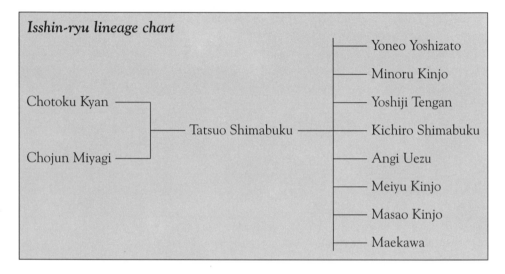

Isshin-ryu lineage chart

Chotoku Kyan ─┐
              ├─ Tatsuo Shimabuku ─┬─ Yoneo Yoshizato
Chojun Miyagi ─┘   ├─ Minoru Kinjo
                                    ├─ Yoshiji Tengan
                                    ├─ Kichiro Shimabuku
                                    ├─ Angi Uezu
                                    ├─ Meiyu Kinjo
                                    ├─ Masao Kinjo
                                    └─ Maekawa

After his father's death, in about 1976, Kichiro Shimabuku closed the old dojo at Agena in Gushikawa city and built the new dojo at Kyan, changing the name of the organisation to its present Isshin-ryu World Karate Association. Although meditation is practised, the special peculiarity of Isshin-ryu is the Thirty Basic Exercises. Fast snap-kicks are also practised, as well as the standing-fist punch which is thought to be faster to deliver than the corkscrew. The chief instructor at the main dojo assured me that three standing fists could be brought home in the same time as two corkscrews and that, since the death of Tatsuo Shimabuku, Kichiro Shimabuku had alternated between the two punches, not being able to make up his mind which one to adopt permanently.

When blocking, Isshin-ryu practitioners use the muscular part of the forearm to cushion the impact because many students used to injure their forearms when using the bony side area. When making a fist, the tip of the thumb is often placed on the first joint of the index finger pronouncing the sinew at the side of the wrist; a handform that many teachers of other styles consider to be detrimental to the health.

Shorin-ryu (Shaolin)
Eizo Shimabuku
In order to differentiate this style of Shorin-ryu from Shorin-ryu (Kobayashi), I have included the word Shaolin in parenthesis, as, in this case, the characters used to write Shorin are the same as those pronounced Shaolin in Chinese. The style was formulated by Eizo Shimabuku (who also pronounces his name Shimabukuro), a chicken farmer who now resides at Kin and runs a small dojo adjoining his home just outside of the main gate at the Camp Hansen Marine Base.

Like his elder brother, the now deceased Tatsuo Shimabuku of Isshin-ryu, Eizo Shimabuku was a student of Chotoku Kyan. He opened his first dojo at Koza (now Okinawa City) in 1948 and over the years since has taken on many American servicemen as students, some of whom have introduced his Shorin-ryu to the United States. Among these is Joe Lewis.

One of Shimabuku's aims is to preserve Kyan's katas intact. However, on his first visit to the United States in 1974, Shimabuku found that the katas he had taught some years earlier had changed significantly. Hoping to rectify the situation, he revisited the United States in 1979 on the invitation of Jerry Gold, a 6th Dan grade who teaches Shorin-ryu in Washington State. Presently, Shimabuku has branch dojos in Iowa, Michigan, Connecticut and Florida, as well as Okinawa.

Lessons are held at the Kin dojo from Monday to Saturday between 8pm and 10pm. Approximately 10–15 students gather nightly, about 80 per cent of whom are US servicemen connected with Camp Hansen; only four or five Okinawan students train regularly. Lessons begin with a series of exercises known as the basic drill:

> squat – loosen thighs
> rotate knees
> 45° side kick (i.e. kick to the knee)
> leg stretch, grasp toe
> bend forwards and backwards
> trunk twist
> straight front kick
> push-ups
> breathing
> hand exercise.

The katas Seisan, Naihanchi Shodan, Naihanchi Nidan, Naihanchi Sandan, Ananku, Wanshu, Pinan Shodan, Pinan Nidan, Pinan Sandan, Pinan Yondan, Pinan Godan, Gojushiho, Chinto, Passai Sho, Passai Dai, Kusanku Dai, Seiunchin and Sanchu are taught; along with the kobudo weapons bo, sai, nunchaku, tunfa and toyei noborikama; with the kobudo katas Bojitsu Ichi, Bojitsu Ni, Sai Ichi and Sai Ni. The toyei noborikama is unique to Shorin-ryu (Shaolin), having been developed from the kama (sickle) by Eizo Shimabuku himself.

Ryukyu Shorin-ryu

Seijin Inamine

Ryukyu Shorin-ryu was formed by a group of five former students of Eizo Shimabuku, namely: Kojun Makishi, Soko Toguchi, Hiroshi Shinya, Ryosho Goya and Seijin Inamine. Seijin Inamine was the first president of their association, the Ryukyu Shorin-ryu Karate-do Association, and at his large modern dojo at Yoshihara he teaches his karate and kobudo to a small group of friendly students.

Between the years 1951 to 1957 Inamine learned the following katas from Tomei Tsuha at Nago: Naihanchi Shodan, Naihanchi Nidan, Naihanchi Sandan, Pinan Shodan, Pinan Nidan, Pinan Sandan, Pinan Yondan, Pinan Godan, Chinto, Rohai and Oyadomari no Passai. At about the age of 30, Tsuha had been a disciple of Shinsuke Kaneshima[9] and used to travel the 65km (40 miles) from Nago to Yonabaru by bus once or twice a week. At one time Tsuha had also been a disciple of Shigeru Nakamura[10] and was described as having been a quiet man.

From 1958 to 1965 Inamine lived at Koza where he became a student of Eizo Shimabuku, relearning the Naihanchi and Pinan katas as well as Chinto. He also learned another form of Passai along with: Seisan, Wanshu, Ananku, Gojushiho, Kusanku; the staff katas, Tokumine no Kun and Sakugawa no Kun; the sai katas, Chatan Yara no Sai and Tawata no Sai; and some sparring techniques.

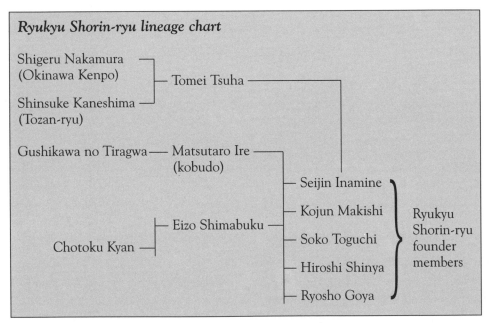

Ryukyu Shorin-ryu lineage chart

Shigeru Nakamura (Okinawa Kenpo) ─┐
                                   ├─ Tomei Tsuha ───────────┐
Shinsuke Kaneshima ─┘ (Tozan-ryu)

Gushikawa no Tiragwa ─── Matsutaro Ire (kobudo) ───┐

                                        ┌─ Seijin Inamine ─┐
                                        ├─ Kojun Makishi   │ Ryukyu
Chotoku Kyan ─┤─ Eizo Shimabuku ─┤─ Soko Toguchi   ├ Shorin-ryu
                                        ├─ Hiroshi Shinya │ founder members
                                        └─ Ryosho Goya ────┘

Inamine had met the other Ryukyu Shorin-ryu Karate-do Association founder members at Eizo Shimabuku's dojo, but in 1966, after a disagreement with the latter (the source of which Inamine did not care to talk about), they all moved on to Matsutaro Ire. Ire, who had been a disciple of Gushikawa Tiragwa (his real name was Higa), taught them kobudo at the Goeku village sacred grove. From him they learned the use of the nunchaku, tonkua and mamori kama (there were two kama katas, Gushikawa Tiragwa Mamori Kama Ichi and Gushikawa Tiragwa Mamori Kama Ni) until his death in 1971 at the age of 92.

Inamine is a quiet, modest and polite electrical worker, worried about Okinawa's political future. When teaching karate he believes that a little imposed discipline is all right, 'but too much can be a bad thing', consequently the atmosphere at his dojo is easy going and the students are self-disciplined. As in many other dojos that I visited, Inamine's dojo has a symbolic shrine and large photographs of deceased teachers. Inamine explained that these help to 'bring the spirits of the teachers to the dojo and give a feeling of reverence'.

Training at the dojo starts and ends with meditation before the shrine. Kata practice is also important: new students start to learn the first kata, Naihanchi Shodan, on their second day of attendance! However, during sparring practice, Inamine believes that one should be free from the rigid kata movements, explaining that in an actual fight 'it is not important how you block, but that you block'.

REFERENCES

[1] See Tomari-te (Matsumora-type tomari-te), page 66.

[2] See Shorin-ryu (Kobayashi), page 91.

[3] See Bugeikan, under Soko Kishimoto, page 137.

[4] See Goju-ryu, page 25.

[5] See Goju-ryu, page 27.

[6] See Matsubayashi-ryu, page 78.

[7] Another organisation, the All Okinawa Karate and Kobudo United Association (see Bugeikan, page 136), also serves as an umbrella association for several karate styles; however, some styles are independent of either association. See Appendix H.

[8] See Goju-ryu, page 28.

[9] See Tozan-ryu, page 109.

[10] See Okinawa Kenpo, page 113.

Chapter 7
Shorin-ryu (Kobayashi);
Kushin-ryu;
Kenwa Mabuni Shito-ryu;
Shinpan Shiroma Shito-ryu;
Tozan-ryu; Okinawa Kenpo

The final group of 'Shorin styles' consists of those that have, to a greater or lesser extent, been influenced by Anko Itosu, who, it is widely claimed, was the originator of what is often termed 'modern karate'.

Shorin-ryu (Kobayashi)
Anko Itosu (1832–1916)
Anko Itosu was born at Yamagawa village, Shuri and from an early age studied karate under Sokon Matsumura. Well-versed in both Chinese and Japanese classics, he became the secretary (or scribe) to the last Ryukyuan king, Sho Tai, until the monarchy was dissolved in 1879. Information concerning the next 20 years of his life is vague, but Katsuya Miyahira told me that during this period Itosu learned karate from Shiroma (Gusukuma) of Tomari and a Chinese who was living at Tomari. 'Later,' Miyahira informed me, 'Itosu simplified Matsumura's kata Naihanchi, developed the Chinese corkscrew punch into its present form and made up the Pinan katas, Shodan, Nidan, Sandan, Yondan and Godan.'

Chozo Nakama told me that Itosu had learned the kata Chiang Nan from a Chinese who had lived on Okinawa, and later remodelled and simplified this into five basic katas, calling them Pinan because the Chinese Chiang Nan was too difficult to pronounce (these became the Heian katas of Funakoshi Gichin's Shotokan at Tokyo). Nakama also told me that Itosu learned the kata Chinto from a teacher called Nakahara. Horoku Ishikawa of Shinpan Shiroma Shito-ryu typically came up with the theory that, 'Itosu had based his five Pinan katas on an analysis of the kata Kusanku Dai'.

In April of 1901 Itosu introduced karate to the Shuri Jinjo Elementary School as part of the physical training curriculum. 'But at first,' Nakama told me, 'karate was considered to be too risky for young children, so Itosu removed the dangerous techniques and simplified his other katas and sparring into mostly punch and block techniques.' In 1905 Itosu became karate teacher at the Prefectural Dai Ichi College and the Prefectural Teachers' Training College. Three years later he wrote a letter for the Prefectural Education Department concerning an idea that led to the introduction of his karate to all Okinawan schools and later its spread to the Japanese mainland, where it eventually played an essential role in the militaristic indoctrination programme. The letter reads as follows:

> Tode did not develop from the way of Buddhism or Confucianism. In the recent past Shorin-ryu and Shorei-ryu were brought over from China. They both have similar strong points, so, before there are too many changes, I should like to write these down.

> 1. Tode is primarily for the benefit of health. In order to protect one's parents or one's master, it is proper to attack a foe regardless of one's own life. Never attack a lone adversary. If one meets a villain or a ruffian one should not use tode but simply parry and step aside.

> 2. The purpose of tode is to make the body hard like stones and iron; hands and feet should be used like the points of arrows; hearts should be strong and brave. If children were to practise tode from their elementary-school days, they would be well prepared for military service. When Wellington and Napoleon met they discussed the point that 'tomorrow's victory will come from today's playground'.

> 3. Tode cannot be learned quickly. Like a slow moving bull, that eventually walks a thousand miles, if one studies seriously every day, in three or four years one will understand what tode is about. The very shape of one's bones will change.

> Those who study as follows will discover the essence of tode:

> 4. In tode the hands and feet are important so they should be trained thoroughly on the makiwara. In so doing drop your shoulders, open your lungs, take hold of your strength, grip the floor with your feet and sink your intrinsic energy to your lower abdomen. Practise with each arm one or two hundred times.

> 5. When practising tode stances make sure your back is straight, drop your shoulders, take your strength and put it in your legs, stand firmly and put the intrinsic energy in your lower abdomen, the top and bottom of which must be held together tightly.

6. The external techniques of tode should be practised, one by one, many times. Because these techniques are passed on by word of mouth, take the trouble to learn the explanations and decide when and in what context it would be possible to use them. Go in, counter, release; is the rule of torite.[1]

7. You must decide whether tode is for cultivating a healthy body or for enhancing your duty.

8. During practice you should imagine you are on the battle field. When blocking and striking make the eyes glare, drop the shoulders and harden the body. Now block the enemy's punch and strike! Always practise with this spirit so that, when on the real battle field, you will naturally be prepared.

9. Do not overexert yourself during practice because the intrinsic energy will rise up, your face and eyes will turn red and your body will be harmed. Be careful.

10. In the past many of those who have mastered tode have lived to an old age. This is because tode aids the development of the bones and sinews, it helps the digestive organs and is good for the circulation of the blood. Therefore, from now on, tode should become the foundation of all sports lessons from elementary schools onward. If this is put into practice there will, I think, be many men who can win against ten aggressors.

The reason for stating all this is that it is my opinion that all students at the Okinawa Prefectural Teachers' Training College should practise tode, so that when they graduate from here they can teach the children in the schools exactly as I have taught them. Within ten years tode will spread all over Okinawa and to the Japanese mainland. This will be a great asset to our militaristic society. I hope you will carefully study the words I have written here.

Anko Itosu. Meiji 41, Year of the Monkey (October 1908).

Itosu's motives are obvious, but it is doubtful whether he could have envisioned the monstrous strength that Japanese militarism would attain, or the years of suffering and devastation his fellow people and homeland would suffer from it.

On investigating Itosu's character, I found that he had been a kind but stern sort of father figure to his students, while physically, he was barrel chested, had a long beard and was the possessor of immense hidden strength. Horoku Ishikawa told me that his own teacher, Shinpan Shiroma, had told him that Itosu was cautious, very strict and, at his dojo in Kubagawa village, Shuri, used spartan-like discipline.

Itosu had a friend called Asato with whom he shared the same given name of Anko. Whilst Asato (a ti expert and brilliant swordsman) believed that the hands and feet should be like bladed weapons and that one should avoid all contact of an opponent's strikes, Itosu held the idea that the body did not have to be so mobile and should be able to take the hardest of blows. Choshin Chibana once said that Itosu indeed did have a very powerful punch, but Matsumura had once said to Itosu: 'With your strong punch you can knock any*thing* down, but you can't so much as touch me.'

Anko Itosu died in 1916 at the age of 85 and in his wake left an impressive list of students (see lineage chart) who later helped to fulfil his dream.

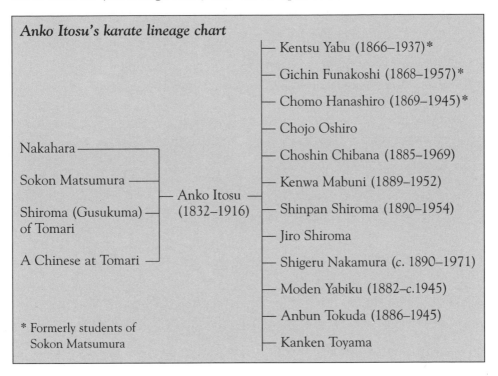

Choshin Chibana (1885–1969)

Among Anko Itosu's students, Gichin Funakoshi is probably the best known on the Japanese mainland, where he did much to popularise his Shotokan karate and encourage its spread throughout the world. On Okinawa, Choshin Chibana energetically taught Itosu's karate and is said to have officially called the style Shorin-ryu in about 1935, adopting the Chinese characters that literally mean 'small wood'. These characters may also be pronounced Kobayashi, so to differentiate this Shorin-ryu from Shorin-ryu (Shaolin), the word Kobayashi has been included in parenthesis.

Most sources agree that Chibana was a native of Torihori village, Shuri and started karate practice (after having been turned away twice) at the age of 15 under Anko Itosu (his only teacher), with whom he remained for a total of 13 years. At the age of 34, Chibana established a dojo at Torihori and taught Itosu's karate without alteration. Later he relocated this dojo to Kumoji village, Naha and in 1929 he moved this to Baron Nakijin's courtyard at Gibo village, Shuri, calling the dojo, The Tode Kenkyu Sho (Tode Research Club).

After the Battle of Okinawa, Chibana found himself on the Chinen Peninsula where he taught karate until 1948, before returning to Shuri and reopening a dojo at Gibo. Later he opened clubs consecutively at Jiku, Asato, Sakayamachi, Mihara (all in Naha) and at Yamagawa village, Shuri, changing from one location to another.

From 1954 to 1958 he was employed as the karate instructor at the Shuri police station. In May of 1956, on the formation of the Okinawa Karate-do Federation (of which he was a founder member), Chibana became the first president. Two years later he resigned and formed the Okinawa Shorin-ryu Karate-do Association and became the first president of that. In 1960 Chibana received the Physical Culture Distinguished Services Award from the *Okinawa Times* newspaper and in 1968 he received the Kunyonto Order of the Sacred Treasure from Emperor Hirohito. During his lifetime Choshin Chibana had performed many demonstrations, and during his last in 1968 he danced to a delighted audience. He died early the following year of facial cancer, from which he had been suffering for some time.

According to Katsuya Miyahira, Choshin Chibana believed that because karate is a martial art it should not be taught as a sport or as a mere physical exercise. 'During practice,' Chibana would say, 'one should forget everything and gather one's spiritual energy together so that the head, eyes, hands and feet become united; the fingers and toes should become like spears so that a single kick or a single punch can kill. To achieve this goal takes long, constant and careful practice; overdoing things will only result in harm.' Miyahira also told me that Chibana believed that one should adapt and develop forms to suit one's own body and temperament. When young, Chibana had wanted to be the strongest, most famous karate-ka of all time and it was this spirit that kept him going into his 80s. 'With age,' he would say, 'the body gets stronger, but on reaching the 50s and 60s one must slow down; then a different kind of strength develops.'

Chibana's most important secret principles were related to me as having been:

1. to understand the katas and measure the improvement in physique so that several times one's normal strength will develop
2. in the martial arts speed is essential
3. with karate kata practice, one's perception will become acute and one's strikes powerful.

Even at the age of 80, Choshin Chibana still believed he had 'a long way to go'.

Katsuya Miyahira

On the death of Choshin Chibana, Katsuya Miyahira became president of the Okinawa Shorin-ryu Karate Association. Miyahira had been a student of Chibana's since the age of 15 and, whilst studying at the Okinawa Prefectural Number One School (now Shuri High School), he also learned karate from the school instructor, Anbun Tokuda, who, like Chibana, had been a disciple of Anko Itosu. While working at Naha, Miyahira had the chance to learn free-fighting from the famous Chokki Motobu who was on one of his return trips from Osaka. Miyahira recalled that Motobu's dojo was at Makishi village, Naha (near where the Mitsukoshi department store now stands) and reminisced how the students there practised on the hardened earth in their bare feet.

During the Second World War Miyahira worked as a school teacher in Manchuria where he also taught self-defence. After the war he returned to Okinawa and taught karate in his garden at Kaneku village in Nishihara, assisting Chibana at Asato. He later moved to Tsuboya in Naha and opened a dojo at Goeku in Koza whilst teaching karate twice a week in the daytime at the University of the Ryukyus in Shuri. At Goeku, Miyahira taught many American servicemen: 'But most of these,' he said, 'did not last long.'

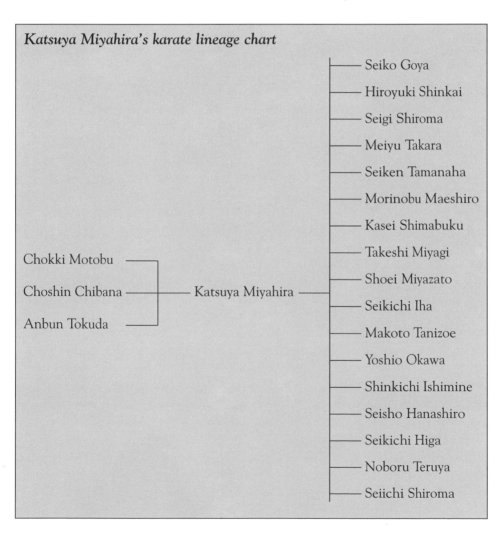

Katsuya Miyahira's karate lineage chart

Chokki Motobu — Choshin Chibana — Anbun Tokuda — Katsuya Miyahira —
- Seiko Goya
- Hiroyuki Shinkai
- Seigi Shiroma
- Meiyu Takara
- Seiken Tamanaha
- Morinobu Maeshiro
- Kasei Shimabuku
- Takeshi Miyagi
- Shoei Miyazato
- Seikichi Iha
- Makoto Tanizoe
- Yoshio Okawa
- Shinkichi Ishimine
- Seisho Hanashiro
- Seikichi Higa
- Noboru Teruya
- Seiichi Shiroma

In 1956, Miyahira built a wooden dojo (called the Shidokan) behind his house in Tsuboya where he has taught karate ever since. He teaches the katas: Naihanchi Shodan, Naihanchi Nidan, Naihanchi Sandan, Pinan Shodan, Pinan Nidan, Pinan Sandan, Pinan Yondan, Pinan Godan, Passai Dai, Passai Sho, Kusanku Dai, Kusanku Sho, Chinto, Okan (or Wankan), Wanshu, Seisan, Jion and Gojushiho.

On Okinawa, Miyahira has about 200 students of first Dan grade or above and has branch dojos in Argentina, Brazil and the Philippines, which he sometimes visits. He believes in teaching his students personally and includes meditation before and after practice. He told me that there are only slight differences between the various Shorin styles taught on Okinawa, but in comparison with the 'Shorin derived' styles in Japan, the diversity is great. The basic forms on the Japanese mainland have varied from the Okinawan forms to such an extent that he considers the punches, blocks and kicks to be virtually ineffective: 'Correct basic form,' he said, 'is of the utmost importance.'

Miyahira went on to say that in the old days it used to be the habit of students to visit various karate teachers in order to learn each one's special techniques and the katas at which they were most adept, but, nowadays, this practice is unfortunately frowned upon. Chibana's teaching had included work on the makiwara, which the students used to make themselves by sawing a thick board of pliable shiza wood diagonally in half.

Miyahira remembered that Chibana would not take on any prospective student of bad character, but such people rarely asked for tuition anyway. He described Chibana as being small, slight and only about 1.62m (5ft 3in) in height; however, his physical size belied his strength. This was the result of 'martial power' or 'spiritual strength', which is 'different from the strength used in carrying a heavy object and comes from the tanden' (i.e. lower abdomen).

The secret principles of karate, as related by Miyahira, depend on the individual: 'One must discover them for oneself, but as such there are no secret principles to show.'

Yuchoku Higa

Yuchoku Higa, to whom fighting is a religion, was a Naha City council member and holds the honorary post of president of the Naha tug-of-war committee. He describes himself as, 'truthful but outspoken' and is consequently 'a source of much embarrassment'. He thought that Katsuya Miyahira's karate was 'too shoulder locked' and said that Shugoro Nakazato's karate was 'useless'. He called Eiichi Miyazato 'a mere boy', stating frankly, 'he tries hard, but what he does is not karate'.

A confident martial artist, at 70 years old Higa still had the skill, power and speed to back up his words. Every morning at 5 o'clock he gets up and jogs a 5km marathon, then skips and goes through three or four katas. One hour before starting his evening teaching sessions (Mondays, Wednesdays and Fridays, 7pm

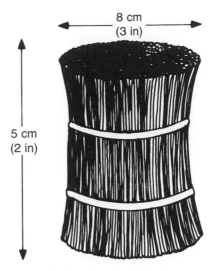

Figure 4 *Higa's 'Daruma exercise'
bamboo sticks*

Figure 5 *The 'grip exercise' rice straw
wad*

to 9pm) he skips and practises katas and, during the Sunday-morning practice session (from 7am) for seniors, to which I was cordially invited, Higa was full of energy and very active; of special note were his circular hip movements which seemed to generate tremendous power. The dedicated attitude of his two senior disciples, who have been with him for over 40 years, left a lasting impression on me.

Before the practice session began, Higa walked up and down striking his entire body with two clusters (one in each hand) of thin, bamboo sticks that he had designed and constructed himself. He calls this ritual 'the Daruma (Dharma) exercise' and performs the sequence once every morning, at midday and in the evening, claiming that it helps in being able to take a blow on any part of the body. During the interview after the session Higa constantly exercised his grip on two small wads of rice straw which he held in his palms (one in each hand) and squeezed with his fingers. These he claimed to have invented when he was a mere schoolboy of 19 and said jokingly: 'They are better and a lot more portable than the pots used in Goju-ryu.'

Yuchoku Higa started his karate training at the age of 17 under Jiro Shiroma, who had been a student of Anko Itosu. Shiroma died when Higa was only 23 years old, so Higa's father, who was a builder at Naha, next introduced him to Jinan Shinzato,[2] who taught him Goju-ryu on a private basis; Chojun Miyagi,[3] who was a friend of the family, sometimes corrected his form. At the same time Higa trained under Seiyei Miyahira, who, besides being well known for his powerful punch, was a calligrapher and noted musician, being well versed in several classical Okinawan instruments. Miyahira, who died in 1958 aged 64, had learned karate from Kiyuna PECHIN (also Chunna TANMEI or Tiji-kun BUSHI, i.e. Closed-fist Knight), who was a master of Shuri-te. Kiyuna had been

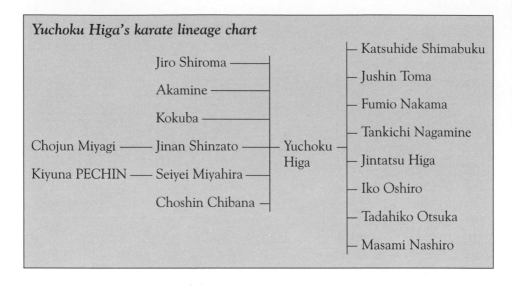

Yuchoku Higa's karate lineage chart

a student of Sokon Matsumura and at one time had been a guard at the Tama Uden royal tombs near Shuri castle. From Seiyei Miyahira, Higa learned the Shuri-te version of the katas Seisan and Sanchin.

Unfortunately, he has forgotten most of the moves of the Sanchin kata, but remembers that it had circular blocks with open-handed, straight (i.e. not corkscrewing) strikes and was practised at normal speed with natural breathing. At the age of 20, Higa had learned the katas Jute and Arakaki-han Sochin, from a karate expert called Akamine, as well as the kata Niseishi, from a karate-ka called Kokuba, but does not teach any of these.

At the age of 29, Higa found a job in the waterworks department of Naha City Hall and was asked by the mayor to form office baseball, karate and judo clubs. Higa was captain of the karate club and taught about 20, at first, enthusiastic members. After a short time only four of these remained; so he decided to hold instruction in his own garden, thus forming his first dojo. Before long Higa left the City Hall and became an Okinawan prefectural office worker where he again started a karate club, this time with about ten members. Jinan Shinzato was the chief instructor there, Higa was the assistant. Directly after the Second World War, Higa lived at Yonabaru where he taught Goju-ryu to the local police. In the evenings he trained under Choshin Chibana who was still at nearby Chinen, and, believing 'the teacher is more important than the style', he remained Chibana's disciple until the latter's death in 1969. From Yonabaru, Higa moved to Tsuboya in Naha where he built his present dojo, the Kyudokan.

The 'hard-soft' circle

'Shorin-ryu,' Higa told me, 'was originally named by Anko Itosu, not Choshin Chibana, and is a natural style, like walking along a road.' He described his karate as 'soft', explaining that the 'hard' is all right for youngsters but not for

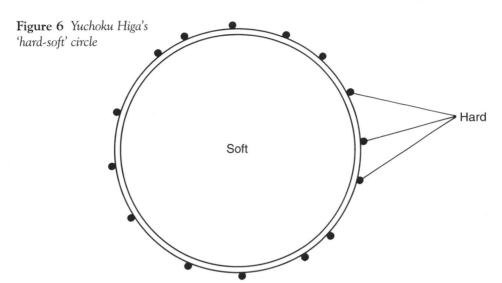

Figure 6 *Yuchoku Higa's 'hard-soft' circle*

those of a mature age. 'Actually,' he went on to say, 'the soft contains hard and is represented by a circle with dots around the circumference; the circle represents the "soft", the dots are the "hard"; this is the principle behind all martial arts.'

Higa believes that both Goju-ryu and Shorin-ryu have strong points. Shorin-ryu has natural stances which allow for freer movement, but does not have the knee kick of Goju-ryu, or the circular blocks. 'In Goju-ryu,' he said, 'there tends to be too much emphasis on body building by weight training, which causes a lack of speed and is not good for the health – that is to say one should never sacrifice health and speed for muscular strength!' (He knew of only one Goju-ryu teacher who had lived to be 80, this was Chojun Miyagi's senior, Juhatsu Kyoda, who taught karate on the Japanese mainland.) Despite his own advice, Higa admitted that when he was young he had made the mistake of purposely developing a massive neck and shoulders until he took on the appearance of a grotesque bull, but feels a lot better now that his shape has 'dropped'.

Teaching points
Nowadays Higa teaches what he considers to be the finer points of both styles in the following ways.

1. Warming-up exercises (jumbi undo). The warming-up exercises are very physical in nature; starting off with five to ten minutes standing in the horse-riding stance, then enough wheelbarrows and push-ups to tire even a young man. During the practice session that I witnessed, the students, two of whom were in their 50s, took all this without a sign of complaint. (It is a dojo policy to keep all the doors and windows shut during the entire workout, the resulting heat of which causes a lot of 'necessary' sweat and, during the humid summer months, many students actually pass out!)

2. Basic – i.e. closed-fist – katas (heishu katas). The basic katas are: Naihanchi Shodan, Naihanchi Nidan, Naihanchi Sandan, Pinan Shodan, Pinan Nidan, Pinan Sandan, Pinan Yondan and Pinan Godan.

3. Advanced – i.e. open handed – katas. The open handed katas are: Passai Dai, Passai Sho, Kusanku Dai, Kusanku Sho, Chinto, Chintei, Unsu, Jion and Gojushiho.

4. Weight training (kojo undo). Weight training is based on Goju-ryu tools and exercises.

5. Meditation (seiri undo). During meditation, which is done either sitting cross-legged or kneeling, the students reflect on their behaviour towards others. Higa enters the self-induced, trance-like state known as 'munenmuso' or 'mushin', a kind of emptiness of mind. 'Thus,' he explained, 'karate is Zen; katas are Zen in motion (doteki Zen). The aim of karate is the aim of life. It is like a mountain with many paths – they all arrive at the same destination; that is, the peak. The martial artist, the priest, the musician, etc., all have the same goal, but they are walking along different paths, so some take longer than others to arrive.'

Although open and friendly with me, Higa admitted that he had lost relatives during the Battle of Okinawa and felt embittered towards Americans; 'But for those with genuine interest,' he smiled, 'I will sweeten up.' He has travelled widely and taught at karate clubs in France, Los Angeles, Hawaii, Peru, Brazil and Argentina. In 1975 he visited Peking and Shanghai, as well as Fukien province, China, where he hoped to locate the Shaolin Temple. Unfortunately, he was not permitted to go near the Fuchou area and could not locate the temple, nor even any good teachers. Once, whilst on a teaching trip to Tokyo, Higa was approached by the then young teachers, Kanazawa and Enoeda, for special tuition. He agreed to instruct Kanazawa, but took a disliking to Enoeda and refused him because he had what Higa termed a 'murderous disposition'.

Higa believes that a serious karate practitioner must practise all his life or, like hot water, 'he will become cold and have to heat up again'. The first step for beginners is to drop the strength from the shoulders and put it in the lower abdomen, because it is from there that true strength develops. Many karate teachers ignore this basic principle, so their students tend to use too much shoulder power. Higa also encourages his students to train with other teachers, so that they will broaden their knowledge of karate; 'Students who stick to just the one teacher,' he explained, 'are sitting on the corner of a table unable to comprehend that there are three other corners.'

The secret principle of karate as related by Higa is: 'A practitioner's own speciality; that is, something that he alone is able to do. But then, when all is said and done, karate should be a spiritual discipline.'

Author's note for the second edition Under a hail of obituaries, Yuchoku Higa died in the late 1980s after a long illness. As a Naha City councillor, he is remembered as having been a huge stimulus to the Okinawan community, especially during its most difficult years. Through his karate teaching, he is also regarded as having been a great cultural asset.

Chozo Nakama

Small in stature, fragile-looking with a faded voice, Chozo Nakama at first seemed to have passed his peak. It was not until I had seen him teaching karate that I realised the hidden power in this seemingly meek Shuri gentleman, who reflected in himself the Ryukyu of old; his karate, as well as his character, exemplifying the once highly developed Okinawan concept of giving way before the superior force.[4] His students also reflected this character trait and, during practice, they worked together or individually of their own accord; there was no imposed discipline and no exertion.

A retired courtroom official, Nakama, unbefitting his former social rank, was living in a tumble-down, tin-roofed hovel approached through a small alleyway. When I visited him there, he told me that he had started karate training during his elementary-school days and, when at middle school, had trained under Anko Itosu, Nago and other teachers, including Kenwa Mabuni.[5] Between the ages of 16 and 17 he learned karate from Choshin Chibana and then spent two years with Chomo Hanashiro and three years under Chokki Motobu, before finally returning to Chibana. Motobu taught Nakama sparring and a rendering of the kata Naihanchi that varied considerably from that of the other teachers, in that the techniques consisted (ti-like) of throws using pressure on vital points.

From about 1935, Nakama taught karate to a few students in his courtyard. After the war, he taught at Onaka in Shuri until 1972, when he relocated his dojo to its present location at the Sakiyama village hall in Shuri, where the average attendance is about ten students. Altogether Nakama has three branch dojos, one of which (being near my house at Ishimine, Shuri) I visited. The head teacher here was Teikichi China (pronounced Cheena), a burly bus driver with

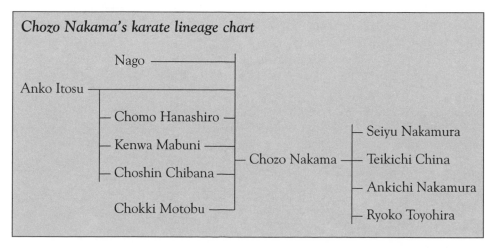

Chozo Nakama's karate lineage chart

Nago ─────────
Anko Itosu ─┬───────
   ├─ Chomo Hanashiro ─
   ├─ Kenwa Mabuni ────┬─ Chozo Nakama ─┬─ Seiyu Nakamura
   ├─ Choshin Chibana ─┤   ├─ Teikichi China
Chokki Motobu ─────┘   ├─ Ankichi Nakamura
                                                └─ Ryoko Toyohira

rumoured (but doubtful) underworld connections, 'who,' I was assured in whispers by some locals, 'used to train guerrilla-like in the surrounding hills'. On mentioning China to Nakama, he merely chuckled and politely explained that all China is good for is 'striking a makiwara'.

Katas

Nakama described Shorin-ryu as a 'fast style with breathing from the tanden'. Beginners at his dojo first learn the movements of the basic kata, Naihanchi Shodan. Then they are told to empty all their strength from their body and relax completely, whilst practising the kata as if dancing. In this way a student's physique becomes naturally adapted to karate, and the intrinsic energy is able to sink to his lower abdomen. Having thus found the correct body dynamics, the student is taught the correct points at which to focus his energy. 'The intrinsic energy,' Nakama told me, 'keeps the body in relaxed tension'; a paradox that he explained by using the analogy of a solid rubber ball that when squeezed and released, returns to its original rounded shape.

After learning Naihanchi Shodan the students move on to: Naihanchi Nidan, Naihanchi Sandan, Pinan Shodan, Pinan Nidan, Pinan Sandan, Pinan Yondan, Pinan Godan, Passai Dai, Passai Sho, Kusanku Dai, Kusanku Sho, Chinto, Wanshu, Seisan and Gojushiho. 'Many of the karate katas taught today,' Nakama explained, 'are simplified versions of the Chinese forms and consist mostly of block-and-then-strike techniques in two separate movements, as opposed to the original Chinese block/strike-in-one-movement techniques.

In the Okinawan arrangements of these Chinese katas, the punching techniques consist generally of the flat (closed) fist type, whereas originally all kinds of handform variations were employed.' He went on to say that Anko Itosu had intended that his corkscrew punch be used with the foreknuckle extended in a foreknuckle strike; but when using it, instead of twisting the fist the whole way, it should strike in a diagonal position, halfway between a standing fist and a full corkscrew. Some extremely vulnerable vital points that were to be attacked with this foreknuckle strike are: the side of the chest, the front of the chest directly below the nipples, the solar plexus, the tanden, a point at the back of the neck, a point between the eyebrows and a point just below the nose.

Although Nakama considers the ball-of-the-foot kick to be ideal for sport karate, he feels that the front kick is most effective when using the tip of the big toe as the weapon. To stop this digit from buckling over on impact with its target, it can be crossed over the second toe. The vital points to strike with this tip-of-the-toe kick are: the tanden, certain points between the floating ribs, and the inside of the legs.

The backfist strike should circle from the side of the head and snap round to the front, attacking between the eyes and the base of the nose.

Less vulnerable vital points to be attacked with the thumb are found along the length of the arms and under the armpit. These are used with ti-derived grappling and throwing techniques that were taught by Chokki Motobu. – A point to note here is that Nakama told me that the effectiveness of vital-point strikes varies with the time of day; a general guide is: morning – head; daytime – body; evening – legs.

More so than all the teachers I visited, Chozo Nakama seemed to express what is often termed 'the traditional Ryukyuan martial spirit'; his genuine humbleness and freedom from materialistic desire clearly reflected his spiritual development and deeply affected my understanding of the fighting arts.

Author's note for the second edition Chozo Nakama sadly passed away in the 1980s; much of his wisdom died with him.

Shugoro Nakazato

Described as a 'one-punch artist' by some of his American students, Shugoro Nakazato has developed his karate sparring to a fine art. A good-natured, likeable showman, he has several large photographs of himself on his dojo wall, which adjudge to his egocentricity; and his many demonstrations on the Japanese mainland, as well as abroad, attest to his popularity. But his greatest claim to fame is his 'many well-known students in the USA', including Tadashi Yamashita, 'who taught nunchaku techniques to the late Bruce Lee'.

On my visiting him at his dojo, Nakazato related that he was born at Samukawa village, Shuri, but his father, who had come from a shizoku background, died when Shugoro was only three years old. He first started karate training in 1935 under Seiichi Iju (a former student of Shinpan Shiroma[6]) at Minato ward, Sakai City, Osaka, staying with him until 1940. At the same time (i.e. 1936–1940), Nakazato trained in the kobudo weapons, sai, bo, nunchaku, tunfa and nichokama, under Seiro Tonaki who was only a little older than himself and had at one time been a student of Sanda Chinen.[7]

Next, Nakazato entered the Japanese army, where he taught bayonet techniques and military discipline to new recruits on the mainland. At first he had wanted to join up, but after a while began to dislike the army life and longed to return to his homeland. At the war's end his dream was fulfilled and he returned to Okinawa to become a disciple of Choshin Chibana, whom he considered to be the 'most eminent karate master of that time'.

In 1951 Nakazato opened a dojo in conjunction with Chibana which he called, fittingly enough, The Chibana Dai Ichi Dojo. Then in 1955, after receiving his Shihan licence from Chibana, Nakazato opened his present dojo at Aja, near Naha, calling it The Shorin-ryu Shorin Kan, Nakazato Dojo; Chibana was headmaster of this in name. In the same year, Nakazato resumed bojitsu training, this time under Seiro Tonaki's teacher's son, Masami Chinen,[8] with whom he stayed until 1958.

Training sessions at the Shorin Kan are held twice daily (except Sundays) from 1pm to 3pm and 6pm to 9pm. On Wednesdays and Friday evenings, weapons training is held. Nakazato teaches the karate katas: Kihon Kata Ichi,

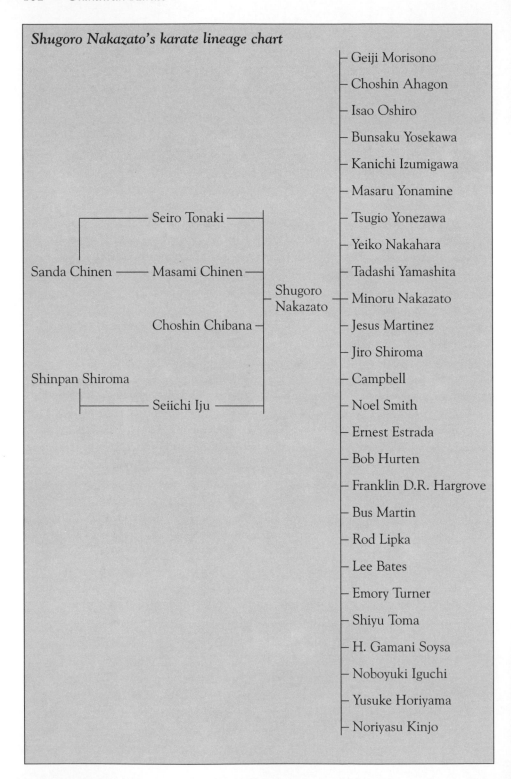

Shugoro Nakazato's karate lineage chart

Kihon Kata Ni, Kihon Kata San, Fukyu Kata Ichi, Fukyu Kata Ni, Fukyu Kata San, Fukyu Kata Yon, Fukyu Kata Go, Naihanchi Ichi, Naihanchi Ni, Naihanchi San, Pinan Ichi, Pinan Ni, Pinan San, Pinan Yon, Pinan Go, Passai Dai, Passai Sho, Kusanku Dai, Kusanku Sho and Gojushiho; as well as the weapons: bo, sai, kama, tunfa and nunchaku. 'Originally,' Nakazato told me, 'Chibana had taught Anko Itosu's style without altering it, however the style had little kumite (sparring).' Nakazato added the Kihon and Fukyu katas and teaches Iju's rendering of Gojushiho.

Assisted by his son Minoru, a police medical examiner, Nakazato keeps strict control in his dojo. His training regimen tends towards the athletic, with high kicks, a lot of sweating and press-ups-on-the-knuckles type of thing. The free sparring (without protectors) is fast and rough, but not unpleasant and there are many dojo competitions. Nakazato is one of the few teachers on Okinawa who actually free-fight with their students, and the students admit that they cannot come close to even striking him because even a slight advantage on their part is met with an instantaneous counter; luckily, Nakazato always pulls his punches. Despite this emphasis on fighting, Nakazato believes that kata practice is more important than sparring and, as in most Okinawan dojos, his grading examinations are based mostly on kata proficiency.

According to one of his students, Nakazato once asked a young American student what he would do if actually attacked by him. The student replied simply, 'RUN'. The seemingly overweight middle-aged Nakazato took up the challenge and, in the ensuing race, easily caught up with and overtook the youngster.

'Nationality,' Nakazato declared, 'is not important. All martial artists are good people; I like Americans, Americans like me.'

Kushin-ryu

Shintaro Yoshizato

The little-known style of Kushin-ryu was formulated at Osaka on the Japanese mainland in 1937 by Kensei Kinjo and Sannosuke Ueshima. Kinjo, an Okinawan who taught karate at Osaka, was a student of Choshin Chibana and had learned some Goju-ryu katas (probably from Chojun Miyagi). Ueshima, a 7th Dan Konshin-ryu jujutsu teacher, came to Kinjo's dojo out of interest to learn some karate. The two decided to pool their knowledge of the fighting arts and called the subsequent style Kushin-ryu, taking the 'ku' syllable from the Chinese character that is pronounced 'kara' in karate and the 'shin' from Ueshima's Konshin-ryu. The style was officially recognised by the Dai Nippon Butokukai in 1939.

Kensei Kinjo's top disciple, Shintaro Yoshizato, introduced Kushin-ryu to Okinawa in 1960 when he opened his present dojo at Ojana, Ginowan City, and he thinks that there is still possibly one other functioning dojo at Osaka. Yoshizato first picked up karate as a young boy by emulating his school seniors. From the age of ten he trained at Tomari[9] under several masters, one of whom

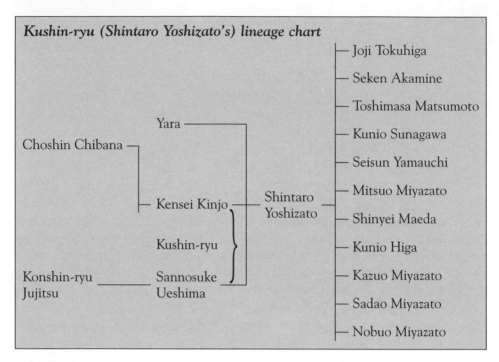

Kushin-ryu (Shintaro Yoshizato's) lineage chart

Choshin Chibana ── Yara ──┐
                          │
                          ├── Kensei Kinjo ── Shintaro Yoshizato ──
                          │
Kushin-ryu ──┐
             ├
Konshin-ryu ──── Sannosuke ──┘
Jujitsu   Ueshima

- Joji Tokuhiga
- Seken Akamine
- Toshimasa Matsumoto
- Kunio Sunagawa
- Seisun Yamauchi
- Mitsuo Miyazato
- Shinyei Maeda
- Kunio Higa
- Kazuo Miyazato
- Sadao Miyazato
- Nobuo Miyazato

was called Yara. In 1935 Yoshizato went to Osaka where he joined Kinjo's dojo and soon became an assistant, remaining with Kinjo during and after the Second World War.

Yoshizato recalled that in the pre-war days, when karate was first being introduced to the Japanese mainland, the standard Japanese kimono was considered to be too restrictive for the physical movements of karate. Karate trainees thus practised naked, except for their loincloths or long cotton underpants – even outdoors during the cold, Osaka winter. However, because the militaristic-minded society of the time revered the emperor and top officials as gods and demigods, the Butokukai, which these officials often attended, required that karate-ka be fully clothed at demonstrations. Karate practitioners on the Japanese mainland thus took to wearing judo training suits and it was not long before local merchants capitalised on the situation and brought out a training suit made of lighter material, which they called the karate-gi. This new trend in training wear spread from the mainland to Okinawa where, even today, the bare chested practitioner is still a common sight and the loinclothed oldster is not totally unheard of.

'Originally,' Yoshizato explained, 'all Kushin-ryu free-sparring was done without protectors. Students were allowed to punch and kick their opponents anywhere, so that they would learn by experience to avoid strikes and develop a natural intuition. The students did in fact receive many nasty knocks that often resulted in bruising, concussion, internal injuries, or even more unpleasant damage!' To minimise these injuries, three basic rules were followed:

1. Only students of a similar standard ever faced each other.
2. The students were first taught to tighten their muscles at the place of impact by regularly practising Sanchin. In this respect, Yoshizato claimed that he had had the ability to take a fully focused kick over his heart without any trouble.
3. The students would not always focus their strikes, so, although there was a stinging pain on the skin, such strikes did not penetrate. – Nowadays, on the advice of Seitoku Higa of the Bugeikan, Yoshizato encourages the use of protectors for those of lesser skill.

Yoshizato thought that karate was probably divided into the various styles when its profit potential was realised. 'Actually,' he said, 'the katas are all very much alike, after all a man has only two hands and two feet, and his movements are very limited.' He would like to erase the 'narrow-minded' attitude of many karate teachers by first discarding the names of the styles, but he admits that, because Kushin-ryu was named by his teachers, propriety inhibits him from taking the first step. 'It is,' he explained, 'not the name, nor the movements of the katas that differentiate a teacher's style, but the interpretation of those moves; i.e. the techniques.'

As a result of Ueshima's influence, Kushin-ryu has many Gyaku-te techniques, but, although his jujitsu contained punches and kicks, these were not adopted. Other techniques were taken from Chinese and Okinawan systems and Yoshizato still encourages his students to research all fighting systems, including Western wrestling and boxing.

The style also contains 'The Eighteen Secret Techniques of Kushin-ryu', but, as yet, Yoshizato has only just started to teach these to three of his most trusted disciples. The Kushin-ryu katas are based on those found in modern-day Goju-ryu and Shorin-ryu, but, because these katas were adopted before the styles were officially named, Yoshizato does not like to say that they came from any particular styles. The katas are namely: Gekisai, Seisai, Sanchin, Sesan, Seyonchin, Sepai, Suparinpa, Passai Dai, Passai Sho, Chinto, Kusanku and Gojushiho.

The secretive Yoshizato's advice on training was: 'The best way to become proficient at karate is to teach it, as watching one's students is like looking into a mirror.'

Kenwa Mabuni Shito-ryu

Kenwa Mabuni (1889–1952)

Two types of Shito-ryu are taught on Okinawa; one was founded by Shinpan Shiroma, the other by Kenwa Mabuni. Shiroma and Mabuni were close friends and brother disciples, having trained together from the age of 13 under the karate teachers Anko Itosu and Kanryo Higaonna.[10] Kenwa Mabuni was among the first Okinawan teachers to introduce karate to the Japanese mainland, where he taught his Shito-ryu at Osaka. According to Kanyei Uechi (not to be confused with Kanyei Uechi of Uechi-ryu, a distant relative), who introduced Kenwa Mabuni Shito-ryu to Okinawa, Mabuni had first called his style Hanko-ryu (i.e. Half-hard-style). Later, in remembrance of his two teachers, he took the Chinese character 'shi' ('ito' in Itosu) and the Chinese character 'to' ('higa' in Higaonna) and combined them to form 'shito', thus Shito-ryu; according to some sources, this was in about 1937.

Kanyei Uechi

When I visited Kanyei Uechi at his small dojo in the southern island fishing town of Itoman, he gave me the impression of being slightly odd, if not a little eccentric. I found it difficult to interview him as he rarely seemed to understand what I was trying to ask. However, after I had somewhat unwillingly performed some Goju-ryu katas, he proudly gave a practical demonstration of his style and, before I left, he kindly gave me a leaflet on the style, which I was able to translate later.

According to this leaflet, Kanyei Uechi was born at Untenbaru on the Motobu Peninsula, the son of a farmer whose family had been of the shizoku class and had migrated from Shuri. As a boy, Uechi had learned Okinawan sumo wrestling and his family's traditional fighting system from his uncle and grandfather. This included the use of the naginata (halberd) and yari (spear). In 1924, at the age of 19, he went to Osaka in search of work, but, due to poor health, he could not keep a steady job and by 1926 was literally flat on his back. On hearing that Kenwa Mabuni had a dojo (the Yoshukan) near his lodgings, Uechi summoned up some strength and enrolled. After learning one or two katas his strength gradually improved until, without realising it, he was quite well again – to such a degree in fact that he was later able to take up judo.

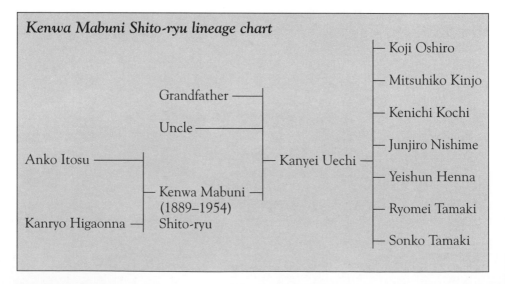

Kenwa Mabuni Shito-ryu lineage chart

Koji Oshiro
Mitsuhiko Kinjo
Kenichi Kochi
Junjiro Nishime
Yeishun Henna
Ryomei Tamaki
Sonko Tamaki

Kanyei Uechi

Grandfather
Uncle

Anko Itosu
Kenwa Mabuni (1889–1954) Shito-ryu
Kanryo Higaonna

In September of 1935, Uechi received his Shihan teaching licence and a 2nd Dan grade. 'This,' he managed to explain to me, 'was the first time that Dans, in imitation of the judo grading system, had ever been given for karate and even a 1st Dan (black belt) was then considered to be a thing of amazement.' Three karate teachers presided over the examination: Uechi's teacher, Kenwa Mabuni, then president of the Kansai Karate-jutsu Research Association; Dr Ryotaro Kanai, honorary president of the Dai Nippon Karate-jutsu Popularisation Society; and Yasuhiro Konishi, president of Shinto Shizen-ryu Karate-do.

Uechi opened his first dojo on 6 January 1937 at Osaka, but closed it three years later in order to return to Okinawa. Back in his homeland, he demonstrated and taught karate at several villages and personally met the 'masters', Chotoku Kyan, Kentsu Yabu and Shigeru Nakamura; however, he did not stay long and returned to Osaka to reopen his dojo. In 1942, at a grading examination overseen by Kenwa Mabuni and Chojun Miyagi, Uechi received a 4th Dan grade in Shito-ryu. Then, in 1948, he returned to Okinawa once more and opened his present dojo, calling it the Shito-ryu Kenpo Karate Dojo.

Among the katas that Uechi teaches are: Sanchin, Seisan, Pinan Ichi, Pinan Ni, Pinan San, Pinan Yon, Pinan Go, Naihanchi, Kusanku, Gojushiho, Passai Dai, Passai Sho, Seyonchin and Seipai. He also teaches the weapons: naginata, yari, bo, sai and nunchaku. Classes are held every day except on Sundays; children from 5pm to 7pm, adults anytime between 10am and 10pm. The techniques he showed me were a simple mixture of judo and karate. The Goju-ryu-derived katas were done, in part, with dynamic tension and 'Sanchin', I remember Uechi having mumbled, 'is not Sanchin unless performed half naked!'

Shinpan Shiroma Shito-ryu
Shinpan Shiroma (1890–1954)
According to Horoku Ishikawa – president of the Shinpan Shiroma Shito-ryu Preservation Society – Shinpan Shiroma was light-footed, thin and possessed explosive strength; he was also extremely adept with his feet and could do an upper front kick inside his outstretched, clasped hands. He was also a bit of an acrobat and had a vice-like grip; his favourite party trick was to handwalk hanging from the housebeams, which he would grip between his thumbs and index fingers, then swing up and sit, monkey-like, on a rafter under the ceiling-less roof. Sometimes young lads would approach him for tuition by asking if he would teach them 'te' ('te' often was, and still is, confused with 'tode'), but Shiroma would always reply: 'No, because you learn with your feet, not your hands.'

Shiroma was born at Taira village, Shuri. When aged 13, he knocked on Anko Itosu's door at the nearby village of Kubagawa and asked for instruction. Itosu agreed, but for the first few weeks made Shiroma cut the grass and do various odd jobs to test the boy's patience. Shiroma later learned Sanchin at Kanryo Higaonna's dojo[11] with his friend and brother disciple Kenwa Mabuni.[12] When

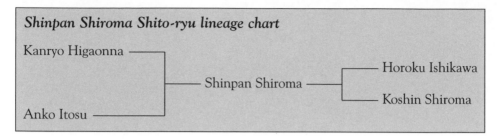

Shinpan Shiroma Shito-ryu lineage chart

Kanryo Higaonna ———

Anko Itosu ———

——— Shinpan Shiroma ———

——— Horoku Ishikawa

——— Koshin Shiroma

aged 18, Shiroma was drafted into the Japanese army but, after his discharge, was able to continue training under Itosu and became a school teacher at the Shuri Dai Ichi Elementary School, where he also taught karate. Later he opened his own dojo at Taira village, Shuri.

Because the Taira dojo was actually Shiroma's tiny back yard, he had to limit his students to five or six who, on rainy days, would practise inside the house! Shiroma was a strict teacher and would even correct the way his students walked along the street; sometimes he would suddenly command a couple of students to race up a steep flight of steps, just to strengthen their legs. During Sanchin practice he would hold his shoulders straight ('To open the chest,' he would explain), rather than rounded, and breathe out in a single short 'huff', rather than with the slow dynamic-tension, double-exhalation of some other teachers; he also kept his front toes pointing forwards, rather than turned in. According to Shinsuke Kaneshima of Tozan-ryu, Shiroma had told Higaonna that he felt more comfortable doing Sanchin this way, to which Higaonna had replied to the effect that it was a good idea.

As far as katas go, Shiroma taught: Sanchin, Pinan Shodan, Pinan Nidan, Pinan Sandan, Pinan Yondan, Pinan Godan, Naihanchi Shodan, Naihanchi Nidan, Naihanchi Sandan, Passai, Gojushiho, Kusanku Dai, Kusanku Sho and Chinto. When asked, Shiroma often admitted to not knowing the technical functions of certain movements and hand forms in the katas and would quite blankly state that Itosu had not known the functions either, merely explaining that they were for 'show'.

During the Battle of Okinawa, Shiroma lost many students but was later able to reopen a dojo at Tera village, Shuri and, for the two years prior to his death in 1954 (at the age of 64), he taught karate at Naminoue in Naha. Despite his moderately short life, Shiroma believed that the aim of karate should be longevity. When anyone happened to mention to him that they knew of a good karate-ka, Shiroma would immediately ask the age of the man in question. If the answer was that he was over 90, Shiroma would openly exclaim: 'Then he must indeed be a good karate-ka.'

Horoku Ishikawa

Horoku Ishikawa first started to learn karate from Shinpan Shiroma when he was a pupil at the Shuri Dai Ichi Elementary School, and remembered doing a karate demonstration before Japanese army officers at the Shuri castle. During his high-school days, Ishikawa trained under Shiroma at the latter's dojo in Taira, but at that time his school instructor had been Anbun Tokuda, who had been Shiroma's junior brother disciple under Itosu. Ishikawa remembered how Shiroma would chuckle at Tokuda's teaching of the Pinan katas, always having to correct the movements of these.

In his adult years, Ishikawa trained continuously under Shiroma except for a brief respite during the Second World War when he spent five years as a school teacher in Tainan, Taiwan. Whilst there, Ishikawa compared his karate katas with the forms of a local Chinese boxer and found them to be almost identical. However, he believes that the standard of fighting arts on Taiwan is higher than that of Okinawa because, 'among other things, the stances of Chinese boxing are lower, leaving the practitioner less vulnerable during an attack'. Ishikawa even went as far as to say: 'Modern kobudo is merely so many weapons' dances and sport karate is not much better.'

At Tainan, Ishikawa learned to speak, read and write Chinese (i.e. Fukien dialect). He told me that in Fukien, Chinese boxing had been called 'kun tao'; Passai, he thought, meant 'eight forts' and Chinto, 'sink and strike'. He also believed that there are many Shaolin temples in China, just as there are Kannondos in Japan or St Peter's in Europe. 'All Okinawan karate,' he stated blankly, 'was derived from Fukien Shaolin boxing which was introduced to Okinawa as tode (Chinese-te) and became labelled as Shuri-te, Tomari-te and Naha-te, then fragmented into the various modern-day karate styles'; he also believed that Gichin Funakoshi was the first to call tode, karate.

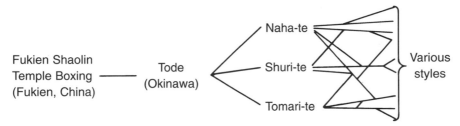

Figure 7 *Diagram representing the introduction of karate from China to Okinawa*

Tozan-ryu
Shinsuke Kaneshima
Shinsuke Kaneshima claims to be the founder and only teacher of Tozan-ryu. At the age of 82, he was healthy, sharp-eyed and full of vibrant energy. He called himself a 'traditional teacher' and I felt that the relaxed atmosphere of his dojo confirmed this. I found his system to be a style of much content, but he flatly refused any photography or note taking with the brief statement: 'Karate should not be commercialised.' Neither did he wish to be represented in this book,

saying that all he told me was for my personal benefit. I was however able to make mental notes of most of what he said and, on returning home, I spent half the night in meditation recalling and jotting down the important points.

I remembered Kaneshima as being totally bald, small and light-footed, with the same look of concealed wisdom that his cousin Shinyei Kaneshima possessed.[13] His karate teacher had gone by the name Toyama (or Tokuyama) from whose name Tozan-ryu had been formed – by using the 'zan' pronunciation of the Chinese character, meaning mountain, that is read 'yama' in Toyama (or of course Tokuyama). Later research came across mention of a Toyama who is said to have formulated a Tozan-ryu and made up (or passed on) the staff kata, Toyama no Kun.

Kaneshima had also learned the kata, Sanchin, from Shinpan Shiroma. However, Yuchoku Higa informed me in all seriousness that the former had been expelled from the latter's dojo because 'he became too powerful'. From Chokki Motobu, Kaneshima had learned free-fighting and the kata Naihanchi. And from Chokki's elder brother, Choyu Motobu,[14] he picked up some Okinawan ti.

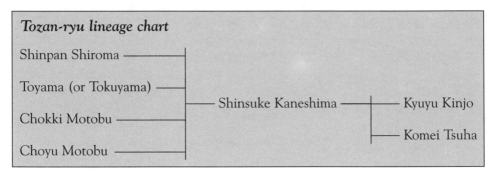

Tozan-ryu lineage chart

Shinpan Shiroma ———

Toyama (or Tokuyama) ——— Shinsuke Kaneshima ——— Kyuyu Kinjo

Chokki Motobu ———

Choyu Motobu ——— Komei Tsuha

Also from the Motobus, Kaneshima learned the secret principles of fighting, namely: kamae is formless, blocking is formless. 'That is to say,' Kaneshima explained, 'one should always be in a state of preparedness to defend oneself from any position, whatever one is doing. To assume a kamae in a challenge fight means almost certain defeat. Likewise one should not think of using a certain technique in a certain way or situation; techniques should be spontaneous and natural, not premeditated.

Another important fact to remember is to never breathe forcefully as in dynamic-tension Sanchin. One should always breathe naturally from the tanden all the time, whether sleeping, walking or talking. This is difficult to accomplish at first, so one must develop a karate physique and then stop breathing with the chest; if one finds oneself continually doing the latter, stop, breathe out with a strong huff and reinhale using the lower abdominal muscles.'

Meditation

Kaneshima also thought that meditation was important and should be practised at all times, firstly by using eye fixation and breath counting to induce a kind of self-hypnotic state. He actually advocated five variations of abdominal breathing which he warned 'should be practised with caution at first, starting with about five breaths a day'. 'During kata and sparring practice one should always remember the fundamentals. These are: concentrate your intrinsic energy in your abdomen, be completely natural, never use force, never become short of breath and do not try to work up a sweat.'

'In my younger days,' Kaneshima told me, 'there was never any talk of Zen, one learned to breathe correctly and meditate without any mention of the word. However, karate works on the same metaphysical principles. If one can enter the trance-like state of "mushin" by self-hypnosis, one can do Zen – it is that simple. Nowadays there is too much philosophical jargon about Zen that is used in commercial gyms as a means of impressing the regular students and prospective new members. True Zen meditation, which originally came to Okinawa from Japan and China, is performed sitting crossed-legged on a cushion; when Okinawans worship at shrines, Buddhist temples or sacred groves, they usually kneel and place their palms together in a similar way to that of Christian worshippers.'

Training and katas

Kaneshima was reared on the tradition that martial arts were for the purpose of defending family, king and country. The Ryukyuan martial code, he thought, was based on a strong sense of propriety or simply just knowing one's place. True martial artists taught or practised in private, telling no one their secrets, except close family members and perhaps a few trusted disciples. They never publicly demonstrated their skills lest a political or other enemy should discover a weakness in their technique and use it to his advantage during a challenge match at Tsuji. Involvement in a fight was never publicised because a strike, although not immediately effective, may have caused death several days or even years later, involving the survivor in costly legal battles.

Figure 8 *Sagi-makiwara*

'Many modern-day teachers who profess to be the "disciple" of a certain "master",' Kaneshima told me, 'actually only learned three or four katas. Traditionally, teachers used to gear a student's training to the particular student's ardour and merits. That is why the same kata learned from a single "old master" often nowadays has several renderings among the various contemporary teachers.'

At Yonabaru, where he was formerly a high-ranking government official, Kaneshima runs a small, wooden dojo (adjoining his house) in which a group of ten dedicated students gather on Mondays, Wednesdays and Fridays. Kaneshima, who has always carefully chosen his students, now refuses to take on any newcomers; his top student, Kyuyu Kinjo, has been with him for 20 years. The training sessions start typically with basics, then group kata practice takes place. This is followed by solo kata practice during which the students' moves are carefully corrected by Kaneshima. Halfway through the lesson the students take a short tea break and are permitted to smoke.

Makiwara training takes place in the small concrete-surfaced courtyard. In the old days, Kaneshima used to practise punching on a sagi-makiwara (lit. hanging punch-bag) that was similar to a modern-day, boxing punching bag but smaller, weighing about 50kg (110lb). It was also very versatile and could be struck with a varied combination of tactics.

At his dojo, Kaneshima teaches Toyama's karate and kobudo katas in their original guise – the kobudo weapons include the bo, sai and tunfua. He told me that originally karate katas took at least a year each to learn and were considered to be more than just a series of dance-like movements; they were a whole meditative process in themselves. He also thought that all karate katas should start and end at the same point and form a balanced pattern.

To help the students in their kata practice Kaneshima's dojo has two clearly marked footprints (in heiko dachi, or parallel stance) in the centre of the dojo floor. Thus, if a student aligns his feet with these at the start of each kata, his feet should end up in exactly the same position on the same marks, at the end. The kiai shout, Kaneshima believes, is not necessary for karate training and if anything its development is he claimed 'An utter waste of time', making clear that kiai, as well as body-hardening exercises, were originally practised for demonstration purposes and are not essential to progress in the martial arts.

Tozan-ryu weight training consists of exercises using the chi-ishi, sashi and kame (i.e. earthenware pots). According to Kaneshima, modern training pots are made with a rim around the neck (to effect a good grip), but in pre-war days the pots used in training had a smooth, tapered, rimless neck and were made to order at the Tsuboya pottery kilns at Naha, according to the size of the customer's own hands.

The gripping of these pots, thus being made all the more difficult, was effected with the fingers closed together and the tip of the thumb bent over. A little sand was put into the pots every day until eventually a trainee, grasping a pot in each hand and walking Sanchin-style, would be carrying more than his own body

Above Line up of karate teachers (*left to right*): Yuchoku Higa, Kanyei Uechi, Katsuya Miyahira, Shugoro Nakazato, Seiki Arakaki, Eisuke Akamine, last three not identified

Okinawa Karate Kobudo Rengokai Members 1968. Upper row (*left to right*): Kanzo Nakandakari, Shian Toma, Shinken Taira, Seitoku Higa, Seikichi Uehara, Shintaro Yoshizato, Eiki Kaneji. Bottom row (*left to right*): Kensei Kinjo, Yoshio Itokazu, Matsutaro Ire, Shosei Kina, Heisaburo Nakamura, Tatsuo Shimabuku

縄空手古武道連合会 第一回称号授興式　1968. 7.

Right Chosin Chibana (*rear centre*) with students at the gate of his Tode Kenkyu Sho (c. 1929)

Below Choshin Chibana with Shugoro Nakazato (1968)

Above left Shugoro Nakazato in 1975; *right* Katsuya Miyahira correcting a student's kata

Above right and right Yuchoku Higa teaching at a Sunday morning session at his dojo

Above left and right Chozo Nakama teaching karate

Katsuya Miyahira's dojo: looking from the inside towards the courtyard

Yuchoku Higa meditating at his dojo. Note the shrine and photographs of deceased teachers

Above left and right Chozo Nakama teaching karate

Left Katsuya Miyahira

Below Training at Shugoro Nakazato's dojo

Shintaro Yoshizato

Kanyei Uechi (of Shito-ryu)
practising Sanchin

Kanyei Uechi demonstrating a grappling technique

Kanyei Uechi demonstrating a Kenwa Mabuni Shito-ryu technique

Shiroma Shinpan (*front row, far right*) with (*from left to right*) Anbun Tokuda, Chojun Miyagi and Chotoku Kyan

Right Kanyei Uechi with students in his dojo

Below right Kenwa Mabuni (*right*) with Yasuhiro Konishi

Below Seitoku Higa of the Bugeikan demonstrating a typical ti technique

Shigeru Nakamura of Okinawa Kenpo

A student of Okinawa Kenpo demonstrates how to punch the makiwara correctly

Shigeru Nakamura

Right Punch bag training
Okinawa Kenpo style

Above Bo (staff) kata of Okinawa Kenpo

Left Eisuke Akamine demonstrating the sai

Masakazu Miyagi (*rear row, second from right*) with some members of his dojo

Above Sanda Kanagusuku

Above right Sanda Chinen

Left Masami Chinen

Sai kata of Honshin-ryu

Eisuke Akamine demonstrating the bo (staff)

Above (from left to right) Kiyo Iha (Kanagusuku's granddaughter), Shosei Kina and Shinyu Isa

Right Shinyu Isa demonstrating kai (oar) kata

Moden Yabiku (*kneeling centre*) with students. Shinken Taira is at Yabiku's right-hand side

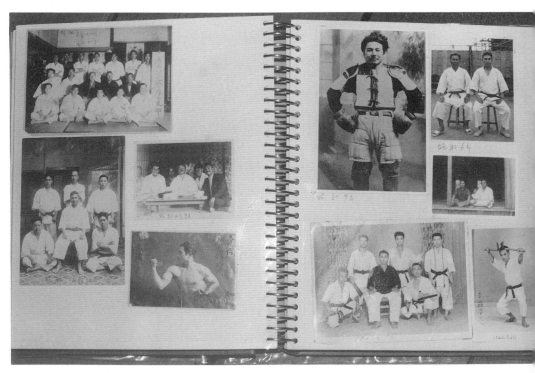

A spread from Eisuke Akamine's photograph album. The large photograph on the right-hand page shows Shinken Taira in 'battle dress'. Below is Shinken Taira with some students

Shinko Matayoshi

Below Interior of the Kodokan. Note the
large mirrors, staff rack and name tags

Seikichi Uehara (*kneeling centre*) with members of his dojo and a display of weapons, May 1977

Above Advanced ti practice

Right Seikichi Uehara performing a typical ti movement

Choyu Motobu

Seitoku Higa with two of his students, in front of the dojo shrine

Left Kiyohiko Higa demonstrating iaijutsu (i.e. sword drawing)

Left and below Seitoku Higa demonstrating empty-hand grappling against a sword

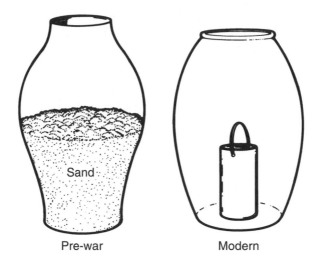

Sand

Pre-war   Modern

Figure 9 *Training pots (kame)*

weight. It was supposedly regular practice in this exercise that gave Shinpan Shiroma his tremendously powerful grip and enabled others to pierce a bundle of bamboo canes with a straight-finger jab, or crush a sugar cane in their bare hands.

Okinawa Kenpo

Shigeru Nakamura (c. 1892–1969)

According to Taketo Nakamura, Shigeru Nakamura, the founder of Okinawa Kenpo, disliked the thought of karate being divided into separate styles. His idea was to form an unrestricted free-fighting system, designed for competitions, using karate katas as a basic core. In this way Nakamura hoped that karate-do would become on a par with the popular Japanese sports of judo and kendo.

As a boy, Shigeru Nakamura had learned a limited amount of ti from his father, Keikichi Nakamura, who unfortunately died when Shigeru was only ten years old. From then on Nakamura trained in karate under his uncle Teiichi Nakamura and the noted teacher Chokki Motobu, who taught him the kata Naihanchi as well as free-fighting. Being close friends, Teiichi Nakamura and Chokki Motobu enjoyed horse riding together and sometimes accompanied each other on expeditions to hawk medicine in the outer islands. Teiichi Nakamura later emigrated to the United States where, as one story has it, the owner of a gloved and muzzled bear challenged him to (on payment of a small fee) up-end his pet for a substantial reward. To the spectators' surprise tiny Teiichi easily threw the bear, but the owner declined to pay up the promised prize money.

Shigeru Nakamura was a bright youth and attended the Prefectural Number One School, where he learned karate from Kentsu Yabu and Chomo Hanashiro.

On graduating from there he attended the Prefectural Teachers' Training College where he became acquainted with many of those in the karate world, and trained under Anko Itosu.

On leaving the college and returning to his home town of Nago, Shigeru Nakamura had the chance to learn karate and kobudo from Shinkichi Kuniyoshi who at that time had a dojo at the nearby village of Miyazato. Kenko Nakaima of Ryuei-ryu told me that Shinkichi Kuniyoshi (or BUSHI Kunishi of Kumoji) was a powerful karate-ka and an expert horseman. He was as well known at Nago as his friend Kanryo Higaonna[15] was at Naha. Kuniyoshi had been a student of Kitoku Sakiyama who had travelled to Fuchou with Norisato Nakaima[16] and trained with him at Ru Ru Ko's dojo. Sakiyama was from Wakuta (now a part of Naha) and nicknamed Taro. He had brilliant leg techniques for which Ru Ru Ko's disciples had envied him very much. When one of Ru Ru Ko's disciples came to Okinawa on official duty, he was grieved to learn that his former brother disciple, Sakiyama, was almost dead from some unknown illness. Thinking that he could cure Sakiyama by using massage techniques, Ru Ru Ko's disciple hurried to his house, but found that he was already dead.

Shigeru Nakamura eventually opened his own dojo at Nago and called his style Okinawa-te, despite the fact that the forms were essentially Chinese-based karate and kobudo katas. During the Battle of Okinawa his house was burned down and he lost many students, but, after the war, he was able to reopen the dojo and renamed his style Okinawa Kenpo.

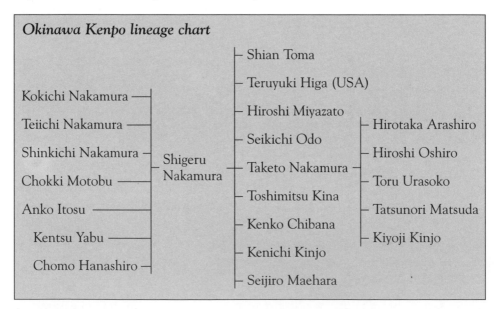

Okinawa Kenpo lineage chart

		Shian Toma	
		Teruyuki Higa (USA)	
Kokichi Nakamura		Hiroshi Miyazato	
Teiichi Nakamura		Seikichi Odo	Hirotaka Arashiro
Shinkichi Nakamura	Shigeru Nakamura	Taketo Nakamura	Hiroshi Oshiro
Chokki Motobu			Toru Urasoko
Anko Itosu		Toshimitsu Kina	Tatsunori Matsuda
Kentsu Yabu		Kenko Chibana	Kiyoji Kinjo
Chomo Hanashiro		Kenichi Kinjo	
		Seijiro Maehara	

Noted for his powerful punch, Nakamura, who spent much time training on the makiwara, was rumoured to be able to flake the bark from a pine tree with a single blow. For this reason he was given the nickname Chiki BUSHI, meaning

Punch Knight. He taught the katas: Naihanchi Shodan, Naihanchi Nidan, Naihanchi Sandan, Pinan Shodan, Pinan Nidan, Pinan Sandan, Pinan Yondan, Pinan Godan, Kusanku Dai, Kusanku Sho, Passai Dai, Passai Sho, Gojushiho and Chinto; as well as Shinkichi Kuniyoshi's katas: Niseishi, Sesan, Anan and Seipa, which is similar to Goju-ryu's Seipai. He also taught the rokushaku bo katas: Tokumine no Kun, Choun no Kun, Sakugawa no Kun, Chikin Bo, Shi Shi no Kun and Kobo; as well as the weapons, hasshaku bo, kyushaku bo, sai, nunchaku, sansetsu kun, kama, tunfa, eku, nunti and katana.

Taketo Nakamura

On Shigeru Nakamura's death, his eldest son, Taketo Nakamura, a strict vegetarian who believes that animals should be left in their natural state, rightly became the next in line for he had always had to work hard to support his father whose only interest was karate. He built the present gym (with a monstrous $60,000 loan) which he justly claims is the 'largest, best equipped karate dojo in Okinawa'.

'Okinawa Kenpo practice,' Taketo informed me, 'consists primarily of free- and fixed-sparring with the use of protectors to prevent bodily injuries.' The style combines speed and agility with strength from the legs and hips. There are several exercises to develop the limb joints, as a practitioner with weak joints will most likely fall over on kicking an opponent. Throws and ti-derived, gyaku te grappling techniques are taught but considered to be too slow for use in actual combat. Breakfall training helps should a student be thrown in a fight.

Figure 10 *Tennis ball on a string for high kicks*

Figure 11 *Nakamura's motor car tyre makiwara*

Because a student must gain enough power to knock down an opponent with a single punch or kick, training with heavy punch bags is encouraged. Extra thick makiwara, which Taketo Nakamura had made out of local wood, are used to harden the knuckles and strengthen the fists. Other training devices peculiar to Nakamura's dojo are: a tennis ball in a cloth bag suspended by a long string, used for practising high kicks, and a small motor car tyre bolted at right angles to a makiwara post.

Although the training is not regimented, students are expected to work hard and consequently sweat heavily. So, to offset the salt loss to the body, they almost ceremoniously eat pinches of salt taken from a readily available stack kept on a table at the end of the dojo. Kneeling meditation (for unity of mind) is done before and after practising each kata. Katas are performed with hard, forceful movements, low hip positioning and powerful focusing that has been refined into a fine art in Okinawa Kenpo.

REFERENCES

[1] Lit. releasing hands.
[2] See Goju-ryu, page 28.
[3] See Goju-ryu, page 27.
[4] Since interviewing Chozo Nakama, he has sadly passed away; he was perhaps the last of the 'old school'.
[5] See Kenwa Mabuni Shito-ryu, page 105.
[6] See Shinpan Shiroma Shito-ryu, page 107.
[7] See Yamani-ryu, page 120.
[8] See Yamani-ryu, page 120.
[9] See Tomari-te, page 65.
[10] See Goju-ryu, page 24.
[11] See Goju-ryu, page 24.
[12] See Kenwa Mabuni Shito-ryu, page 105.
[13] See Ishimine-ryu, page 62.
[14] See Motobu-ryu, page 130.
[15] See Goju-ryu, page 24.
[16] See Ryuei-ryu, page 19.

Part III

The kobudo and the ti styles

Chapter 8
Honshin-ryu; Yamani-ryu; Uhuchiku kobudo; Ryukyu kobudo; Matayoshi kobudo

On Okinawa, kobudo is taught along with and has been incorporated into many karate styles. As mentioned in the introduction, an outline of the five styles that have influenced, or still influence, the development of kobudo is thus included here to give the reader a more comprehensive view of Okinawan karate.

Honshin-ryu
Masakazu Miyagi
The Honshin-ryu Karate and Kobudo Hozon Kai is a non-profit-making society dedicated to the preservation of kobudo as a cultural asset. I visited the president and founder, Masakazu Miyagi, at the quiet Motobu Peninsula town of Toguchi (situated near the Okinawa Oceanographic Exposition site) one evening in late summer. The air was humid and still; silence was broken only by the sounds of shamisen and the laughter of young girls as they tried to learn their dances in time for the Toguchi dance festival. Even the odd rain shower did not dampen their enthusiasm. Miyagi explained that the dance festival is a big event for the town and is held alternately every third, then fourth year, with the added attraction of a tug-of-war every seventh.

Honshin-ryu students take an active part in the festival by displaying kobudo katas and kumi dances – i.e. a dance kata performed to the sound of brass gongs by two exponents who block and strike each other's weapons in a fixed sequence of moves. Other Motobu Peninsula towns and villages hold their own dance festivals at regular intervals, at which the locals display the kumi dances peculiar to their area. Although the rokushaku bo (182cm (6ft) staff) kumi dances are by far the most common (in Toguchi alone Miyagi has recorded over 80), other weapons sometimes seen include the tunfa, sai and tinbei.

'According to local tradition,' Miyagi told me, 'the history of the staff katas on the Motobu Peninsula is traced back to sometime after the Satsuma invasion of 1609[1] when, for reasons unknown, many Okinawans of shizoku descent fled from the area to the Shaolin Temple at Fuchou in China where they stayed for about ten years, before returning to Motobu to take up farming. At the Shaolin Temple these Okinawans learned the use of the staff and other weapons; then, on returning to Motobu, they made up katas and kumi dances based on the Shaolin Temple techniques, for display at the village festivals.' Miyagi thought that these Okinawans learned the use of the staff out of personal interest and he knew of no evidence to suggest that kobudo was developed as a means of repulsing the Satsuma overlords.

The total number of those who visited China for study of the martial arts is not certain. However, in the latter half of the 19th century four people from Motobu are recorded as having visited Fuchou for that purpose. One of these was Matsuda of Henachi hamlet[2] who is remembered for his skill with the Chinese halberd; he once demonstrated this to a Satsuma samurai who later tried unsuccessfully to manoeuvre the weighty weapon with one hand.

Before the Second World War, in preparation for the Toguchi village festivals, all young boys and stout young ladies were made to learn bo katas and kumi dances by their village youth organisation seniors; but nowadays, although all the village oldsters are skilled in the use of the staff, most youngsters take little interest. Some of the oldsters still even remember how to make a good, strong, straight staff.

Masakazu Miyagi started his karate career by studying Uechi-ryu at Koza, and at the headquarters dojo at Futenma. He later learned karate and kobudo from various teachers including the sai expert Shinyei Kyan, a student of Matsubayashi-ryu karate. Later, at Toguchi, Miyagi became the disciple of a local teacher called Heisaburo Nakamura who had learned karate, kobudo and some kumi dances from Shinkichi Kuniyoshi.[3]

Heisaburo Nakamura was headmaster of the Toguchi High School and thus had many students to whom he taught karate katas (one such kata was Chisochin), bo katas and kumi dances. In 1975, on Nakamura's death at the age of 81, Miyagi became his successor.

Miyagi teaches the weapons: bo, sai, tuiha and kama; as well as the bo katas: Kunishi Bo and Kunishi Kumi Bo, which were made up by Shinkichi Kuniyoshi

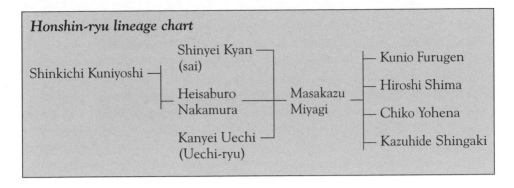

Honshin-ryu lineage chart

Shinkichi Kuniyoshi — Shinyei Kyan (sai) / Heisaburo Nakamura / Kanyei Uechi (Uechi-ryu) — Masakazu Miyagi — Kunio Furugen / Hiroshi Shima / Chiko Yohena / Kazuhide Shingaki

and are unusual in that they use an elongated version of the regular Sanchin stance. Beginners and children first learn Miyagi's own closed-fist rendering of the karate kata Sanchin along with Naifuanchi and two katas of his own design, called Soshin and Soshin Dai Ni.

Staff katas
Shinkichi Kuniyoshi intended his bo katas to be weapon dances for demonstrations by children at Motobu Peninsula village festivals, and Miyagi believes that many of the kobudo katas taught today as weapon systems originally had the same purpose. On close investigation I was surprised to find that many villages in the Ryukyu Islands still have their own weapon dances (some of which have a semi-religious function), the bo being the most popular weapon. I also recorded the use of the kai, kama, tinbei, katana, naginata and yari. The history of the introduction of these weapon dances to the villages can usually be traced and can be divided into two main categories with two subdivisions each.

1. Introduced by: (A) Shuri shizoku who settled in or near the villages as farmers after 1724, or (B) political outcasts who were deported from Shuri to the outer islands and took up residence with the villagers.
2. Introduced from overseas by: (A) Okinawans who had learned weapon systems or dances abroad, or (B) foreigners who visited the islands by chance or design.

Historically (i.e. prior to 1879), nothing has been found to suggest that weapons were regularly, if ever, used by country folk for personal protection, or in an organised resistance movement against Satsuma. Although there were instances of the staff being used after 1879 by members of village youth groups in protecting their villages against what they considered to be unwelcome intruders.

The question of what exactly constitutes the difference between kobudo katas and weapon dances is one that few, if any, teachers could answer adequately. Careful observation shows that the forms and movements of the dances are exactly the same as the katas, although the dances are accompanied by the sound of musical instruments (cymbals, gongs and/or drums) whereas the katas are not. Also, most of those teachers with commercial gyms, who include weapons practice in their curriculum, claim to teach kobudo as a fighting art, and it is a point to note that analysis of technique (bunkai) is rarely taught by members of the village youth organisations during weapon dance or kumi dance instruction. Visual appeal (or looks) is nowadays considered to be important when performing both the dances and kobudo katas which have consequently become quite thrilling to watch. This trend has added to their popularity and helped in their recognition as a major Okinawan art form and an important part of the Prefecture's cultural heritage.

Yamani-ryu

Masami Chinen (1898–1976)

Yamani-ryu (also Yamane-ryu) was formed by Masami Chinen who taught boju-tsu (the art of the staff) on a private basis at his home in Tobaru village, Shuri. The style ceased to exist after Chinen's death, but some of his katas are preserved by Seitoku Higa of the Bugeikan and Shugoro Nakazato of Shorin-ryu. Chinen named the style in honour of his father and bojutsu teacher, Sanda Chinen, who died at the age of 82 and was also known as Yamani USUMEI (also Yamane TANMEI). Sanda Chinen had in turn learned bojutsu from his father Chinen PECHIN (Yamagusuku Andaya) and Shichiyanaka Chinen. According to Eisuke Akamine of Ryukyu kobudo, Chinen PECHIN had been a student of Sakugawa SATUNUSHI (Tode Sakugawa) who had learned Chinese boxing from Kusanku and had studied bojutsu as well as other fighting arts in China.

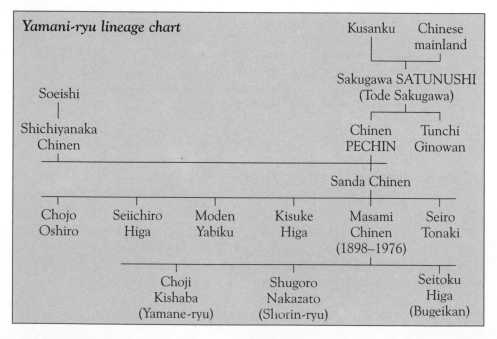

Yamani-ryu lineage chart

Although little is known about Masami Chinen's life, Horoku Ishikawa of Shinpan Shiroma Shito-ryu told me that Chinen had been a policeman and, being a relative, had spent the period of the Second World War with him in Tainan, Taiwan (this was later confirmed after an interview with Chinen's wife). Whilst there Chinen had learned the use of the sai from a local Chinese; he had also collected many interesting weapons, but was not permitted to take these back to Okinawa and left them in charge of a local temple.

Seitoku Higa told me that Chinen had had a large callous on his left side caused by constant daily practice of the staff movements with which he is said to have been so skilful that, after performing a diagonal strike, his staff would be seen to quiver and remain for some time in this vibrant state, even after he had placed it on the floor. Once during a bojutsu demonstration, because there was no staff readily available, he used a spear but twirled the weapon so fast that the metal tip came flying off and stuck fast in a wooden pillar just above a bewildered spectator's head.

The Yamani-ryu bojutsu katas were: Sakugawa no Kun, Soeishi no Kun, Choun no Kun, Chinen Shichiyanaka no Kun, Yonegawa no Kun, Shirotaro no Kun, Sushi no Kun, Tsuken Bo, Sunakaki no Kun, Sueyoshi no Kun and Shimajiri Bo. From information written in Shinken Taira's book *Ryukyu Kobudo Taikan*, it is possible to discern that the first of these katas to have become part of the Chinen family bojutsu system was Sakugawa no Kun, devised by Sakugawa SATUNUSHI more than 100 years ago.[4] Soeishi no Kun and Choun no Kun were devised over 100 years ago by Soeishi of Ona village, Shuri. Shichiyanaka Chinen had been employed by Soeishi as a manservant but, being fond of martial arts, Chinen often spied on his master's bojutsu practice. Soeishi found Chinen out one day and, being impressed by his enthusiasm, took him on as a student. Shichiyanaka Chinen is said to have later made up the kata Chinen Shichiyanaka no Kun about 100 years ago.

Shimajiri Bo came from Southern Okinawa and was probably introduced into Yamani-ryu by Masami Chinen. Shimajiri was the southernmost of the three districts into which Okinawa was formerly divided – the other two districts were Nakagami and Kunigami; the boundaries of these three districts roughly coincided with the three former feudal states of Nanzan, Chuzan and Hokuzan.

Evidence suggests that Yamani-ryu had more besides the basics and katas. Preserved at the Bugeikan is Masami Chinen's favourite kata, Sushi no Kun (also Suji no Kun) which he practised every day almost until the day he died. This is the only Yamani-ryu kata that contains several movements suggestive of ti forms, despite its supposed Chinese origin. The kata is short but sweet and said to be difficult to master as it contains in its compactness a number of unusual techniques. Seitoku Higa believed that the Sushi no Kun taught in other styles is a lengthened version of this Sushi no Kun (minus the ti-like movements) that Sanda Chinen made up especially for display at demonstrations. It seems likely that Masami Chinen knew weapon techniques based on Okinawan ti, but usually taught only the katas based on Chinen's style. In fact Seitoku Higa and others once saw him do a ti stick dance during which his hand movements were so skilful that none of the spectators could see the stick.

Author's note for the second edition It has been brought to my notice that Yamani-ryu, going by the name Yamane Ryu, has surfaced under the auspices of Chogi Kishaba, but it appears that the latter is rather secretive on such matters. He is reportedly pretty disgusted with 'what some Western teachers are doing with the style' and information is hard to come by. Chogi Kishaba's student, Toshihiro Oshiro, has promulgated a popular version of Yamane Ryu that has been modified for tournament competition, and he has produced a video tape that includes some general information. His address is: Oshiro's Karate Dojo, 917 Main Street, Redwood City, CA 94063 (tel: 415 364 7653, fax: 415 364 1338). Teruo Chinen (of Goju-ryu fame, *see* page 33) claims that he has close ancestral links with the Chinen family and is in possession of some rare photographs. Evidently he practises Yamane Ryu privately and, reflecting his martial arts skill in general, his kata is said to be superb. Whenever anyone asks him about Yamane Ryu, however, he is reportedly often quoted as stating that he is 'not qualified' to practise, teach or discuss the subject.

Uhuchiku kobudo

Sanda Kanagusuku (c.1841–1921)

Uhuchiku kobudo is a modern style, founded and taught by Shinyu Isa at Okinawa City. However, the roots of the style can be traced back to one Sanda Kanagusuku (also Saburo Kinjo, Kinjo UHUCHIKU or Kani USUMEI), a former gentleman of Shuri.

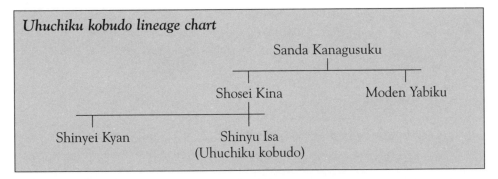

Uhuchiku kobudo lineage chart

Sanda Kanagusuku

Shosei Kina   Moden Yabiku

Shinyei Kyan   Shinyu Isa
(Uhuchiku kobudo)

The father of five sons (Matsu, Unta, Sanda, Kanaa and Taruu) and two daughters (Tsuru and Kami), it was surprising to find out that Kanagusuku has only one surviving relative, a grand daughter, Kiyo Iha, who was born to his daughter Tsuru; the rest of his offspring having tragically died whilst young without having given birth to heirs. I found Kiyo Iha at her home in Tobaru, Shuri where she resides alone. Then in her late 70s, she remembered how she had grown up with her grandfather Sanda (her father having died when she was still a baby) and had actually looked upon him as a father.

'In his later years,' Iha told me, 'Sanda Kanagusuku taught kobujutsu during the evening in the courtyard of his home at Gibo village, Shuri to a few pupils, as well as my mother Tsuru. He was very easy going, rarely if ever consumed alcohol and often told us stories about ghosts which he had actually seen.' When younger, in 1879, having been until that time a martial arts instructor and body-guard to the king Sho Tai, Kanagusuku was entrusted to take the deposed king's royal pony to Tokyo on a junk, but, because the revered animal got seasick and refused to eat, Kanagusuku, in true proprietous fashion, refused to eat also. After his return to Okinawa, Kanagusuku was made senior chief inspector (UHUCHIKU)[5] and reputedly brought about the popularity of his favourite weapon, the sai. He died from a cold at about the age of 80.

Shosei Kina

A Christian who never drinks tea or coffee, Shosei Kina at 90 years of age is the only surviving student of Sanda Kanagusuku. Born at Shimabukuro village (now in Kitanakagusuku ward), near present-day Okinawa City, Kina was the second son among nine brothers and sisters. From the age of 24, Kina started to learn kobudo under Kanagusuku whilst attending the teachers' training college at Shuri. On approaching Kanagusuku for tuition the first time he was politely refused, but he was later accepted when he asked Kanagusuku a second time. He remained the latter's disciple for a total of five years, learning the use of the sai, as well as other weapons.

Kina remembered how Kanagusuku had often emphasised the spiritual aspects behind kobudo with such statements as: 'The secret principle of weapons' practice is to be found in the heart and mind (kokoro)' or: 'To take the spiritual aspects of the martial arts seriously, is the prerequisite of weapons' training.' Kanagusuku would usually teach attack and strike techniques, but always cautioned that the heart of the martial arts lies in defensive tactics not in autocratic behaviour, with the statement: 'A true teacher will never need to attack.'

From the age of 25, Kina became an elementary school teacher and, after retirement at the age of 55, he became a council member for the old Nakagusuku ward (now comprising Kitanakagusuku and Nakagusuku wards). During the Battle of Okinawa his fellow villagers, panic stricken at the sight of approaching American soldiers on patrol, naturally came to Kina for advice. He, heart beating rapidly, boldly stepped out in front to face the 'enemy' saying: 'You American gentleman, me Okinawan Christian.' A Japanese-American interpreter, going by the name Thomas Higataro, recognised Kina as his old school teacher and had a somewhat strange reunion to the delight of the villagers who, at that time, thought they had been spared certain death.

The story of Kina and his village spread across the United States and he received many letters and monetary donations from sympathisers the world over.

After the Second World War, Kina taught kobudo, especially the sai, to among others, Shinyu Isa and the local politician, Shinyei Kyan, but, although still in good health, he admits that he would barely be able to lift a heavy sai. Although kobudo may have played a part, Kina believes that his long, illness-free life is due to his policy of not drinking or smoking and always eating regularly.

Shinyu Isa

A Buddhist priest by profession, Shinyu Isa claims to be a third-generation kobudo teacher, tracing his martial-arts lineage back through Shosei Kina to Sanda Kanagusuku (see lineage chart). Isa started his karate training at the age of three under his grandfather, later moving on to Kina and a now deceased teacher called Saburo Tokashiki, as well as Seikichi Uehara of Motobu-ryu.

Having graduated from the Shingon sect Somotosan Denpo Monastery at Kyoto, Japan, Isa became a priest at the Futenma Kannondo (Kwannon) Temple in Ginowan City, Okinawa, which is run by a relative of his. He teaches his brand of Shorin-ryu karate and kobudo at his small wooden dojo, the Shudokan. It is situated at Yamazato, Okinawa City and is open from 8.00pm every evening except Sundays, but, due to Isa's priestly activities, he is not usually in attendance himself. Among the weapons taught at the Shudokan are the sai, kai, manji no sai, tunfa, nunchaku, kama, rokushaku kama, tecchu (wooden) and rokushaku bo.

Ryukyu kobudo

Moden Yabiku (1882–c. 1945)

The Ryukyu Kobudo Hozon Shinkokai (Society for the Promotion and Preservation of Ryukyuan Kobudo) is nowadays presided over in Okinawa by Eisuke Akamine who teaches kobudo and karate in his small dojo near Naha, and kindly provided most of the following information. The association was originally known as the Ryukyu Kobujutsu Research Association and had been founded in about 1911 by Moden Yabiku who taught kobudo on the Japanese mainland. Yabiku had learned karate from Anko Itosu, Yamani-type bojutsu from Sanda Chinen, as well as kobudo from Tawata PECHIN (Tawata nu Meigantu) and the sai expert Sanda Kanagusuku. Yabiku's organisation disbanded on his death, some time during the Second World War.

Shinken Taira (c.1897–1970)

After the war, one of Moden Yabiku's disciples, Shinken Taira, who had been teaching kobudo and karate on Okinawa since 1940, formed the Ryukyu Kobudo Hozon Shinkokai. Shinken Taira was born on the tiny island of Kume and, when a young man, went to the Japanese mainland where he trained in karate under Gichin Funakoshi (from 1922) and Kenwa Mabuni, learning kobudo from Moden Yabiku. On his death bed Taira named his disciple Eisuke Akamine as his successor.

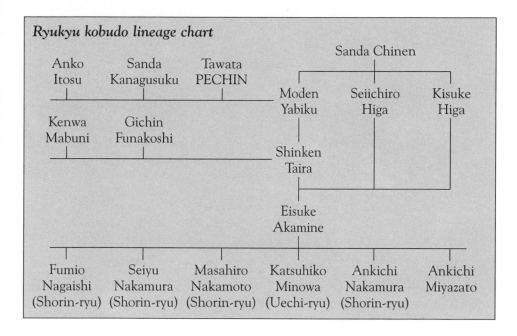

Ryukyu kobudo lineage chart

Eisuke Akamine

From the age of 24, Eisuke Akamine learned Yamani-type bojutsu from Sanda Chinen's disciples, Seiichiro Higa and Kisuke Higa. Akamine became a student of Shinken Taira in 1959, and by 1965 had received his teacher's licence. In 1971 he opened his first dojo, the Shinbukan, which now has branches in Miyazaki Prefecture, Shizuoka Prefecture, Kumamoto Prefecture and the United States.

Akamine teaches the weapons: rokushaku bo, sai, manji no sai, tunfa, kama, nunchaku, sanbon nunchaku, kai, suruchin, tekko, tinbei and ticchu. His bo katas are: Sushi no Kun Dai, Sushi no Kun Sho, Sakugawa no Kun Sho, Yonegawa no Kun, Shirotaro no Kun, Choun no Kun, Chinen Shichiyanaka no Kun, Sueyoshi no Kun, Soeishi no Kun, Tsuken Sunakaki no Kun, Urasoe no Bo, Chatan Yara no Kun and Sesoko no Kun. The sai katas being: Tsuken Shitahaku no Sai, Chatan Yara no Sai, Tawata no Sai, Hamahiga no Sai, Yaka no Sai, Hantagawa Koragwa no Sai, Jigen no Sai and Kojo no Sai. He also teaches the katas: Hamahiga no Tunfa, Chatan Yara no Tunfa, Taira no Nunchaku, Tsuken Sunakaki no Kai and Nichokama no Kama.

Akamine holds the theory that historically, spurned by the weapon edicts and subjugation by the Satsuma clan, the upper classes at Shuri utilised farmers' tools and developed a new form of armed self-defence which became known as kobu-jutsu – the Ryukyuan peasant classes most certainly not having been permitted to practise any form of martial art. He also believed that most kobudo katas received their names from well-known Shuri teachers who either developed a particular kata or made it their speciality. Other katas are named after islands or villages where they were preserved for demonstration purposes at the various festivals.

The bo kata, Urasoe no Bo, and the sai kata, Hantagawa Koragwa no Sai, were passed on by the teacher Koragwa Tsuken who had formulated Koragwa saijutsu. Yara Chatan, who was born in Shuri and moved to Chatan to become a pioneer farmer, gave his name to bo, sai and tunfa katas. The kata, Jigen no Sai, suggests possible connections with the Japanese system known as Jigen-ryu that Yara Chatan is thought to have studied. The nunchaku kata used in Ryukyu Kobudo, Taira no Nunchaku, was made up by Shinken Taira and was thus given his name, i.e. the Nunchaku of Taira.

Matayoshi kobudo

Shinko Matayoshi (1888–1947)

Although this system of kobudo is commonly known on Okinawa as Matayoshi kobudo, its official name is Shadan Hojin: Zen Okinawa Kobudo Renmei (All Okinawa Kobudo Federation: Incorporated Body). The system was originally put together by Shinko Matayoshi who spent a total of 13 years in China studying Chinese weaponry, boxing and medicine. Matayoshi was born into a shizoku family at Kakinohana village, Naha and grew up in Shinbaru village, Chatan where his family became well known for their work in sugar cane culture experiments.

At Chatan, Matayoshi learned bojutsu, saijutsu, kamajutsu and iekujutsu from Gushikawa no Tiragwa (Higa TANMEI) as well as nunchakujutsu and tunkuajutsu from Jitude Moshigwa Ire who was a senior of Matsutaro Ire.[6] At the end of the Meiji era, about 1911, Matayoshi travelled north through Japan to Hokkaido and crossed over, via the island of Sakhalin, to Manchuria, where he joined a gang of mounted bandits and learned horse riding, the lasso, shurikenjutsu and the bow and arrow.

After his return to Japan, Matayoshi was given the chance to perform his tonkuajutsu at a demonstration with Gichin Funakoshi at Tokyo in 1915. In 1921 Matayoshi, who had by that time received the nicknames Kama nu Ti Mateshi and Chikara Mateshi, performed 'Ryukyuan Kobudo' at a demonstration with the karate teacher Chojun Miyagi before Prince Hirohito who was visiting Okinawa.

Matayoshi next travelled to Shanghai where he learned suruchinjutsu, nunteijutsu, tinbeijutsu, herbal medicine, acupuncture and a form of Shaolin Temple boxing known as Kingai-noon that is considered to be a sister style of Kanbun Uechi's Pangai-noon, as they both have the same Sesan kata and differ in name only by the first Chinese character. Before finally returning to Okinawa in 1934, Matayoshi learned another form of Shaolin at Fuchou. He died in 1947 aged 59 and is remembered as having been a fine, but somewhat short-lived, martial artist.

Shinpo Matayoshi

Before his second trip to China, Shinko Matayoshi had sired a son called Shinpo who is now headmaster of the Matayoshi Kobudo Headquarters Dojo, Okinawa and president of the Federation. Between the ages of eight and eleven, Shinpo Matayoshi learned karate from Chotoku Kyan and in 1934 started kobudo training under his own father. From 1935 Matayoshi learned White Crane from Gokenki[7] at Naha and from 1945 he taught kobudo at Kawasaki in Kanagawa

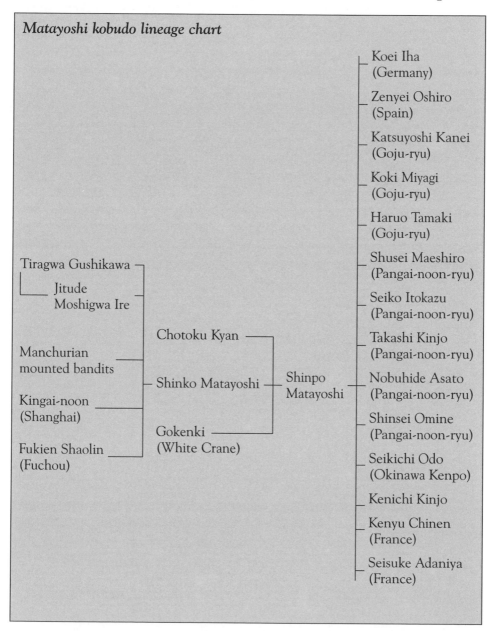

Matayoshi kobudo lineage chart

Koei Iha
(Germany)

Zenyei Oshiro
(Spain)

Katsuyoshi Kanei
(Goju-ryu)

Koki Miyagi
(Goju-ryu)

Haruo Tamaki
(Goju-ryu)

Shusei Maeshiro
(Pangai-noon-ryu)

Seiko Itokazu
(Pangai-noon-ryu)

Takashi Kinjo
(Pangai-noon-ryu)

Nobuhide Asato
(Pangai-noon-ryu)

Shinsei Omine
(Pangai-noon-ryu)

Seikichi Odo
(Okinawa Kenpo)

Kenichi Kinjo

Kenyu Chinen
(France)

Seisuke Adaniya
(France)

Tiragwa Gushikawa

Jitude
Moshigwa Ire

Manchurian
mounted bandits

Kingai-noon
(Shanghai)

Fukien Shaolin
(Fuchou)

Chotoku Kyan

Shinko Matayoshi

Gokenki
(White Crane)

Shinpo
Matayoshi

Prefecture. Later, on his return to Okinawa in 1960, he became kobudo instructor at Seiko Higa's Goju-ryu dojo. By 1969 Shinpo Matayoshi had his own dojo which he called the Kodokan (Enlightened Way), in honour of his father Shinko, whose name means True Light. In 1970 he formed and became president of the Ryukyu Kobudo Renmei, which in 1972 was reorganised into his present organisation.

Matayoshi presently has branch dojos in Miyagi Prefecture, Fukuoka Prefecture, Yamanashi Prefecture, Kanagawa Prefecture, Yamaguchi Prefecture, Fukushima Prefecture, Tokyo, Osaka, Kagoshima Prefecture, Miyazaki Prefecture, Aiichi Prefecture and Saitama Prefecture, as well as in France, Germany, Spain and Mexico. At his dojo he teaches the weapons: bo (sanshaku, yonshaku, rokushaku and hasshaku), sai, tonkua, suruchin, nuntei, nunchaku kun, sanchaku kun, kai, tecchu, tinbei, kama, kuwa and tekko. His bo katas are: Sushi no Kun, Shishi (Sueyoshi) no Kun, Chikin (Tsuken) no Kun and Choun no Kun. He also teaches the kai kata, Tsuken Akachu no Kai.

Matayoshi does not teach karate or Chinese boxing, although he still practises some of the katas, recently having performed White Crane at a demonstration at Naha. One of Matayoshi's students visited Fuchou in 1977 where he found that, although Chinese boxing was not taught commercially, it was thriving in state educational institutions; he also noted that kobudo there was almost identical to Matayoshi's.

Feeling that kobudo is more than beneficial to society, Matayoshi has given demonstrations at local institutional homes since 1971 and, in 1973, demonstrated kobudo in Europe and the USA. He believes that kobudo is not just a means of fighting, but also a weapon of peace.

Author's note for the second edition Shinpo Matayoshi died in September 1997. Since those memorable early days of my training under him (at a dingy Naha dojo, near Sogenji gate) and my later writing of *Okinawan Karate*, until his death, he achieved his dream of seeing his kobudo practised around the globe. With the likes of my old training partner and senior, Kenyu Chinen, in France, along with a large following in San Diego under Franco Sanguinetti (Bushikan Karate and Kobudo Dojo, 760 744 5560) and many others elsewhere, his aims have been more than fulfilled. Evidently, after Matayoshi's death, Yoshiaki Gakiya, a long-serving and respected senior at the main Kodokan dojo, was selected to carry on spearheading Matayoshi's life work.

REFERENCES
1 He did not know exactly how long after. Most evidence points to about 200 years after.
2 Another was Kanbun Uechi. See Uechi-ryu, page 38.
3 See Goju-ryu under Kanryo Higaonna, page 26, and Okinawa Kenpo, page 114.

[4] Other estimates put the time at as much as 200 years ago. The author estimates it to have been no more than 150 years ago.

[5] According to Shinyu Isa the police grades at that time consisted of:

Okinawan	Japanese equivalent	British equivalent
UHUCHIKU	KEIBUHO or KEISHISEI	Senior Police Inspector
WAKISAJI	KEIBU	Police Inspector
CHIKUSAJI	JUNSA BUCHO	Police Sergeant
SAJI	JUNSA	Police Constable

[6] See Ryukyu Shorin-ryu, page 86.

[7] See Goju-ryu, page 27.

Chapter 9
Motobu-ryu; Bugeikan

The two styles in this last chapter have been designated the 'ti styles' and, although a lengthy discourse would be needed to describe ti in its entirety, a basic introduction will have to suffice for this work.

Motobu-ryu
Choyu Motobu (died: 1926)
Motobu-ryu is based on the 'secret' Motobu UDUN family ti system, that was passed down through this family by the eldest sons for eleven generations to Choyu Motobu. The Motobu family line is traced back to Prince Sho Koshin, the sixth son of the Ryukyuan king Sho Shitsu, who reigned from 1648–1669.

Choyu Motobu was the ti instructor to the last of the Ryukyuan kings, the young Sho Tai, who lived from 1841 to 1901 and reigned from 1848 to 1879. Some years after the king's abolition, Motobu opened a dojo at Naha and in 1924 helped form and presided over the Okinawa Tode Research Club based at Nami no Ue, Naha, formed for the purpose of discussion and development of tode and the other fighting arts. Among the members were such other notables as: Chojun Miyagi, Kenwa Mabuni, Kentsu Yabu, Chotoku Kyan, Chojo Oshiro and Chokki Motobu.

Choyu Motobu had hoped that his second son, Chomo, would follow in the Motobu tradition and become the successor to the family ti system (his eldest son seems to have died early in life), but Chomo was not interested and went to work in Wakayama Prefecture. However, the then 20-year-old tea boy at the Okinawa Tode Research Club, Seikichi Uehara, who had been a student of Choyu Motobu for seven years and had trained with the unwilling Chomo at the Naha dojo, eventually became Motobu's next in line. About three years after Choyu Motobu's death in 1926 the Okinawa Tode Research Club folded and interest in Motobu ti was kept alive only by the ambitious Uehara.

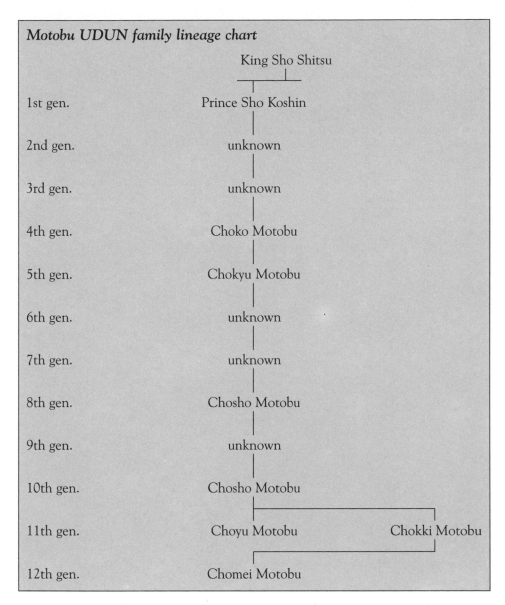

Motobu UDUN family lineage chart

	King Sho Shitsu
1st gen.	Prince Sho Koshin
2nd gen.	unknown
3rd gen.	unknown
4th gen.	Choko Motobu
5th gen.	Chokyu Motobu
6th gen.	unknown
7th gen.	unknown
8th gen.	Chosho Motobu
9th gen.	unknown
10th gen.	Chosho Motobu
11th gen.	Choyu Motobu / Chokki Motobu
12th gen.	Chomei Motobu

Seikichi Uehara

In 1947 Seikichi Uehara named the style Motobu-ryu in remembrance of his teacher and organised several demonstrations in an attempt to popularise it. By 1964 the style had begun to become known and Uehara gave a demonstration at the Okinawa Festival in Kumamoto Prefecture, then finally the Motobu-ryu Kobujutsu Association was formed by Uehara in 1969 as a branch of the All Okinawa Karate and Kobudo Combined Association.

Motobu-ryu is still a fairly unknown style and more often than not misunderstood or dismissed as 'a silly version of aikido'. In actual fact the style has a depth that cannot be easily grasped by observing the odd demonstration. One of Uehara's top disciples, Takao Miyagi, who has researched and written to some extent about ti, said that Motobu-ryu's secret principles are simple: 'Relax the body and throw your opponent with softness.' By 'throw', he actually meant neutralise and by the term 'with softness', he meant that one should utilise the hardness and force of an opponent so that he actually defeats himself; for the aggressor this can be like attacking a vacuum or diving into an empty swimming pool that he thought was filled with water. One could say that ti combines the finer points of the three most acclaimed internal Chinese boxing styles and more, having within its various guises the swift, straight-lined attack of Hsing-i, the softness of T'ai-chi and the everchanging circular defence of Pa Kua.

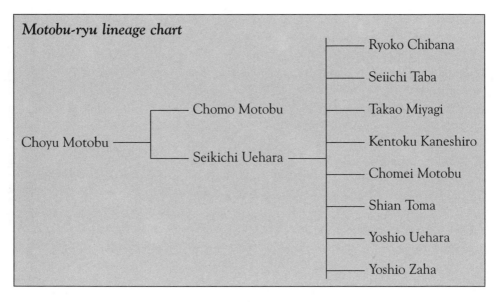

Motobu-ryu lineage chart

Choyu Motobu —— Chomo Motobu / Seikichi Uehara ——

- Ryoko Chibana
- Seiichi Taba
- Takao Miyagi
- Kentoku Kaneshiro
- Chomei Motobu
- Shian Toma
- Yoshio Uehara
- Yoshio Zaha

'The ultimate aim of ti as a means of self-defence,' Uehara told me, 'is to nullify a nasty situation without reverting to the physical and, if actually attacked, to lead the aggressor in such a way that he realises his own deficiencies and becomes a better person; as massage is also an intricate part of ti, he may also get a health massage into the bargain. But be most assured, ti, being a martial art, can also become a deadly weapon within a fraction of a second or with a minute change in body positioning. To put it another way, "In attack there is defence, in defence there is attack".'

The style

Ti is thus complex in its simplicity and is by no means easy to learn. For this reason Motobu-ryu exponents start off by learning the basic principles with a soft version of the Sanchin kata known as Moto-te Sanchin. From practising this, students who have been brought up on karate are taught to lose the habit of hunching up and learn how to stretch out and gain maximum reach from their limbs; Moto-te Sanchin also aids in blood and intrinsic energy circulation.

Next, the basic foot movements are mastered. These differ from karate basics in that the heels are kept off the floor with the weight distributed on the balls of the feet. The foot movements thus become light, flexible and quite ballet-like. The basic closed-fist punch and the toe-tip kick are then taught using exercises that are combined with the foot movements. When punching, the fists are kept in front of the body (one fist held near the elbow of the other arm) and are snapped out in concordance with the forward momentum. For kicking, the forward foot is usually used in conjunction with forward momentum.

Despite popular belief, ti is primarily an open handed system and rarely incorporates the closed fist in advanced techniques. The main striking tool is the thumb which is used in two fundamental hand forms. In the first, which is the most commonly used, the tip of the thumb is aligned with the middle finger and about 3–4 cm (1–1½in) away from it. The thumb is used for lightly striking or pressing vital points during grappling or massaging. Obvious places to strike (which should be avoided at all times) are the eyes, the temples, the spaces between the lower floating ribs and the side of the windpipe. In the second hand form the tip of the thumb is used to lightly strike the vital points of the body in preparation for grappling.

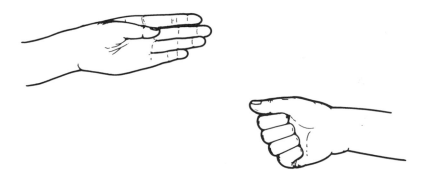

Figure 12 *Hand form one (left) and hand form two (right)*

Katas and dance

As in karate (karate katas are taught as part of Motobu-ryu in Uehara's branch dojos) any part of the body may be used to strike an opponent, but in ti these strikes are not necessarily an end in themselves and are used to gently goad the opponent into a submissive state. For example, the elbow can be used during grappling to lightly strike (or touch) the vital points at the side of the chest and below the nipple. The inner side (palm side) of the index finger knuckle is used to bring pressure on vital points of the wrist during grappling or throwing and in a form of health treatment using similar techniques. The tips of the fingers can be used to flick the eyes prior to grappling, to cause temporary loss of vision, or to apply pressure at vital points on the side of the neck when throwing.

Grappling, combined with throwing, makes up a large part of the curriculum of Motobu-ryu and, when mastered, Seikichi Uehara claimed, can be used to overpower an opponent with a never-ending series of techniques that flow from one to the other. These techniques are known generally as odori-te (dance-hand); some of the techniques being: kaeshi-te (return-hand), tori-te (take- or release-hand), nage-te (throw-hand), tori-te kaeshi (take- or release-hand reversal), nage-te (throw-hand).

When combined, these techniques originally formed a kind of kata known as Anji Kata no Mekata (The Dance Kata of the Lords) that was the pinnacle of the art and was passed down in secret through the Motobu family. Uehara unfortunately failed to learn Anji Kata no Mekata, but all is not lost. Takao Miyagi is among those who believe that several similar dance katas have been preserved as 'onna odori' (ladies' dances) that were originally danced by men in women's clothing: a major Okinawan classical art form that stresses slow, balanced postures performed to music whilst in a trance-like state. Indeed the similarities between ti and onna odori are remarkable. To name but a few:

1. the stances and movements are the same
2. the way of looking is the same
3. the hand movements of the dances correspond exactly with ti techniques
4. the phraseology used in teaching is the same (for example, 'hold your arms as if water will run off them', or, 'feel as if the top of your head is suspended by a fine thread')
5. the dances, like ti, are divided into a series of movements that bear names such as, tsuki-te (strike-hand), harai-te (parry-hand), ago ate (chin strike), kamae (ready position), choun-te (white cloud-hand), tsuki mi-te (watching the moon hand), and the previously noted nage-te (throw hand), etc.

Indeed, the comparison between the fighting arts and dance is a common theme in Okinawan culture. Sokon Matsumura wrote that practitioners of court instructors' styles bear the appearance of ladies dancing; Shinpan Shiroma once said that when he taught a lady dancer the difficult Goju-ryu mawashi (circular) block she picked it up after only three goes. Shoshin Nagamine, in *The Essence of Okinawan Karate-do*, recalls that Ankichi Arakaki once said: 'Both karate and Ryukyuan dancing show similarities in their movements from the point of view of dynamics.'

Seiki Arakaki of Matsumura Orthodox Shorin-ryu told me that dance is a good thing because it 'softens you up', but Arakaki thought himself to be too hard to even attempt dancing. And, returning to Choyu Motobu, the botanist Shinju Tawata remembered that when he was a boy he saw a ti demonstration by Choyu Motobu in which Motobu seemed to be dancing and was totally relaxed, but whenever anyone closed in on him, he would immediately throw them without interrupting the flow of his dance. In comparison, Uehara thought that Chokki Motobu's techniques were crude.

Thus, as Takao Miyagi claims, it seems likely that ti and classical dance were originally one and the same. So, for this reason, Motobu-ryu includes dance as part of its curriculum. In fact, the ever searching Miyagi has even gone one step further and points out that Motobu-ryu odori-te and classical dance can be whittled down into three distinct sets of movements:

rising – ogami-te (prayer-hand)
reversing – coneri-te (twist-hand)
lowering – oshi-te (push-hand).

These three hand forms are mentioned in the Omoro Soshi (often referred to as the Okinawan bible) and, used in combination, can be seen to have a direct relationship to meditative dance forms used by Okinawan priestesses during prayer ceremonies.

Weapons

Although ti is also a weapons' system incorporating both bladed and non-bladed weapons, it is not likely that any of these were used in an organised resistance movement against Satsuma, except during the actual invasion of 1609. Following the Satsuma weapons edicts (which do not seem to have been very strictly enforced on a personal basis), there were no organised Ryukyuan armies and ti became merely a means of personal self-defence for the nobility, rather than a military discipline. In ti, virtually any object can become a weapon and, because the empty hand techniques and movements correspond exactly to those used in weapons practice, it is not difficult for the ti expert to arm himself effectively. Also, advanced ti practice includes ways of disarming an assailant armed with any weapon.

Motobu-ryu includes practice with the traditional bladed weapons of the ti armoury, katana (sword), naginata (halberd), yari (spear) and tanto (short sword) which, although similar in name and shape to their Japanese counterparts are, according to Seikichi Uehara, employed in a fashion unique to Okinawa. Other weapons taught in Motobu-ryu are: nichokama, rokushaku bo, jo, goshaku jo, nijotanbo, uchibo, santo, toifua, eku and sai.

Choyu Motobu had taught Seikichi Uehara the secrets of ti with the hope that his ti system would eventually return to the Motobu family. It is an interesting sequel to note that, although Choyu Motobu's dream came true, it was Chokki Motobu's eldest son Chomei who actually made it a reality. A former police officer by profession, Chomei Motobu is now a specialist in judo injuries and teaches karate at Kaizuka City, Osaka. He came to Uehara's dojo in August of 1978 to receive special training and hopes eventually to become the successor to Motobu UDUN ti.

Bugeikan

Seitoku Higa

The Bugeikan was founded by Seitoku Higa, an influential man in the Okinawan karate world who, as founder member and president (for ten years) of the All Okinawa Karate and Kobudo United Association, has done much to help the spread of kobudo and the establishment of the lesser-known karate styles.

Seitoku Higa first started karate training at the age of five under his father Miinshiin Higa, who had learned Tomari-te from Kokan Oyadomari and was remembered for his ability to break a large earthenware pot with his spear hand, a technique that he developed from constantly thrusting his extended fingers into a container filled with sand. From the age of 12, Seitoku Higa started ti training under his life-time teacher, Soko Kishimoto, who had been a student of a little-known ti expert named Takemura. In 1940 Higa did a demonstration on the mainland at Kawasaki with Kanken Toyama, who later promoted Higa to the grade of Shihan. In 1943 Higa received his teacher's licence from Soko Kishimoto and in 1944 he was drafted into the Japanese army and posted to Sumatra where he remained until 1946, teaching karate at the offshore island of Sabang.

Returning to Japan in 1947 Higa received his 7th Dan from The All Japan Karate Association and in 1948 he opened a karate dojo at Kikuchi in Kumamoto Prefecture. Then, in the same year, he became vice-president of the Japanese Karate-do Popularisation Association. Returning to Okinawa in 1950 Higa taught his brand of ti and karate at Akahira village, Shuri and in 1951 opened a dojo at the present site of the Bugeikan at Gibo in Shuri.

Between 1952 and 1958, Higa took on the task of visiting several well-known Okinawan teachers in an effort to learn and preserve as much of the Okinawan martial arts as possible. In 1956 he started to learn Yamani-ryu bojutsu from Masami Chinen who gave Higa the Shihan grade in bojutsu four years later. With help from the Ryukyuan government, Higa formed the Okinawan Kobudo Association in 1961 with the aim of popularising the, at that time, little-known art of bojutsu and, during the same year, he became a student of Seikichi Uehara from whom (for a period of five years) he learned Motobu-ryu ti and the use of the associated weapons.

In 1968 Higa's dojo adopted the nonpartisan name of Bugeikan (Martial Arts Hall) so as not to become affiliated with or classed as any style in particular. Ti, various karate katas, kobudo katas, as well as aikido and ti, are taught as separate systems under the same roof.

According to Seitoku Higa, the Okinawan Kobudo Association was remoulded into the All Okinawa Karate and Kobudo United Association in 1967 as an umbrella organisation and means of centralising various karate and kobudo styles. Shihan grades were first granted in 1964 to, among others, Zenryo Shimabukuro of Chubu Shorin-ryu and Hohan Soken of Matsumura Orthodox Shorin-ryu.

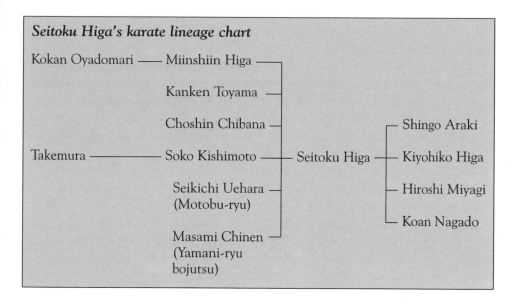

Seitoku Higa's karate lineage chart

Other masters graded by Seitoku Higa were Kenko Nakaima of Ryuei-ryu, Shinpo Matayoshi of Matayoshi Kobudo and Shinsuke Kaneshima of Tozan-ryu.

The grading system is similar to that of the All Okinawa Karate-do Federation, being based on ten Dan, or black-belt grades, starting with 1st Dan (Shodan) and working up to 10th Dan (Judan). The Shihan (master) grade is usually considered to be 4th or 5th Dan, a 6th Dan is equivalent to a Renshi; 7th Dan to a Kyoshi; 8th Dan to Tasshi; 9th and 10th Dan to a Hanshi. The higher grades (6th Dan and above) are generally given on the basis of age, prestige and number of years of practice, rather than on skill or performance. Kyu (beginner grades) and lower Dan grades (1st to 5th) are usually given by the respective headquarters dojo. Kyu grades range from 9th to 1st (in that order) and are usually divided amongst white, green and brown belts.

Soko Kishimoto (1862–1945)

In his book *Kenpu Shukuya, Dai Ichi Bu*, Keihan Ono gives a detailed description of the life and times of Soko Kishimoto as remembered by Seiken Shukumine, head of Taido Kyokai in Tokyo who, at the age of 15, became a student of Soko Kishimoto and thus a junior disciple to Seitoku Higa. According to Ono, at that time Kishimoto had long, white hair, ate herbs and lived with his wife in a tiny thatch-roofed hut surrounded by fields at Agarie, near Nago. There was little furniture in the hut apart from a Buddhist shrine and a pair of sai displayed in the tokonoma.

Shukumine remembered that when he first approached Kishimoto for tuition he introduced himself to the master who just sat staring at him for some time from across the tiny room. Then without warning Kishimoto picked up the poker from a charcoal brazier and lobbed it at the young Shukumine's stomach.

Shukumine adroitly dodged the flying implement that lodged itself in the slatted bamboo wall behind him. Thereon Kishimoto agreed to teach the lad providing he keep the instruction secret.

Soko Kishimoto was born at Yabu on the Motobu Peninsula in 1862 and grew up in the nearby village of Awa. He was slight of build, extremely agile and when young was often referred to as a very human-like monkey. He is said to have been able to do all kinds of tricks with his legs and feet, one of which was to hang upside down from a tree by clasping a branch between his prehensile big and second toes.

In his book Ono says that Shukumine told him that Kishimoto had no martial arts teachers and actually (though dubiously) gained his fighting ability from avoiding wild boars when out collecting firewood in the Motobu hills and from challenging village youths. He is also said to have picked on visiting karate exponents in order to steal their techniques. However, it should be pointed out that Kishimoto described his style as an old form of Shuri-te and could have probably spread the no teacher rumour to conceal his true teacher's (i.e. Takemura's) identity. Be that as it may, Kishimoto seems to have been in love with scrapping and, although small in stature, had a strong will to win. He was also said to have been noted for his skill with the staff as well as the sai and often walked around with a pair of sai held concealed up his kimono sleeves.

Seitoku Higa often spoke to me about Kishimoto and the picture he painted in my mind was quite different from that expressed by Ono. 'Soko Kishimoto,' Higa told me, 'actually came from a well-known martial arts family; he was nicknamed Nago no Agarie and bore the honorary title of Uezu ANJI. A Buddhist by religion, Kishimoto spent much of his time in meditation and as a result gained highly developed extra-sensory powers.

Once, whilst leaning with his back to a limestone crag, a young man named Kencho Miyagi crept up along a ledge and attempted to strike Kishimoto full force from the rear with a heavy stick. Kishimoto, sensing danger, spun round like a top and caught the stick just as it was about to come home. In the next instant the surprised Miyagi found himself disarmed and facing Kishimoto who fatherly rebuked him with the words, "Be a good boy now and don't play with sticks". Some time later, not being satisfied with one scolding, Miyagi again decided to try his luck and boldly entered Kishimoto's house whilst the latter was sitting cross-legged and seemingly totally immersed in the joysome process of eating his lunch. Without saying a word, Miyagi launched an all out attack, but the unperturbed Kishimoto merely pinned the miscreant's wrist to the table with his chopsticks whilst continuing to sip his bowl of miso soup. Miyagi retained a mark on the wrist for several days after the episode.'

Once, in his later years, whilst he was walking in a grove of fukugi trees one moonless night, Kishimoto instinctively avoided a surprise attack from the rear. Seitoku Higa was so impressed by this act that he asked his teacher how it was done. Kishimoto replied simply: 'I can see the shadows.' On contemplating this answer, Higa came to the conclusion that by 'shadows' Kishimoto had actually been referring to psychic phenomena and had actually meant the shadows or disturbances caused by the attacker's mind.

Although Kishimoto died from a wound caused by a stray bullet during the Battle of Okinawa, he had actually developed some resistance to being pierced by sharp implements. A traditional doctor, who had been enjoying a pleasant stay with Kishimoto, wanted to return the favour and offered to cure any aches and pains from which Kishimoto might be suffering. Kishimoto stated smilingly that he sometimes felt a pain in his back and shoulders, so the doctor, taking an acupuncture needle in his thumb and forefinger, attempted unsuccessfully to pierce a fleshy part of Kishimoto's shoulder. Thinking that his needle must be blunt, the doctor had another go but still could not penetrate Kishimoto's flesh. Perplexed, the doctor resorted to moxibustion treatment.

Takemura

Kishimoto most assuredly did have a teacher who was even more legendary than himself. Going by the name of Takemura (or BUSHI Tachimura) he had been a tax collector prior to 1879 and, although remembered as being honest, strict and to have never indulged in extortion, he was, for reasons known only to the peasants, very unpopular. Once, at the age of 55, whilst on a tax collecting trip to a small island, Takemura was attacked at the local wharf by about 20 of the village males. Eyewitnesses stated that he somehow managed to avoid all of the offenders' attacks with circular movements and that now and again his right foot would be seen to sweep up and scuff the head of an attacker who would run clutching his head in an attempt to replace a flap of skin and hair that had been removed by Takemura's extraordinary 'scalping kick' – luckily perhaps, this rather gruesome technique has not been passed down to the present generation.

Some of the villagers, who were crew members during Takemura's return voyage, disguised their identities and plied him with liquor. When he had fallen asleep in a drunken stupor near the tiller, the miscreants pinned Takemura to the deck by his four limbs and attempted to scalp and dismember him. On waking just in the nick of time and realising what was happening, Takemura gave one mighty shake, bounced the assailants off of himself and threw them all into the sea. On landing, he was seen to have makeshift bandages tied haphazardly around his head, arms and legs. An official investigation failed to trace the offenders, and Takemura, feeling that his job was becoming a little too dangerous, resigned and later migrated from Shuri to become a farmer in the north of the island where he taught ti to Kishimoto and eventually died at the ripe old age of 85.

Takemura and the elderly master Sokon Matsumura had been good friends. Once (again according to Seitoku Higa) whilst they were drinking together in the garden of a country estate at Shikina near Shuri, Takemura teased

Matsumura by saying that he was too old to do anything. A friendly match thus being provoked, Takemura started to rise from his cross-legged sitting position and had just raised one knee when Matsumura attempted to scoop his leg, but instead of being thrown, Takemura floated gracefully through the air, did a perfect back somersault and landed gently on a small stone bridge over a carp pond. Matsumura was so taken aback at seeing this exhibition of levitation that he ran into his house and failed to reappear for the rest of the evening.

The style
At the Bugeikan, karate, kobudo and ti are taught on Mondays, Wednesdays and Fridays (children from 6pm to 8pm, adults from 8.30pm to 10.30pm). Because Seitoku Higa is not always present, his son Kiyohiko Higa, who also teaches aikido on Tuesdays, Thursdays and Saturdays, is usually in charge of the adult practice sessions.

Lessons are divided into six stages:

1. Karate kata practice
The karate katas taught at the Bugeikan are: Naihanchi, Pinan Shodan, Pinan Nidan, Pinan Sandan, Pinan Yondan, Pinan Godan, Sesan, Sochin, Jitti, Niseshi, Chinto, Passai Dai, Passai Sho, Passai Chu, Jion, Ananku, Kusanku (old type), Kusanku (Takemura-type), Gojushiho, Moto-te Sanchin, Matsu Sanchin, Jichin, Suchin, Rufua, Nidanbu Dai, Nidanbu Sho, Sanpabu Ichi and Sanpabu Ni. Of these katas, Seitoku Higa learned Naihanchi and Kusanku (Takemura-type), as well as the Nidanbu and Sanpabu katas from Soko Kishimoto; all four having been passed down from Takemura. Although the Nidanbu and Sanpabu katas are like normal karate katas in appearance and structure, they are actually made up of ti techniques and incorporate ti footwork. The Pinan katas came from Kanzo Nakandakari and are distinguished from the Pinan katas of many Shorin styles in that they consist of block and punch techniques in one action rather than two. Sesan, which Higa describes as an old Naha-te kata based on a Chinese prototype, came from both Arakaki no TANMEI of Naha and Kyochoku Chitose of Chito-ryu on the Japanese mainland. Higa also learned Chinto from Chomo Hanashiro and Gojushiho from Chozo Nakama of Shorin-ryu (Kobayashi). At the Bugeikan, karate kata practice is considered essential for beginners and children, but as exponents mature in their ability they may discontinue the practice of these. Katas may be performed with soft or snappy movements, depending on the student.

2. Basic ti punches and kicks
The ti basics are almost identical to those of Motobu-ryu; however, Higa emphasises greater body mobility which necessitates a lighter, springier type of footwork. For kicking, the ball of the foot, the tip of the big toe or the outer side of the foot may be used.

3. Ti body manipulation

Ti body manipulation exercises are based on the idea that the first and most important thing to do when attacked is to get out of the way. To help students understand the importance of this aspect a type of fixed-sparring (against one or several attackers) has been developed in which the attacker or attackers uses either his foot, fist or a rubber knife. The opponent has to avoid all contact with the attacker's implement by learning to flow in the direction of the oncoming force and then to guide the attacker into a submissive state without causing him any harm. Rubber knives allow for complete safety whilst illustrating the essential reality to those karate-ka who have transferred from other schools and have been brought up on the slogan: 'I can take a blow on any body surface.'

4. Ti techniques practice, both with and without weapons

All the previous exercises help the student to gain an in-depth understanding of the ti techniques which, in Higa's words, 'Use pressure on vital points, wrist locks, grappling, strikes and kicks in a gentle manner to neutralise an attack'. Maiming and killing techniques are taught, but never resorted to; 'safe', simplified variations of these are practised in the dojo. The throwing techniques, which are said to be uncountable, enable the thrower to be in complete control of his victim and, although graceful in appearance, can actually be quite nasty. 'Unlike karate katas,' Higa told me, 'ti takes a long time to master. True softness cannot be found in the rigid karate forms, so the practice of the flowing ti techniques gives the student an idea of this aspect.' Breathing is natural and done with the tanden, but the abdomen should not be moved. Higa summed it up like this: 'When you move, be like running water so that the soft overwhelms the hard.' The empty hand ti techniques are used to disarm assailants armed with traditional implements and the principles behind the empty hand forms are incorporated in weapon v. weapon combinations – e.g. staff v. staff, staff v. sai, sai v. sword combinations.

5. Kobujutsu katas practice

Kobujutsu katas form the basis of weapons practice. These are namely: the Bo katas, Suji no Kun, Sunakaki no Kun Dai, Sunakaki no Kun Sho, Sakugawa no Kun, Ufugushiku no Bo, Tsuken Bo and Tsuken Dai Kun. Other katas are: Tonfua no Kata, Sai Dai, Sai Sho, Nunchaku Dai and Nunchaku Sho. Other weapons taught are: katana, naginata, yari, kama, jo, nijo tanbo, tanto, kai and suruchin.

The techniques found in the kobujutsu katas are actually quite different from ti weapons techniques and the katas are taught to help students get used to handling the weapons, as well as for their historical and cultural value. Higa told me that the kobujutsu katas are based on Chinese forms and the oldest date back only 200 years, whereas ti weapons training has been practised on Okinawa for over 1,000 years. Also, although the wearing of bladed weapons was banned by the Satsuma overlords, the king, princes and lords were in fact permitted to keep and practise with such weapons in their homes.

6. Free practice

Free practice at the Bugeikan takes many forms, including one-punch free-, or fixed-sparring (without protectors), sport type free-sparring with full protectors (helmet, breastplate and gloves) and practice with the punch bag. Makiwara training is not encouraged.

Meditation at the Bugeikan is encouraged. Before each lesson commences the students perform a breathing exercise that, I am assured, is good for the health. This consists of two types of breathing performed in a kneeling position with the back held straight. When doing the first, inhale slowly from the lower abdomen. As you inhale expand the abdomen, then, as you slowly exhale, hollow your abdomen and expand your chest. Next, as you slowly exhale, depress your chest and expand your abdomen. Perform this exercise ten times a day.

I was able to join the small group of students at the Bugeikan, where I eventually remained for several years. Although the training seemed easy to grasp at first, I only began to realise the complexity and depth of ti after several months of hard work. Indeed, having previously trained in karate, judo, aikido and internal forms of Chinese boxing, I can safely say that ti opened up a whole new vista in my understanding of the martial arts and I regret that, due to the secrecy in which ti has been enshrouded, it has not as yet been taught as an independent system outside of Okinawa.

Author's note for the second edition Since my return to England in 1990, I have been teaching ti as well as its related shiatsu (massage) techniques. All my work has been accepted enthusiastically by a martial arts community that knew more about competition and rigidity than it did about subtlety and healthful longevity. Many a damaged martial artist has been nurtured back to full strength and a better lifestyle through ti, alternative exercises and shiatsu. My own style of ti is naturally a synthesis of the Okinawan schools at which I trained extensively, along with a detailed study of Chinese boxing and classical Okinawan dancing (see *Zen Kobudo, Mysteries of Okinawan Weaponry and Te*). There were many other scattered sources too, like the teachers I interviewed on Okinawa and spontaneously trained under. So much ti was covertly stored in the techniques and philosophy of these karate greats, like coloured jewels at the bottom of a vast, confused sea of change – yet so many consciously knew not of it.

Seitoku Higa's continued demands that I participate in his religious ordinances, made it impossible for me to remain in contact with the Bugeikan. However, Higa has gone on to formulate his beliefs into a school of thought that he calls Seido, or 'Way of Life'. From my point of view, this has shamanistic and cultist overtones that are not conducive to healthy spiritual development.

Appendices

Appendix A
Maps of the Ryukyu Islands and of Okinawa and surrounding islands

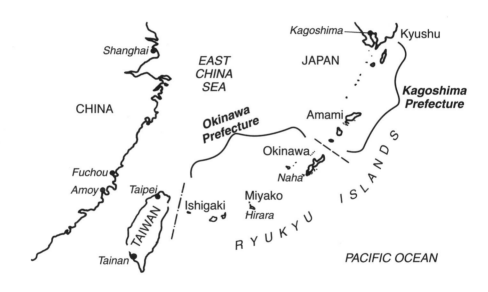

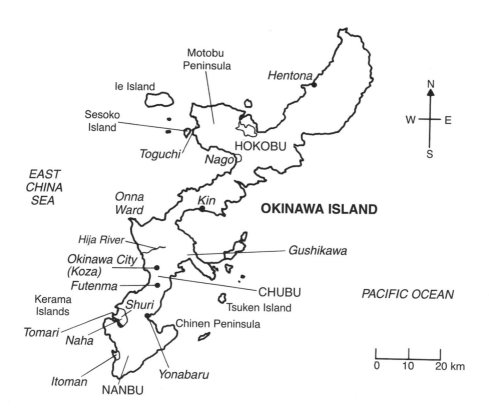

Appendix B
Glossary of Japanese, Okinawan and Chinese words used in the text

Aikido: A Japanese martial-art-based sport incorporating much grappling.

Anji: An Okinawan feudal lord. See SHIZOKU.

Awamori: A potent Okinawan rice wine.

Bugei: Martial arts.

Bushi: A samurai or warrior. Previously used in Okinawa to denote someone of notoriety in the martial arts, or a man possessing abnormal strength.

Chi-ishi: Also CHIKARA ISHI: Lit. power stone. A training device used in karate.

Chikara: Strength. Often confused with the Okinawan CHII KARA, which has the same meaning as the Chinese CH'I and Japanese KI; meaning intrinsic energy, psychic energy or spirit. Equivalent terms used on Okinawa are: KI NO CHIKARA, BURYOKU, TE NO OMOMI or BU NO CHIKARA.

Chikara Ishi: See CHI-ISHI.

Chikusaji: A former police sergeant.

Chuan: A Chinese word meaning boxing or fist.

Dan: A black belt grade, from 1st to 10th.

Do: Lit. way, as in KARATE-DO, i.e. the way of karate. DO usually indicates the modern sport form of a martial-art-based sport, as in aikido and judo.

Dojo: A training hall or gym. On Okinawa the term also has the meaning of a group of students involved in karate training, or the location at which they train.

Dojo Kun: The dojo rules.

Gi: A training suit.

Gyaku Te: Lit. reverse hand. Grappling or arm locking techniques.

Hachimaki: A small towel or cloth used as a headband.

Honbu: Headquarters; as in HONBU DOJO, i.e. headquarters gym.

146

Judo: A Japanese martial-art-based sport.

Jujutsu: A Japanese martial art said to be the forerunner of judo and aikido.

Jutsu: Lit. art or skill, as in karate-jutsu, i.e. the art of karate. Jutsu usually indicates the more traditional form of a martial art, as in kobujutsu or jujutsu.

Ka: As in KARATE-KA or JUDO-KA; a person who practises that particular art or sport.

Kamae: A posture or ready-to-fight position.

Kame: Pots; used in karate training.

Karate: Also karate-do or karate-jutsu. An Okinawan martial art, fighting art or martial-art-based sport (depending on the style), developed from Chinese boxing.

Kata: A series of offensive and defensive karate movements arranged into a set geometrical pattern.

Ken: A closed-fist, as in kenpo. Also, a sword.

Kendo: A Japanese martial-art-based form of sport fencing.

Kenpo: Lit. fist method.

Ki: Intrinsic energy. See CHIKARA.

Kobudo: Also KOBUJUTSU. Okinawan weapons' practice.

Kumi Odori: A weapons' dance performed by two or more exponents.

Kumite: Sparring. JIYU-KUMITE is free-sparring; YAKUSOKU-KUMITE is fixed-sparring.

Kyoshi: A grade for a teacher.

Kyu: A grade for beginners.

Makiwara: A striking post.

O: Polite term of respect, used with Okinawan surnames, to denote an old man.

Odori: Dance.

Oyakata: See UEKATA.

Pechin: A former Okinawan rank (for military officer), equivalent to the Japanese middle samurai. See SHIZOKU.

Reigi: Courtesy.

Ryu: Style.

Ryukyu: The name of the kingdom that historically encompassed the Ryukyu Islands.

Sashi: Stone training weights used in karate.

Satunushi: A former Okinawan rank (page boy). See SHIZOKU.

Sempai: A senior.

Sensei: Teacher.

Shihan: A karate grade equivalent to master, usually from 4th to 5th DAN.

Shizoku: Former (pre-1879) upper-class families. On Okinawa there were nine ranks: ANJI, UEKATA, PECHIN, SATUNUSHI-PECHIN, CHIKUDUN-PECHIN, SATUNUSHI, WAKA-SATUNUSHI, CHIKUDUN, CHIKUDUN-ZASHIKI.

Tanden: A point on the body, just below the navel.

Tanmei: Polite suffix, used with Okinawan surnames, to denote old man.

Ti: Also TE. Indigenous Okinawan martial art incorporating empty-handed and weapons' practice.

Te: Lit. hands. See TI.

Tode: Also TUTI. Lit. Chinese te, or Chinese boxing; the forerunner of karate.

Torite: Hand releasing techniques.

Tuti: See TODE.

Udun: A family of the ANJI rank. See SHIZOKU.

Uekata: Also OYAKATA. A former rank, equivalent to the Japanese upper samurai. See SHIZOKU.

Uhuchiku: Formerly, a senior police inspector.

Usumei: Polite suffix, used with Okinawan surnames, to denote an old woman.

Zen: A Buddhist sect, or religious meditation.

Appendix C
List of karate katas

Abbreviations

RYU. Ryuei-ryu
KOJ. Kojo-ryu
ISH. Ishimine-ryu
CHU. Chubu Shorin-ryu
KOB. Shorin-ryu (Kobayashi)
KMS. Kenwa Mabuni Shito-ryu
MOT. Motobu-ryu
GOJ. Goju-ryu
RYS. Ryukyu Shorin-ryu
SHA. Shorin-ryu (Shaolin)
HON. Honshin-ryu

MAT. Matsumura Orthodox Shorin-ryu
SHO. Shorinji-ryu
ISS. Isshin-ryu
KUS. Kushin-ryu
SHS. Shinpan Shiroma Shito-ryu
OKK. Okinawa Kenpo
RYK. Ryukyu Kobudo
BUG. Bugeikan
UEC. Uechi-ryu
MAB. Matsubayashi-ryu
MAK. Matayoshi Kobudo

Names of kata	*Styles incorporating katas*
Anan[a]	RYK. OKK.
Ananku[a]	SHO. MAB. CHU. RYS. BUG. SHA.
Aran[a]	CHU.
Chi no kata[a]	KOJ.
Chintei[a]	KOB.
Chintou, Chinto[a]	MAT. KOB. KUS. SHS. SHO. MAB. CHU. RYS. BUG. RYK. OKK. SHA.
Fukyu Kata Ichi[b]	MAB. KOB.
Fukyu Kata Ni (see Gekisai Ichi)	
Fukyu Kata San[b]	KOB.
Fukyu Kata Yon[b]	KOB.
Fukyu Kata Go[b]	KOB.

Gekisai Ichi, Fukyu Kata Ni[b]	GOJ. MAB. KOB.
Gekisai Ni[b]	GOJ. KUS.
Gojushiho[a]	SHO. MAB. CHU. RYS. BUG. RYK. MAT. KOB. KUS. KMS. SHS. SHA. OKK.
Hako[a]	KOJ.
Hakuryu[a]	KOJ.
Hakutsuru, Hakaku[a]	MAT. MAK. KOJ.
Heiku[a]	RYU.
Jichin[a]	BUG.
Jion[a]	KOB. BUG.
Jute, Jitti, Jittei[a]	KOB. BUG.
Kanchin[b]	UEC.
Kanshiwa[b]	UEC.
Kanshu, Dai Ni Sesan[b]	UEC.
Kihon Kata Ichi[b]	KOB.
Kihon Kata Ni[b]	KOB.
Kihon Kata San[b]	KOB.
Kuma-te Sanchin, Kuma-di Sanchin[a]	ISH.
Ku no Kata[a]	KOJ.
Kururunfua[a]	GOJ.
Kusanku Dai, Kusanku, Kosokun Dai[a]	MAT. KOB. KUS. KMS. SHS. SHO. MAB. CHU. RYS. BUG. RYK. OKK. SHA.
Kusanku Sho, Kosokun Sho[a]	KOB. SHS. RYK. OKK.
Kusanku (Takemura-type)[a]	BUG.
Matsu Sanchin[b]	BUG.
Moto-te Ichi, Mutu-di Sanchin, Moto-te Sanchin[b]	MOT. BUG.
Moto-te Ni[b]	MOT.
Moto-te San[b]	MOT.
Moto-te Yon[b]	MOT.
Moto-te Go[b]	MOT.
Naihanchi Shodan, Naihanchin, Naihanchi Ichi, Naifuanchi[a]	MAT. KOB. KMS. SHS. MAB. HON. SHO. CHU. RYS. ISH. BUG. RYK. OKK. SHA.
Naihanchi Nidan, Naihanchin Nidan, Naihanchi Ni[a]	MAT. KOB. SHS. MAB. CHU. RYS. RYK. OKK. SHA.
Naihanchi Sandan, Naihanchin Sandan, Naihanchi San[b]	MAT. KOB. SHS. MAB. CHU. RYS. RYK. OKK. SHA.

Nidanbu Dai[b]	BUG.
Nidanbu Sho[b]	BUG.
Niseshi, Niseishi[b]	RYU. OKK. KOB. BUG.
Ohan[a]	RYU.
Pachu[a]	RYU.
Paiho[a]	RYU.
Paiku[a]	RYU.
Passai Dai, Passai, Tawata no Passai[a]	MAT. KOB. KUS. KMS. SHS. OKK. BUG. SHO. MAB. CHU. RYS. ISH. RYK. SHA.
Passai Chu[a]	BUG.
Passai Sho[a]	MAT. KOB. KUS. KMS. SHO. CHU. BUG. RYK. OKK. SHA.
Pinan Shodan, Pinan Ichi[b]	MAT. KOB. KMS. SHS. MAB. CHU. RYS. BUG. RYK. OKK. SHA.
Pinan Nidan, Pinan Ni[b]	MAT. KOB. KMS. SHS. MAB. CHU. RYS. BUG. RYK. OKK. SHA.
Pinan Sandan, Pinan San[b]	KOB. KMS. SHS. MAB. CHU. RYS. BUG. RYK. OKK. SHA.
Pinan Yondan, Pinan Yon[b]	KOB. KMS. SHS. MAB. CHU. RYS. BUG. RYK. OKK. SHA.
Pinan Godan, Pinan Go[b]	KOB. KMS. SHS. MAB. CHU. RYS. BUG. RYK. OKK. SHA.
Rohai Jo, Rohai[a]	MAT. MAB. RYS.
Rohai Chu[a]	MAT.
Rohai Ge[a]	MAT.
Rufua[a]	BUG.
Saifua[a]	GOJ.
Sanchin[a]	RYU. GOJ. UEC. KUS. KMS. SHS. HON. ISS.
Sanchu[a]	SHA.
Sanseru, Sanseiru, Sanseryu[a]	RYU. GOJ. UEC.
Sanpabu Ichi[b]	BUG.
Sanpabu Ni[b]	BUG.
Sechin[b]	UEC.
Seisai[a]	KUS.
Seryu[a]	UEC.
Sesan, Seisan[a]	RYU. GOJ. UEC. MAT. KOB. SHA. SHO. CHU. BUG. OKK. RYS. KUS. KMS.
Sepai, Seipa Seipai[a]	GOJ. KUS. OKK. KMS.

Seyonchin, Seiyonchin, Seienchin, Seiunchin[a]	RYU. GOJ. KUS. SHA. ISS. KMS.
Shisouchin, Shisounchin, Shisochin, Chisochin[a]	GOJ.
Sochin, Arakaki Han Sochin[a]	BUG. KOB.
Soshin[b]	HON.
Soshin (Dai Ni)[b]	HON.
Suchin[a]	BUG.
Sunsu[a]	ISS.
Suparinpe, Pachurin, Suparinpa[a]	GOJ. KUS.
Ten no Kata[a]	KOJ.
Tensho[a]	GOJ.
Unsu[a]	KOB.
Wankan, Okan[a]	KOB. MAB.
Wanshu, Wansu[a]	KOB. SHO. MAB. CHU. RYS. SHA.

[a] Chinese origin
[b] Okinawan origin

Appendix D
List of kobudo weapons

Weapon names	Description
Jo, tsue, sutiku, sanshaku bo, yonshaku bo:	A stick, approx. 91–120cm (3–4ft) long.
Goshaku jo:	A stick, approx. 152cm (5ft) long.
Rokushaku bo, kon, kun, bo:	A staff, approx. 182cm (6ft) long.
Nanashaku bo:	A staff, approx. 213cm (7ft) long.
Hasshaku bo:	A staff, approx. 243cm (8ft) long.
Kyushaku bo:	A staff, approx. 274cm (9ft) long.
Tankon:	A short stick, approx. 60cm (2ft) long for one-handed use.
Gusan, gusan jo:	A heavy, ovoid-cross-sectioned stick, approx. 1.2m (4ft) long.
Gekiguan:	A stick, approx. 1.2m (4ft) long, with a weighted chain attached to one end.
Tanbo, nijotanbo:	A pair of short, stubby sticks.
Dajio:	Two wooden rods, approx. 15cm (6in) long, joined by a long length of rope.
Nunchaku, nunchiku, nuchiku, nunchaku kun:	A flail-like, wooden weapon, consisting of two long rods joined by a short length of rope.
Renkuwan, uchibo:	A flail-like, wooden weapon, consisting of one long and one short rod joined by a short length of rope or chain.
Sanchaku kun, sanbon nunchaku:	A flail-like, wooden weapon, consisting of three short rods joined by two short lengths of rope or chain.
Sansetsu kun:	A flail-like, wooden weapon, consisting of three long rods joined by two short lengths of rope or chain.

Tunfa, tonfa, tuifa, taofua, tuiha, tunfua, tonfua, toifua, tonkua, tunkua:	A wooden rod, approx. 40cm (1ft 4in) long, with a handle fixed at right angle; used in pairs.
Kai, ieku, eku, ueku:	A long, paddle-like oar.
Kuwa, kue:	A broad-bladed, mattock-like agricultural hoe.
Sai:	A three-pronged, metal truncheon, approx. 40cm (1ft 4in) long, usually used in pairs.
Manji no sai:	A metal weapon, similar to a sai.
Nuntei, nunti:	A staff (approx. 213cm (7ft) long), with a manji no sai-like implement attached to one end.
Suruchin:	A long piece of rope or chain, weighted at both ends.
Tekko:	A metal knuckle duster; usually used in pairs.
Ticchu, tecchu, techu:	A short metal rod (approx. 10cm (4in) long), tapered at both ends, with a swivel ring attached at the centre. Also wooden variation.
Kama, nichokama, mamori kama:	A sickle; usually used in pairs.
Kusarigama:	Two sickles joined by a long length of rope or chain.
Tinbei, tinbe:	A short-handled spear or long machete, used in conjunction with a light shield or straw hat.
Tanto:	A short sword or a long knife.
Katana:	A single- or double-edged sword.
Yari, hoko:	A hand spear.
Toyei noborikama:	A staff (approx. 1.7m (5½ft) long), with a hatchet-shaped, iron blade fixed to one end.
Rokushaku kama:	A staff (approx. 182cm (6ft) long), surmounted by a large sickle blade.
Naginata, bisento:	A halberd or glaive.

Appendix E

Map chart of related historical development of the styles

See following double page spread.

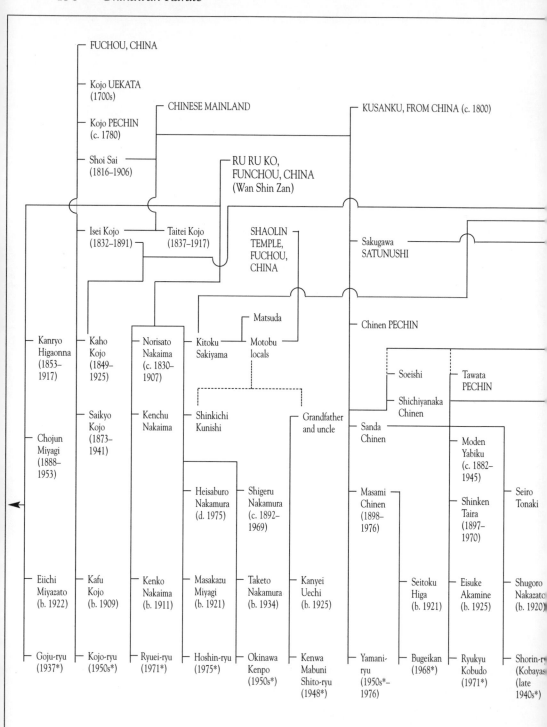

FUCHOU, CHINA

Kojo UEKATA
(1700s)

CHINESE MAINLAND

KUSANKU, FROM CHINA (c. 1800)

Kojo PECHIN
(c. 1780)

Shoi Sai
(1816–1906)

RU RU KO,
FUNCHOU, CHINA
(Wan Shin Zan)

Isei Kojo
(1832–1891)

Taitei Kojo
(1837–1917)

SHAOLIN
TEMPLE,
FUCHOU,
CHINA

Sakugawa
SATUNUSHI

Matsuda

Chinen PECHIN

Kanryo
Higaonna
(1853–
1917)

Kaho
Kojo
(1849–
1925)

Norisato
Nakaima
(c. 1830–
1907)

Kitoku
Sakiyama

Motobu
locals

Soeishi

Tawata
PECHIN

Shichiyanaka
Chinen

Saikyo
Kojo
(1873–
1941)

Kenchu
Nakaima

Shinkichi
Kunishi

Grandfather
and uncle

Sanda
Chinen

Moden
Yabiku
(c. 1882–
1945)

Seiro
Tonaki

Chojun
Miyagi
(1888–
1953)

Heisaburo
Nakamura
(d. 1975)

Shigeru
Nakamura
(c. 1892–
1969)

Masami
Chinen
(1898–
1976)

Shinken
Taira
(1897–
1970)

Eiichi
Miyazato
(b. 1922)

Kafu
Kojo
(b. 1909)

Kenko
Nakaima
(b. 1911)

Masakazu
Miyagi
(b. 1921)

Taketo
Nakamura
(b. 1934)

Kanyei
Uechi
(b. 1925)

Seitoku
Higa
(b. 1921)

Eisuke
Akamine
(b. 1925)

Shugoro
Nakazato
(b. 1920)

Goju-ryu
(1937*)

Kojo-ryu
(1950s*)

Ryuei-ryu
(1971*)

Hoshin-ryu
(1975*)

Okinawa
Kenpo
(1950s*)

Kenwa
Mabuni
Shito-ryu
(1948*)

Yamani-
ryu
(1950s*–
1976)

Bugeikan
(1968*)

Ryukyu
Kobudo
(1971*)

Shorin-ry
(Kobayas
(late
1940s*)

Map chart (simplified) showing the introduction and development of the major karate and weapon-based systems into Okinawa, plus the modern-day derivative karate, as well as kobudo styles.

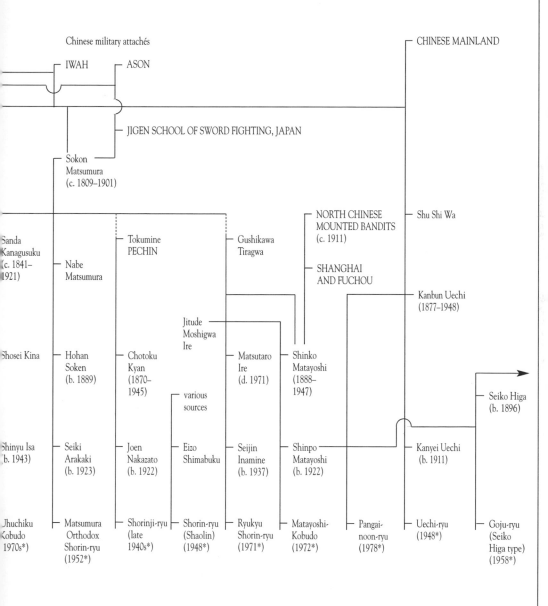

Chinese military attachés

IWAH   ASON   CHINESE MAINLAND

JIGEN SCHOOL OF SWORD FIGHTING, JAPAN

Sokon
Matsumura
(c. 1809–1901)

					NORTH CHINESE MOUNTED BANDITS (c. 1911)	Shu Shi Wa
Sanda Kanagusuku (c. 1841–1921)	Nabe Matsumura	Tokumine PECHIN		Gushikawa Tiragwa	SHANGHAI AND FUCHOU	Kanbun Uechi (1877–1948)
			Jitude Moshigwa Ire			
Shosei Kina	Hohan Soken (b. 1889)	Chotoku Kyan (1870–1945)		Matsutaro Ire (d. 1971)	Shinko Matayoshi (1888–1947)	Seiko Higa (b. 1896)
			various sources			
Shinyu Isa (b. 1943)	Seiki Arakaki (b. 1923)	Joen Nakazato (b. 1922)	Eizo Shimabuku	Seijin Inamine (b. 1937)	Shinpo Matayoshi (b. 1922)	Kanyei Uechi (b. 1911)
Jhuchiku Kobudo (1970s*)	Matsumura Orthodox Shorin-ryu (1952*)	Shorinji-ryu (late 1940s*)	Shorin-ryu (Shaolin) (1948*)	Ryukyu Shorin-ryu (1971*)	Matayoshi-Kobudo (1972*)	Pangai-noon-ryu (1978*)	Uechi-ryu (1948*)	Goju-ryu (Seiko Higa type) (1958*)

* approximate year of formation
---------- probable link-up

Appendix F
Table of introduction of Chinese boxing from China to Okinawa

* Chinese national
† Okinawan/Ryukyuan

Kojo UEKATA; Ko Sai† (*c.* 1700s): Born in Kume village (the 'China Town' of Okinawa), he was a descendant of the '36 Families' who immigrated from China in 1393. He learned Chinese weaponry, grappling and other forms in China. On returning, he taught these to Kojo family members.

Kusanku; Ku Shanku; Koso Kun* (*c.* 1700s–early 1800s): First recorded Chinese martial arts teacher to have travelled from China to Okinawa. Earliest date given is 1761. His name survives in three karate katas found in several styles.

Sakugawa SATUNUSHI; Tode Sakugawa† (*c.* 1700s–1800s): Okinawan from Akata village, Shuri. He studied the staff in Fuchou, China, and learned tode from **Kusanku**. Among his students was **Sokon Matsumura**. The staff kata, Sakugawa no Kun, was devised by him in about the mid-1800s.

Sokon Matsumura; Buseitatsu; Unyu; Bushi Matsumura† (*c.* 1809–1901): As a bodyguard to three Ryukyuan kings, he visited China twice and trained under the Chinese military attachés **Iwah** and **Ason**. In Satsuma he trained in Jigen-ryu sword, under Yashichiro Ijuin. Founder of the Shuri-te (Shorin) styles, with many students.

Anan* (1800s): Southern Chinese (possibly from Taiwan) who was stranded on Okinawa and lived like a derelict at Tomari. Notable students of his were Kosaku Matsumora, Kokan Oyadomari and Gusukuma, all of Tomari. Tomari-te stemmed from this liaison.

Iwah* (1800s): Chinese military attaché who once stayed at Kume village, Naha, and instructed, among others, Bushi Maezato. In Fuchou, China, he taught Chinese boxing to **Sokon Matsumura**, **Isei Kojo** and his son **Kaho Kojo**.

Ason* (1800s): A Chinese military attaché who instructed **Sokon Matsumura** in Fuchou, China. On a visit to Okinawa with **Wan Shu**, he reportedly taught **Sakiyama**, Gushi and Tomoyore.

Wan Shu; Wansu; (Wan Shin Zan?)* (1800s): Chinese military attaché who journeyed to Okinawa with **Ason**. At Tomari he taught the kata Wanshu to Kosaku Matsumora (1829–1898) and contemporary Kokan Oyadomari, who together formulated Tomari-te.

Wan Shin Zan; Wai Shin Zan; (Wan Shu?)* (1800s): Possibly one and the same as **Wan Shu**. He too was a military attaché and journeyed to Okinawa where he taught a form of Shaolin. He was the chief instructor under a Ryu Ryo Ko (or Ru Ru Ko) who had a dojo in Fuchou. Okinawans known to have trained there were: **Norisato Nakaima**, **Taitei Kojo** and **Kanryo Higaonna**. He had other students too.

Shoi Sai; Seijin Tanmei† (1816–1906): Member of the Kojo family. He spent some time in Fuchou, China, where he learned grappling as well as Chinese weaponry, before returning to Okinawa. Introduced sword concealing techniques to the Kojo family system. Retired penniless in Fuchou.

Isei Kojo† (1832–1891): Between the years 1848 and 1868, went to Fuchou with his father **Shoi Sai**. Studied weaponry there, particularly hand spear, bow and arrow. **Iwah** taught him Chinese boxing, which became known as Kojo-ryu on Okinawa.

Taitei Kojo† (1837–1917): Cousin of **Isei Kojo**, with whom he travelled to Fuchou, China. Trained in Chinese boxing there under **Wan Shin Zan**. On returning to Okinawa, he brought back weapons and a martial arts book.

Kaho Kojo† (1849–1925): Son of **Isei Kojo**. Born on Okinawa but taken to Fuchou, China, by **Iwah**, from whom he learned Chinese boxing. Later opened a dojo at Fuchou himself. Introduced stick to the family system.

Matsuda†: Hailed from Henachi hamlet on Okinawa's Motobu peninsula. Evidently travelled to China in the late 1800s and trained in the use of the Chinese halberd. Taught this on returning to Okinawa.

Norisato Nakaima; Nakaima PECHIN† (1850–1907): Spent five years in China, mostly in Fuchou. He was a student there of **Wan Shin Zan**'s teacher, Ru Ru Ko. On returning to Okinawa, he taught the style to his son Kenchu. It later became Ryuei-ryu.

Kitoku Sakiyama; Taro†: A colleague of **Norisato Nakaima** who travelled to

Fuchou with him and trained under Ru Ru Ko. His place of birth was the Naha village of Wakuta and, like many Okinawans, he was noted for his te-based footwork. A student of his was Shinkichi Kuniyoshi.

Kanryo Higa(shi)onna; Moshi; Ushi-chi; Shin Zen Enko† (1853–1917): Travelled to Fuchou, China, between 1876 and 1885 (or 1893). Trained under **Ryu Ryo Ko** and his disciple **Wan Shin Zan**. On returning home he taught, among others, **Chojun Miyagi**. His style was called Shorei-ryu, or Naha-te, but became known as Goju-ryu under Miyagi in 1937, with some alteration.

Kanbun Uechi† (1877–1948): Between 1897 and 1909 he learned a form of Chinese boxing at Fuchou, China, that was similar to Shorei-ryu and called Pangai-noon. His teacher was a medicine hawker called Shu Shi Wa. The style was originally introduced to Okinawa through Kanbun's son Kanyei Uechi, in about 1940, as Uechi-ryu.

Matsu Kinjo; Machiya Buntoku† (*c.* late 1800s–early 1900s): Practised a dance-like form of Chinese boxing (probably T'ai-chi Chuan) that he had learned in Fuchou, China. He lived at Itoman in Southern Okinawa, but had no students and hated having his photograph taken.

Gokenki; Yoshikawa* (1886–1940): An ethnic Chinese, from China, who immigrated to Okinawa and adopted Japanese nationality. He was a tea importer and lived in Naha, where he taught a Southern form of White Crane Boxing to **Chojun Miyagi** and others. This affected the development of Shorei-ryu (Naha-te) into Goju-ryu.

Chojun Miyagi† (1888–1953): A disciple of **Kanryo Higaonna**, he visited Fuchou and Shanghai with his friend **Gokenki** but learned little there. **Gokenki** taught him some White Crane, which Miyagi incorporated into his Goju-ryu.

Shinko Matayoshi† (1888–1947): Twice visited China (*c.* 1911–1915 and *c.* 1923–1924). The first trip, to Manchuria, involved him with mounted bandits; the second trip saw him in Shanghai and Fuchou. He learned various weaponry, Chinese boxing and medicine. Passed his knowledge on to his son, who teaches what is generally known as Matayoshi Kobudo.

Masami Chinen† (1898–1976): Founder of Yamani-ryu. He spent the War years in Tainan, Taiwan, as a Japanese policeman. Here he learned, among other things, the use of the 'sai' (small trident baton) from a local Chinese.

Eiji Kinjo; Saburo† (1899–1995): A Japanese administrator in Taiwan during the War. He trained there in T'ai-chi sword, a form of Fukien Shaolin and other styles. Combining this knowledge with his family te and shiatsu, he (with the author) founded 'Ryukyu Bugei' and later 'Sogo Bugei no Kai'.

Horoku Ishikawa† (*b.* 1900): Founder of Shinpan Shiroma Shito-ryu. Lived in

Taiwan as a school teacher for five years, where he observed, rather than trained in, Chinese boxing.

Akio Kinjo† (*b.* 1936): Started his karate training in Goju-ryu. Later, in Taiwan, he learned Jukendo from the Golden Dragon, or Kinryu. Jukendo is made from seven Chinese styles, including Pa kua and Fukien Shaolin. Kinjo teaches it on his native Southern Ryukyu island of Miyako.

China† (*b.* 1930s): Teaches Taikyoken Tode (T'ai-chi Chuan Karate) on Okinawa, at Ginowan and Naha. Made several long study trips to Fukien Province, China, in the 1980s. The first person to teach T'ai-chi commercially on Okinawa. Includes sword and other weaponry.

Appendix G
Vital points chart

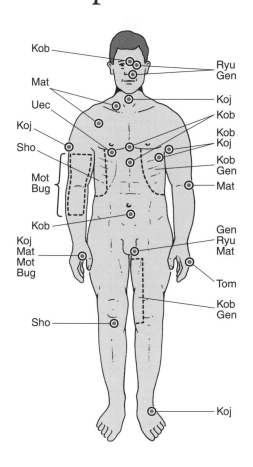

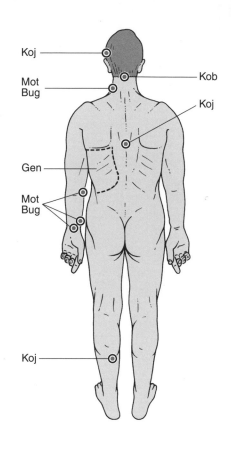

Key

Gen general usage
Bug Bugeikan
Kob Shorin-ryu (Kobayashi)
Koj Kojo-ryu
Mat Matsumura Orthodox Shorin-ryu

Mot Motobu-ryu
Ryu Ryuei-ryu
Sho Shorinji-ryu
Tom Tomari-te
Uec Uechi-ryu

162

Useful information and postal addresses

Abbreviations:

style:	Name of style
org.:	Organisation
N. of P.:	Name of President
rank:	Rank of President
D. of B.:	Date of Birth
P. of B.:	Place of Birth
occ.:	Occupation
N. of D.:	Name of dojo
P.A.:	Postal address
a	Member of Zen Okinawa Karate Kobudo Rengokai (All Okinawa Karate and Kobudo United Association).
b	Member of Zen Okinawa Karate-do Renmei (All Okinawa Karate-do Federation).
c	Independent.

style:	*Jukendo*
org.:	Nihon Zenkoku Jukendo Kyokai (All Japan Jukendo Association)[c]
N. of P.:	Akio Kinjo
rank:	Tasshi, 8th Dan
D. of B.:	2 Nov 1936
N. of D.:	Kensei Budokan
P.A.:	804 Shimozato, Hirara City, Miyako, Okinawa

style: *Ryuei-ryu*
org.:   Ryuei-ryu Karate-do, Kobudo Hozonkai (Ryuei-ryu Karate, Kobudo Preservation Society)[c]
N. of P.:   Kenko Nakaima
rank: Hanshi, 10th Dan
D. of B.:   2 Dec 1911
P. of B.:   Kume, Naha, Okinawa
occ.:   School headmaster (retired)
N. of D.:   Ryuhokan Honbu
P.A.:   166 Miyazato, Nago City, Okinawa Prefecture
     Tel. 0980-53-2468

style: *Goju-ryu*
org.:   Okinawa Goju-ryu Karate-do Kyokai (Okinawan Goju-ryu Karate-do Association)[c]
N. of P.:   Eiichi Miyazato
rank: Kyoshi, 8th Dan
D. of B.:   5 Jul 1922
P. of B.:   Higashimachi, Naha, Okinawa
occ.:   Company director
N. of D.:   Jundokan
P.A.:   433 Asato, Naha City, Okinawa Prefecture
     Tel. 0988-32-0011

style: *Goju-ryu*
org.:   Zen Okinawa Karate-do Goju-ryu Gojukai (All Okinawa Goju-ryu karate-do, Goju Association)[b]
N. of P.:   Meitoku Yagi
rank: Hanshi, 10th Dan
D. of B.:   6 Mar 1912
P. of B.:   Kume, Naha, Okinawa
occ.:   Karate instructor
N. of D.:   Meibukan
P.A.:   20–14 Banchi, 2 Chome, Kume, Naha City, Okinawa
     Tel. 0988-68-2098

style: *Goju-ryu*
org.:   Kokusai Karate Kobudo Renmei (International Karate and Kobudo Federation)[c]
N. of P.:   Choboku Takamine
rank: Hanshi
D. of B.:   24 Mar 1908
P. of B.:   Ozato, Itoman, Okinawa
occ.:   Karate instructor

N. of D.: Shodokan
P.A.: 174 Yosemiya, Naha City, Okinawa Prefecture

Name: Seikichi Higa
rank: Hanshi
D. of B.: 10 Feb 1927
P.A.: 323 Yogi, Naha City, Okinawa Prefecture
Tel. 0988-32-5471

style: *Goju-ryu*
org.: Itokazukei Goju-ryu Kenkyukai (Itokazu-type Goju-ryu Research Association)[a]
N. of P.: Yoshio Itokazu
rank: Hanshi, 10th Dan
D. of B.: 2 Oct 1896
P. of B.: Near Naha
occ.: Karate instructor
N. of D.: Shinkokan
P.A.: 967 Funakoshi, Tamaki Ward, Okinawa Prefecture

style: *Uechi-ryu*
org.: Uechi-ryu Karate-do Kyokai (Uechi-ryu Karate-do Association)[b]
N. of P.: Kanyei Uechi
rank: Hanshi, 10th Dan
D. of B.: 26 Jun 1911
P. of B.: Izumi, Motobu Cho, Okinawa
occ.: Karate instructor
N. of D.: Shubukan
P.A.: 166 Futenma, Ginowan City, Okinawa Prefecture
Tel. 0988-92-2409

style: *Kojo-ryu*
org.: Kidokai Kojo-ryu[c]
N. of P.: Kafu Kojo
rank: Hanshi
D. of B.: 13 Feb 1909
P. of B.: Kakinohana, Naha, Okinawa
occ.: Retired
N. of D.: Kobukan (temporarily closed)
P.A.: 2–318 Makishi Cho, Naha City, Okinawa Prefecture
Tel. 0988-55-4471

style: *Matsumura Orthodox Shorin-ryu*
org.: Shorin-ryu Matsumura Seito Okinawa Kobudo Kyokai (Matsumura Orthodox Shorin-ryu and Okinawa Kobudo Association)[c]
N. of P.: Hohan Soken

rank: Hanshi, 10th Dan
D. of B.: 25 May 1889
P. of B.: Gaja, Nishihara, Okinawa
occ.: Farmer
N. of D.: Soken Dojo
P.A.: 104 Gaja, Nishihara Ward, Okinawa

style: *Matsumura Orthodox Shorin-ryu*
org.: Matsumura Shorin-ryu Karate-do Kyokai (Matsumura Shorin-ryu Karate-do Association)[b]
N. of P.: Seiki Arakaki
rank: Kyoshi, 8th Dan
D. of B.: 1 Dec 1923
P. of B.: Gaja, Nishihara, Okinawa
occ.: Company director
N. of D.: Shinbukan
P.A.: 662 Kiyuna, Ginowan, Okinawa
Tel. 0988-92-3326

style: *Ishimine-ryu*
org.: Ishimine-ryu Karate-do Hozon Kai (Ishimine-ryu Karate-do Preservation Society)[a]
N. of P.: Shinyei Kaneshima
rank: Hanshi
D. of B.: 22 Sep 1900
P. of B.: Samukawa, Shuri, Okinawa
occ.: Lawyer (retired)
P.A.: 1–16, Samukawa Cho, Shuri, Naha City, Okinawa
Tel. 0988-34-1705

style: *Oyadomari-type Tomari-te*[c]
N. of P.: Seikichi Hokama
D.of B.: 11 Sep 1896
P. of B.: Tomari, Okinawa
occ.: Retired
P.A.: 2–17 Makishi, Naha City, Okinawa Prefecture

style: *Shorinji-ryu*
org.: Zen Okinawa Shorinji-ryu Karate-do Kyokai (All Okinawa Shorinji-ryu Karate-do Association)[b]
N. of P.: Joen Nakazato
rank: Kyoshi, 8th Dan
D. of B.: 13 Apr 1922
P. of B.: Chinen, Okinawa
occ.: School teacher (deputy headmaster)

N. of D.: Nakazato Dojo
P. A.: 589 Chinen, Chinen Ward, Okinawa Prefecture
Tel. 0989-47-2253

style: *Matsubayashi-ryu*
org.: Sekai Matsubayashi-ryu Karate-do Renmei (World Shorin-ryu Karate-do Federation)[b]
N. of P.: Shoshin Nagamine
rank: Hanshi, 10th Dan
D. of B.: 15 Jul 1907
P. of B.: Tomari, Naha
occ.: Karate instructor
N. of D.: Matsubayashi-ryu Honbu Dojo (Kodokan)
P.A.: 3-14-3, Kumoji, Naha City, Okinawa Prefecture
Tel. 0988-33-3413

style: *Chubu Shorin-ryu*
org.: Chubu Shorin-ryu Karate-do Kyokai (Chubu Shorin-ryu Karate-do Association)[b]
N. of P.: Zenpo Shimabukuro
D. of B.: 11 Oct 1943
P. of B.: Chatan, Okinawa
occ.: Businessman
N. of D.: Seibukan
P.A.: 1003 Yoshihara, Chatan Ward, Okinawa Prefecture
Tel. 0989-38-0997

style: *Isshin-ryu*
org.: Isshin-ryu Kokusai Karate-do Renmei (Isshin-ryu World Karate Association)[c]
N. of P.: Kichiro Shimabuku
rank: Hanshi
D. of B.: 15 Feb 1938
occ.: Karate instructor
P.A.: 829 Kyan, Gushikawa City, Okinawa Prefecture
Tel. 0989-72-4185

style: *Ryukyu Shorin-ryu*
org.: Ryukyu Shorin-ryu Karate-do Kyokai (Ryukyu Shorin-ryu Karate-do Association)[a]
N. of P.: Seijin Inamine
rank: Renshi, 6th Dan
D. of B.: 2 Jan 1937
P. of B.: Nago, Okinawa
occ.: Electric company employee

N. of D.: Inamine Dojo
P.A.: 261, Yoshihara, Chatan Ward, Okinawa Prefecture
      Tel. 0989-38-3249

style: *Shorin-ryu* (Kobayashi)
org.: Okinawa Shorin-ryu Karate-do Kyokai (Okinawa Shorin-ryu Karate-do Association)[c]
N. of P.: Katsuya Miyahira
rank: Hanshi, 9th Dan
D. of B.: 16 Aug 1918
P. of B.: Kaneku, Nishihara, Okinawa
occ.: Naha City Hall departmental chief
N. of D.: Shidokan
P.A.: 210–1, Tsuboya, Naha City, Okinawa Prefecture
      Tel. 0988-32-2413

style: *Shorin-ryu* (Kobayashi)
N. of P.: Chozo Nakama
D. of P.: 1 Dec 1899 (now deceased)
former occ.: Courthouse employee
N. of D.: Sakiyama Village Hall
P.A.: 13–2 Chome, Tonokura, Shuri, Naha City, Okinawa Prefecture

style: *Shorin-ryu* (Kobayashi)
org.: Shorin-ryu Kyudokan Shinkokai (Kyudokan Shorin-ryu Promotion Society)[b]
N. of P.: Yuchoku Higa
rank: Hanshi, 10th Dan
D. of B.: 8 Feb 1910
P. of B.: Wakasa, Naha, Okinawa
occ.: Naha City councillor
N. of D.: Kyudokan
P.A.: 60, Tsuboya, Naha City, Okinawa Prefecture
      Tel. 0988-32-4307

style: *Shorin-ryu* (Kobayashi)
org.: Okinawa Karate-do Shorin-ryu Shorinkan Kyokai (Okinawa Shorin-ryu Karate-do Shorinkan Association)[c]
N. of P.: Shugoro Nakazato
rank: Hanshi, 9th Dan
D. of B.: 14 Aug 1920
P. of B.: Yamagawa, Shuri, Okinawa
occ.: Karate instructor
N. of D.: Shorin Kan
P.A.: 218 Aja, Naha City, Okinawa Prefecture
      Tel. 0988-61-2502

style: *Kushin-ryu*

org.:   Kushin-ryu Karate-do Kenkyukai (Kushin-ryu Karate-do Research Society)[a]

N. of P.:   Shintaro Yoshizato

rank: Tasshi

D. of B.:   20 Jun 1913

P. of B.:   Itoman, Okinawa

occ.:   Self-employed

N. of D.:   Kushin-ryu Karate Dojo

P.A.:   101–2, Ojana, Ginowan City, Okinawa Prefecture
            Tel. 0988-97-3340

style: *Kenwa Mabuni Shito-ryu*

org.:   Shito-ryu Kenpo Karate-do Kai (Shito-ryu Kenpo Karate-do Association)[a]

N. of P.:   Kanyei Uechi

rank: Hanshi

D. of B.:   3 Feb 1904

P. of B.:   Untenbaru, Motobu, Okinawa

occ.:   Karate instructor

N. of D.:   Shito-ryu Kenpo Karate Dojo

P.A.:   1333–3 Banchi, Minami Ku, Itoman City, Okinawa Prefecture
            Tel. 0988-92-3850

style: *Shinpan Shiroma Shito-ryu*

org.:   Shinpan Shiroma Kei Shito-ryu Karate Hozon Kai (Shinpan Shiroma Type Shito-ryu Karate Preservation Society)[a]

N. of P.:   Horoku Ishikawa

D. of B.:   27 Jul 1922

P. of B.:   Tera, Shuri, Okinawa

occ.:   School teacher

P.A.:   4–105, Torihori, Shuri, Naha City, Okinawa Prefecture
            Tel. 0988-34-2741

style: *Tozan-ryu*

N. of P.:   Shinsuke Kaneshima

D. of B.:   1896

P. of B.:   Shuri, Okinawa

occ.:   Retired

P.A.:   Yonabaru, Okinawa Prefecture

style: *Okinawa Kenpo*

org.:   Okinawa Kenpo Renmei (Okinawa Kenpo Federation)[c]

N. of P.:   Taketo Nakamura

rank: 6th Dan

D. of B.:	2 Jan 1934
P. of B.:	Nago, Okinawa
occ.:	Mechanic
N. of D.:	Nakamura Dojo
P.A.:	481, Nago, Nago City, Okinawa Prefecture

style:	*Honshin-ryu*
org.:	Honshin-ryu Karate Kobudo Hozon Kai (Honshin-ryu Karate and Kobudo Preservation Society)[a]
N. of P.:	Masakazu Miyagi
rank:	Hanshi
D. of B.:	25 Sep 1921
P. of B.:	Motobu, Okinawa
occ.:	Dental technician
N. of D.:	Motobu Kan
P.A.:	3–21 Toguchi, Motobu, Okinawa Prefecture Tel. 0980-47-2984

style:	*Uhuchiku Kobudo*
org.:	Shorin-ryu Karate Kobudo Uhuchikuden (Shorin-ryu and Uhuchiku-type Kobudo)[c]
N. of P.:	Shinyu Isa (as well as Shosei Kina)
rank:	Shihan
D. of B.:	1943
P. of B.:	Nr Kadena, Okinawa
occ.:	Buddhist priest
N. of D.:	Shudokan
P.A.:	Yamazato, Okinawa City, Okinawa Prefecture Tel. 0989-37-3908

style:	*Ryukyu Kobudo*
org.:	Ryukyu Kobudo Hozon Shinkokai (Society for the Promotion and Preservation of Ryukyuan Kobudo)[b]
N. of D.:	Eisuke Akamine
rank:	Kyoshi, 8th Dan
D. of B.:	1 May 1925
P. of B.:	Kakazu, Tomigusuku, Okinawa
occ.:	Businessman
N. of D.:	Shinbukan
P.A.:	677, Nesabu, Tomishiro Ward, Okinawa Prefecture Tel. 0988-57-3160

style:	*Matayoshi Kobudo*
org.:	Shadan Hojin: Zen Okinawa Kobudo Renmei (All Okinawa Kobudo Federation: Incorporated Body)[c]

N. of P.: Shinpo Matayoshi
rank: Hanshi
D. of B.: 16 Jan 1922
P. of B.: Kumoji, Naha, Okinawa
occ.: Businessman
N. of D.: Kodokan
P.A.: 34–342, Sobe, Naha City, Okinawa Prefecture
Tel. 0988-34-7866

style: *Motobu-ryu*
org.: Motobu-ryu Kobujutsu Kyokai (Motobu-ryu Kobujutsu Association)[a]
N. of P.: Seikichi Uehara
rank: Hanshi, 10th Dan
D. of B.: 24 Mar 1904
P. of B.: Oroku, Okinawa
occ.: Businessman
N. of D.: Seidokan
P.A.: 419–1, Ojana, Ginowan City, Okinawa Prefecture
Tel. 0988-97-2651

style: *Bugeikan*
org.: Bugei no Kai (Martial Arts Association)[a]
N. of P.: Seitoku Higa
rank: Hanshi, 10th Dan
D. of B.: 20 Jan 1921
occ.: Notary Public
N. of D.: Bugeikan
P.A.: 43-1-2 Chome, Gibo, Shuri, Naha City, Okinawa Prefecture
Tel. 0988-32-8620

Bibliography

Draeger, Donn F. and Smith, Robert W. *Asian Fighting Arts*, Tokyo: Kodansha International Ltd., 1969

Funakoshi, Gichin. *Karate-do Kyohan*, Tokyo: Kodansha International Ltd., 1973

Funakoshi, Gichin. *Karate-do, My Way of Life*, Tokyo: Kodansha International Ltd., 1975

Haines, Bruce A. *Karate's History and Traditions*, Rutland, Vt: Charles E. Tuttle Co. Inc., 1968

Miyazato, Eiichi. *Okinawan Goju-ryu Karate-do*, Tokyo: Jitsugyo no Sekai Sha, 1978

Mattson, George E. *The Way of Karate*, Tokyo: Charles E. Tuttle Co. Inc., 1963

Murakami, Katsumi. *Karate-do to Ryukyu Kobudo*, Tokyo: Seibido Sports Library, 1977

Nagamine, Shoshin. *The Essence of Okinawan Karate-do*, Tokyo: Charles E. Tuttle Co. Inc., 1976

Ono, Keihan. *Kenpu Shukuya, Dai Ichi Bu*, Tokyo: Nihon Taido Kyokai, 1972

Smith, Robert W. *Chinese Boxing, Masters and Methods*, Tokyo: Kodansha International Ltd., 1974

Smith, Robert W. *Secrets of Shaolin Temple Boxing*, Rutland, Vt: Charles E. Tuttle Co. Inc., 1964

Taira, Shinken. *Ryukyu Kobudo Taikan, Hozon Ryukyu Kobudo Shinkokai*, Okinawa: published privately

Uechi, Kanyei. *Seisetsu Okinawa Karate-do, Sono Rekishi to Giho*, Okinawa: published privately, 1978

Index